COLLECTED POEMS

COLLECTED POEMS

Peter Redgrove

edited by Neil Roberts

CAPE POETRY

Published by Jonathan Cape 2012

2 4 6 8 10 9 7 5 3 1

First published in Great Britain in 2012 by
Jonathan Cape
Random House, 20 Vauxhall Bridge Road,
London SW1V 2SA

www.randomhouse.co.uk

Addresses for companies within The Random House Group Limited
can be found at: www.randomhouse.co.uk/offices.htm

The Random House Group Limited Reg. No. 954009

A CIP catalogue record for this book is available from the British Library

ISBN 9780224090278

The Random House Group Limited supports The Forest Stewardship
Council (FSC®), the leading international forest certification organisation.
Our books carrying the FSC label are printed on FSC® certified paper. FSC
is the only forest certification scheme endorsed by the leading environmental
organisations, including Greenpeace. Our paper procurement policy can be
found at www.randomhouse.co.uk/environment

Typeset by Palimpsest Book Production Limited, Falkirk, Stirlingshire

Printed and bound in Great Britain by
the MPG Books Group

to Penelope Shuttle

CONTENTS

Introduction

IV

At the White Monument (1963)

V

The Force (1966)

X
From Every Chink of the Ark (1977)

XI
The Weddings at Nether Powers (1979)

XII

The Apple-Broadcast (1981)

XIII

The Working of Water (1984)

XIV

The Man Named East (1985)

XV

The Mudlark Poems & Grand Buveur (1986)

XVI

In the Hall of the Saurians (1987)

XVII
The First Earthquake (1989)

XVIII
Dressed as for a Tarot Pack (1990)

XIX
Under the Reservoir (1992)

XXIV
Orchard End (1997)

XXV
From the Virgil Caverns (2002)

XXVI
Sheen (2003)

XXVII

A Speaker for the Silver Goddess (2006)

XXVIII

The Harper (2006)

INTRODUCTION

Peter Redgrove's work is exceptionally of a piece. He had one great theme, a transformed vision of the world which is at the same time an affirmation of neglected human powers. He explored this theme with extraordinary dedication and intensity, and at the same time his writing is an unusually complete revelation of the man. His voice is educated, even scholarly, well-mannered but with a note of what Philip Fried called 'disciplined wildness'.[1] Both in person and in writing he had a genial, at times wicked, and at times bizarre sense of humour. His career was a sustained and heroic commitment to the creative imagination and his poetic style, matching the vision of which it was the expression, was at once exuberant and precise, fantastic and scientific. Unorthodox and challenging ideas are matched by minute and exact observation. So in one poem, characteristically titled 'In the Pharmacy', he asks his reader to entertain the idea that a 'pupa cogitates', but at the same time reveals the 'floury wings' and 'fernleaf tongue' of the moth. He once said that anyone who described him as a surrealist could never have looked through a microscope.

As a young boy he wanted to be a scientist. He had his own laboratory in the family home and when he left school, just short of his eighteenth birthday, he had won a State Scholarship and an Open College Scholarship to read Natural Sciences at Cambridge. But this image of conventional success and promise was delusive. The young man was already troubled by obsessions that would, within months of leaving school, shatter the youthful scientist and, over the next few years, remake him as a poet.

Before going to university he had to subject himself to military service and, under the stress of the harsh regime of basic training, he had a nervous breakdown. Sexual obsessions, originating in his superficially conventional but deeply conflicted family life, and phobias about his health and sanity, overwhelmed him. He was diagnosed as schizophrenic and, at that time, there was only one treatment for schizophrenia: Deep Insulin Coma Therapy. He escaped the army, but at the cost of a more extreme ordeal: daily injections of insulin, inducing a coma from which he was brought back by injections of glucose. He was subjected to this – later discredited – treatment fifty times.

The following year he went up to Cambridge but it became apparent that he no longer had any enthusiasm for pursuing a degree in science. During his years at Cambridge what absorbed him was not science but

---

1 Philip Fried, 'Scientist of the Strange: An Interview with Peter Redgrove', *Manhattan Review* 3.1, p.6

poetry. By his own, perhaps self-mythologising, account it was his first sexual experience that made him a poet. After making love a peace and silence came into his head, and into this silence his first poem, 'The Collector', which became the title-poem of his first collection.[2] An even more important poem of his Cambridge years was 'Lazarus and the Sea', which encodes the transformative effect of his insulin coma treatment. During those comas he had vivid dreams, in one of which he was 'dead, and dissolved into the soil'.[3] When, setting out as a poet, he asked himself what authority he had, he remembered this experience:

I could say nothing of where I had been,
But I knew the soil in my limbs and the rain-water
In my mouth, knew the ground as a slow sea unstable
Like clouds and tolerating no organisation such as mine
In its throat of my grave.

Written at the age of twenty-one, 'Lazarus and the Sea' is an astonishingly authoritative and resonant poem, which may well have inspired Sylvia Plath to follow the example of using the figure of Lazarus in her poem inspired by aggressive psychiatric treatment, 'Lady Lazarus'.

Redgrove was not isolated as a poet at Cambridge. Early in his second year he joined a poetry group run by a freshman, Philip Hobsbaum. Hobsbaum was soon convinced that his new friend was a genius, and Redgrove in turn credited Hobsbaum with having 'that genius as a teacher that welcomes people on their own terms'.[4] It was also at Cambridge that Redgrove began his lifelong friendship with Ted Hughes. He later told Hughes's biographer that from the start he looked up to Hughes as 'a senior poet',[5] but this was modesty born of their later contrasting fortunes: by the time he left Cambridge he had published ten poems, including one in the *TLS*, and started his own magazine, *Delta*, whereas Hughes published nothing under his own name, and did not even tell his closest friends that he wrote poetry until shortly before he graduated. Many years later Hughes wrote warmly to Redgrove of 'how important you've been to me. You've no idea how much – right from the first time we met.'[6]

---

2 Peter Redgrove, *The Colour of Radio*, ed. Neil Roberts, Exeter, Stride Books, 2006, pp.70, 142
3 Peter Redgrove, *In the Country of the Skin*, London, Routledge, 1973, p.39
4 *The Colour of Radio*, p.19
5 Elaine Feinstein, *Ted Hughes: The Life of a Poet*, London, Weidenfeld & Nicholson, 2001, p.31
6 Neil Roberts, *A Lucid Dreamer: The Life of Peter Redgrove*, London, Cape, 2012, p.83

Redgrove left Cambridge without taking a degree, but was able to marry the woman who had inspired him to poetry, Barbara Sherlock, a sculptor, and settle in London with a well-paid job in the publicity department of Odham's Press. Thus began a long period of stress in which he attempted to reconcile the vocation of poetry, on which his life was centred, with earning a living in the commercial world. His father was a successful advertising man, and the jobs in publicity, journalism and advertising that Redgrove took during the next seven years were attempts to appease or emulate this domineering model of conventional masculinity who, Peter's psychiatrist had shrewdly noted, did not understand, though he did his best materially to help, the son he loved. Peter's loyalty had always been to his capricious, imaginative and sexually rebellious mother, though she had contributed materially to his psychological difficulties by confiding in him at puberty about her adulteries and abortions.

Philip Hobsbaum also settled in London when he graduated in 1955 and the student poetry group was revived to become The Group, a collection of poets who gathered weekly to discuss each other's poetry with a critical rigour that Hobsbaum had learned from his Cambridge tutor, F. R. Leavis. As well as Hobsbaum and Redgrove, Peter Porter, Martin Bell, George MacBeth, Edward Lucie-Smith and Alan Brownjohn were to be the mainstays. Although no-one else wrote quite like Redgrove, the Group provided him with a world of fellow-poets, and Hobsbaum, Porter and Bell were particularly supportive friends.

Despite working full-time (apart from a period of seven months in 1957 when he escaped to Spain with the help of a legacy) he wrote prolifically, as he was always to do – enough for him to bring out two volumes in quick succession: *The Collector* (1960) and *The Nature of Cold Weather* (1961). He wrote some wonderful and varied poems during this period: the haunting evocation of longing for a child, 'Bedtime Story for My Son', the poignant elegy for his brother who was killed in an accident, 'Memorial', the high-spirited comic dialogue 'The Play' and perhaps above all the prose monologue 'Mr Waterman', in which anxieties about sexuality, mental stability and the forces of nature are given memorably comic expression.

However, there is a sense that, for all the energy and commitment that he was putting into being a poet, Redgrove was marking time during this period: there is no clear advance on his undergraduate work, and he had still not written a poem better than 'Lazarus and the Sea'. His circumstances changed in 1962 when he won a Gregory Fellowship at the University of Leeds. At Leeds he ran a poetry group, but for three years he was paid mainly to get on with his own work, and the result of this freedom was that he began writing with a consistently greater clarity, fluidity and coherence, and began more deeply to explore the preoccupations which drove him to poetry. Nowhere is this development more evident than in the long poem 'The Case', which draws on his personal experience of an Oedipal family situation to dramatise a consciousness torn in conflict between the mother-world of nature and the masculine-coded idea of God. Ted Hughes was one who detected in *The Force* (1966), and in 'The Case' especially, a new level in Redgrove's writing: 'the best & biggest thing you've done by far – in an altogether new dimension'. He singled out this passage as 'a wonderfully sustained piece of truly musical writing'[7]:

And I swam in the thunderstorm in the river of blood, oil and
    cider,
And I saw the blue of my recovery open around me in the water,
Blood, cider, rainbow, and the apples still warm after sunset
Dashed in the cold downpour, and so this mother-world
Opened around me and I lay in the perfumes after rain out of
    the river
Tugging the wet grass, eyes squeezed, straining to the glory,
The burst of white glory like the whitest clouds rising to the
    sun

And it was like a door opening in the sky, it was like a door
    opening in the water,
It was like the high mansion of the sky, and water poured from
    the tall French windows.
It was like a sudden smell of fur among the flowers, it was like
    a face at dusk
It was like a rough trouser on a smooth leg. Oh, shame,
It was the mother-world wet with perfume. It was something
    about God.

As an adolescent Redgrove had rolled in mud in a thunderstorm, the sensitivity of his skin exquisitely enhanced by the electricity in the atmosphere. He called this being 'raped by thunder',[8] and it was the beginning of a troublingly fetishistic sexuality (which probably had its psychological roots in his mother's intrusive revelations and his rejection of his father's domineering masculinity) but also of a belief in the possibilities of visionary awakening through enhanced senses. Something of this secret life had found expression in 'Lazarus and the Sea', but 'The Case' takes the visionary experience, and the religious questioning, much further, and marks Redgrove's arrival as a major poet.

---

7 *A Lucid Dreamer: The Life of Peter Redgrove*, p.144
8 *A Lucid Dreamer: The Life of Peter Redgrove*, p.23

Something else happened at Leeds which affected the direction of Redgrove's poetry. For ten years he had been loyal to Barbara, and striven to reconcile what were for him the often conflicting demands of poetry and family life. In Leeds he had his first affair, with Dilly Creffield, the wife of Dennis Creffield, the Gregory Fellow in painting and a close friend. In 1966 Redgrove moved with Barbara and their children to Falmouth, to take up a teaching post at the School of Art. This seemed to signal the end of the affair and a determination to repair the marriage – in the first poem that he wrote in Cornwall, 'The Moon Disposes', his companion is Barbara and the hoofprints signify the broken ring that they are trying to mend. But shortly afterwards he was writing poems with a very different significance, featuring a dangerously alluring woman who is also a muse – 'Young Women With the Hair of Witches and No Modesty' is the most accomplished of these.

Although he now had a salaried job again, his work for the School of Art suited and stimulated him, at least in the early years. It was a small, very 'sixties' institution in which it was possible for all the staff and students to know each other, and for a creative spirit such as Redgrove to be given his head. Many students later testified to the inspiration they drew from him. But, as his poems inspired by Dilly testify, his life was still divided, he was drinking heavily, and still troubled by his aberrant sexual preoccupation with mud and dirt. He later attributed the saving of his sanity to an unorthodox Jungian therapist, John Layard, who had recently settled in Cornwall. He heard Layard lecture, and his notes suggest that it spoke to some of his deepest preoccupations: Layard spoke of God feeding on our sins, and the serpent telling Mary that she was too clean. In a book based on one of his own case-histories he had written, 'that which has hitherto been most feared or despised may be . . . transformed into spiritual strength'.[9] This was exactly what Redgrove wanted to hear, and shortly afterwards, on a sleepless night journey to London, he drafted the first poem that directly celebrates his own dark secrets, perhaps the most important poem in his oeuvre, 'The Idea of Entropy at Maenporth Beach'. The author's personal investment in the subject is superficially disguised by the fact that the protagonist is a glamorous blonde woman in a white dress. Does the speaker identify with the woman, or is he a voyeur, aroused by the sight of the woman covered in mud? The answer is both: Redgrove was a heterosexual man who desired to be a woman, for him personally the 'Game', as he called his dirt-fetish, was a route to escape from oppressive gender-identity; but above all, of course, the poem works beyond its author's personal

9 John Layard, *The Lady of the Hare, A Study of the Healing Power of Dreams* (1944), Boston and Shaftesbury, Shambhala, 1988, p.18

psychology, as an achieved metaphor for the acceptance of the darker side of the self:

> Drenched in the mud, pure white rejoiced,
> From this collision were new colours born,
> And in their slithering passage to the sea
> The shrugged-up riches of deep darkness sang.

Redgrove underwent therapy with Layard for eighteen months. He worked mainly by dream analysis but also, in the spirit of his first mentor the idealistic libertarian Homer Lane, encouraged his patient not only to act out his 'Game' but to sleep with as many women as he could. Not surprisingly the marriage didn't survive.

But perhaps even more important than Layard was Redgrove's meeting with the young poet and novelist Penelope Shuttle. Their relationship began in 1969, shortly before Redgrove and Barbara separated, and early the following year she moved in with him and one of the great literary partnerships began. Shuttle was the inspiration of Redgrove's experimental novel, *In the Country of the Skin* (1973), which won the Guardian Prize for fiction, they published the joint poetry collection *The Hermaphrodite Album*, but most importantly they worked together on Redgrove's first non-fiction work, *The Wise Wound*. This book was inspired by Shuttle's own menstrual distress, but its subject was paradoxically to be more significant to him than to her. For the first time his poetic and scientific selves worked in harmony. He had always evaded the question of 'discourse' in poetry, claiming that it was something which could not be argued about, but now his poetry entered a new phase in which it was structured by a coherent vision, and he insisted on a continuity between it and his prose work. Moreover, while menstruation seems a bizarre preoccupation for a male writer (and it remained one for Redgrove till the end of his life), his work on the validation of this despised aspect of female sexuality helped him to develop a similarly ideological attitude to his own sexuality: menstruation was an equivalent for his 'Game'.

His work became even more prolific and, especially in the late seventies and early eighties, with *The Apple-Broadcast* and *The Man Named East*, remarkably consistent in quality. His finest work combines a profound subjectivity, highly developed sensuous responsiveness and a scientist's awareness of the natural world, with a syntactical fluidity that moves between these levels to create a multi-dimensional perspective:

> The wireless at midnight gives out its hum
> Like a black fly of electricity, folded in wings.

A moth like a tiny lady dances to the set,
The hum is light to her, a boxed warm candle,

This set has inner gardens full of light.
Our baby, like a moth, flutters at its mother,

Who mutters to her baby, uttering milk
That dresses itself in white baby, who smiles

With milky creases up at the breast creating
Milky creases, and milk-hued water

Hangs in the sky, waiting for its clothes,
Like a great white ear floats over us, listening

To the mothy mother-mutter, or like a sky-beard smiles
And slips into its thunderous vestry and descends

In streaming sleeves of electrical arms
To run in gutters where it sucks and sings.
('The White, Night-Flying Moths Called "Souls"')

And there is always a current of humour, quiet in these lines, more
uproarious in 'Pheromones', where the poet imagines that he has the
olfactory powers of a dog and can distinguish the smell of all the users
of the pub gents, including a tennis champion:

my own genius mingles with that
Of the champion and the forty-seven assorted
Boozers I can distinguish here in silent music,

In odorous tapestries. In this Gents
We are creating a mingled
Essence of Gent whose powers

To the attuned nose
Are magnificent indeed
And shall affect the umpires

Who shall agree with what their noses
Tell them strides viewless from the urinal
Where the gentlemen sacrifice into stone bowls

In silent trance.

The productivity and consistency of his writing in this period were enhanced by a highly developed working method, which ensured that he never got stuck – as Philip Larkin once did for a whole year – on a single poem. He kept a journal in which records of his intimate life and dreams were interspersed with passing phrases and observations. He called these 'germs'; examples are 'The sparkling well: Fenten ow Clyttra' and 'Horus comes to meet you through this oil', which developed into 'From the Life of a Dowser' and 'The Proper Halo' respectively. He practised 'sealed writing', not revisiting his journals for several months, then writing out and developing, in a separate notebook, imagery that struck him as promising. This book he would seal again before developing the imagery further into prose and finally verse drafts. By this method the composition of a single poem might cover several years, and he was always at work on different stages of numerous poems simultaneously.[10]

From his first collection through to the mid-1980s he had been published by Routledge, a mainly academic publisher with a small poetry list who took a very hands-off approach to editing, and allowed him to design his collections more or less as he wished. However, for many years he was dissatisfied with Routledge's marketing of his work, and when he learned that Robin Robertson, the editor at Secker, was interested in recruiting him he jumped at the chance. He felt that with Secker (*In the Hall of the Saurians, The First Earthquake, Under the Reservoir*) and subsequently Cape when Robertson moved there (*My Father's Trapdoors, Assembling a Ghost, From the Virgil Caverns* and the posthumous *The Harper*) his books were more professionally handled. However, Robertson took a much more active role as editor than Redgrove was used to, and was decisive in his preferences. The last four Routledge books had each been over 130 pages long; the Secker and Cape books were less than half this length, and many of the poems Redgrove submitted were rejected. So from the late eighties onward he formed the habit of bringing out supplementary collections with Rupert Loydell's Exeter-based Stride Books: *Dressed as For a Tarot Pack, The Laborators, Abyssophone, Orchard End* and *Sheen*. Penelope Shuttle continued this tradition after his death, when she published the overspill from *The Harper* with Stride as *A Speaker for the Silver Goddess*. Redgrove developed the idea that his work could only be fully appreciated by following this 'alternative stream' as he called it, as well as the Secker/Cape collections. He cherished the idea of a 'Collected Poems' in which both sides of his work would be represented. By selecting from every verse collection that he published, this volume tries to honour that wish.

---

10 See *The Colour of Radio*, Chapter 4, pp.58–62

In his last years he was still experimenting, and began casting his poems as what he called 'stepped verse', essentially the same as William Carlos Williams's 'variable foot', with each line divided into three rhythmic units. He believed that this form had both aural and visual effects, controlling the breath when reading aloud, and carrying the reader's eye forward to anticipate the narrative of the poem. He also believed that each column of verse could be read independently, though few readers have found much profit in this. Regardless of how one responds to the new form, Redgrove's poetry retained its imaginative verve and precision to the last. 'Reservoirs of Perfected Ghost', which imagines a field of bluebells as 'heaven is so full of sky/ it cannot hold it', or 'The Harper' in which the circular ripples created by water-beetles are conceived as musical improvisations – 'The music bends/ turning over and over/ in its helicals' – are just two examples of how his imaginative vitality and freshness of vision persisted to the end of his life.

Neil Roberts

I

EARLY UNCOLLECTED POEMS
(1953–54)

PHLEBAS THE PHOENICIAN

A footprint in snow is not more impermanent
Than the haste and facility in dressing that the sea
    accomplishes.
The mermaid tresses are disposed, the sands patted
Into place, the necklace shells bestowed on the nape of the
    beach,
In less time than it takes the muscles of the wind
To turn. The gray lady or the sparkling blonde
The clear salt that runs in her veins
Her cold lips lying on the shore, the beat
Of her heart against the ribbed and inverted chest
That brave men launch on her icy motherhood:
All these are at your disposal, and with these
A holy simplicity of small-voiced currents that would rinse
Your dead mouth and nostrils clean of any human
    conversations
Should you fail to please.

DR IMMANUEL RATH

Stamped with authority, a scholar,
This man of integrity, slow in the flesh
But painstaking in mental application, required his life
Consolidated by small ceremonies. Time to make sure
Of a sufficient amount of sugar in his tea, the canary fed,
Of the small pocket notebook carrying his list of daily
    requirements.
Time in fact to provide for
Duties and the slow exactness of his bodily movements; all
In order that a portion of the day might be set aside for
Study without guilt, delight without distraction.

　　For he was slow from the flesh,
　　But fresh as a schoolboy clambering on a loom,
　　His bastions of rubbish were earthworks
　　Where heroes turned to fight and classify.
　　Sunk in small echoes, handfuls of advice,
　　He bred his applications in the warmth he made,
　　Caressed and planted them like velvet pile;
　　For he loved his words and tied them to his fingertips

To glance and dazzle at his weakening eyes,
Trail through the sand, smear honey on his lips,
And weigh his teaching in a golden scale.

We know he took his pinch of dust and let it fly
To be a mote in sunlight no pupil there could see;
And before this angel came to spoil
His breviary, and to crack his seal,
He loved his words, no woman flowered for him,
Sheer multiplicity chuckled in his loins.

GUARDIAN

He was a good husband to his family
And to his home; a fine business-man certainly,
He saw to his property and to his solid home; his family
    life
He saw to it first, provided first
Of all for his family and for his wife.
There was no question that he married without love,
It was incumbent on him (he saw to it first)
To the community in which he had settled his life,
A proper duty to these children and their kindly mother
The full-rigged ship for his last adventure,
This settlement, the correct furniture
Without which he could not plant the dedicated grove.

Hunched in his black coat like the agricultural crow
He haggled over property and bought the ground,
He had his background of experience and there he found
That his family would never dare to follow.
Rare in this age, a tradition of service,
(The king's gardener, son man and boy),
He gladly assumed their ancient responsibility
In the twilight of his life, by his own choice.

Dragged in the portly soil the seed of green
By the virtue of his own and the sun's green fingers
A harmless hobby reared the nodding stately assembly,
A place in whose service fine wits grew lean,
In which no breath of mechanism ever lingered.

In time a god grew there, and spoke to him sometimes
From the tall temples. From his own image
Of a glimmer of white collar in a dark patronage
Of shuttered leaves; or of a black fly busied on a green pane;
He brought himself to see the thickness of a great tree
Rippling out through time like a rod thrust into water,
A marrow to these segmental days and hours
Passed in the world through his aged body,
Like a backbone scaled through thin fingertips.

They now regarded it all as an intolerable folly
In the domestic shade; and at pain of his liberty
They would constrain him to tell his sacred story.
But when he would tell, the tender god hid
And would not be discovered again among the flowers.

He would have mourned the trees like flutes to his lips:
– Broad-chested against the wind of the morning,
    Sewn out of dirt, green capes against the weather,
    White birds among trees, seen in the springtime,
    Hung out on a bodice of black branches,
    Consorts to the white fountains sobbing in the garden,
    Shaped and sharpened by the departed form
    Stand my trees, emptied of godhead. –

But most cruelly beset the frost of such enquiry
Chilled the red rose of brain which grew
Cradled in the snow-white bower of his dedicated bone.
And so it passed that the sound of his last expiration
Should be content with this sorry evasion:
– Lay me like a sword in my own garden,
    Among the turning leaves; I wish to remain
    A monument to the proper action of sun and of rain. –

II

THE COLLECTOR

(1960)

AGAINST DEATH

We are glad to have birds in our roof
Sealed off from rooms by white ceiling,
And glad to glimpse them homing straight
Blinking across the upstairs windows,
And to listen to them scratching on the laths
As we bed and whisper staring at the ceiling.
We're glad to be hospitable to birds.
In our rooms, in general only humans come,
We keep no cats and dislike wet-mouthed dogs,
And wind comes up the floorboards in a gale,
So then we keep to bed: no more productive place
To spend a blustery winter evening and keep warm.
Occasionally a spider capsizes in the bath,
Blot streaming with legs among the soap,
Cool and scab-bodied, soot-and-suet,
So we have to suffocate it down the pipe
For none of us'd have dealings with it,
Like kissing a corpse's lips, even
Through the fingers, so I flood it out.
In our high-headed rooms we're going to breed
Many human beings for their home
To fill the house with children and with life,
Running in service of the shrill white bodies,
With human life but for sparrows in the roof,
Wiping noses and cleaning up behind,
Slapping and sympathising, and catching glimpses
Of each other and ourselves as we were then,
And let out in the world a homing of adults.

And if there ever should be a corpse in the house
Hard on its bedsprings in a room upstairs,
Smelling of brass-polish, with sucked-in cheeks,
Staring through eyelids at a scratching ceiling,
Some firm'd hurry it outdoors and burn it quick –
We'd expect no more to happen to ourselves
Our children gradually foregoing grief of us
As the hot bodies of the sparrows increase each
    summer.

THE PREGNANT FATHER

Where have we come to now, pausing on our walk
To consider a few paltry roses in the hedge,
A dung-hued thrush, and across the grass
The murder-cheerful cuckoo's hoot.
The sun is shining – and last night there was
A petty skirmish on the sea that choked
And strangled with white cords the landing-stage.
Certainly the sun is shining, but what of it?

We're on our way to tea to stuff
The shallow organs of our sense with buns.
Let's get it over quick, and have a sleep,
Not loiter round these oft-repeated flowers.
I dare not whisper anything like this to you
As you shine with such delight at flowers
And are replete with the outcome of our love:
The start of one love and ending of another.

Well, well, we start back; and the world turns round.
We leave soft footprints in the dust
While waves yawn and crack each others' backs
And that thrush snaps a worm short at the turf.
I feel my dung, and want to get back quick.
You feel your child, and want to muse your flowers.
I really want to weep. Where is our love
When you watch your belly like that with your tears?

Where is my love? It's why I do not speak
Moods like this one, fleshy with its death.
I wait, and watch the sea, and sneer at that,
Excoriate myself with thoughts of cuckooed homes,
Disregard the crosslike uncrossed rose
And russet-throated thrush, or sneer at that,
But in all my recollection never mock
Your heaped-up belly and your heavy walk.

LAZARUS AND THE SEA

The tide of my death came whispering like this
Soiling my body with its tireless voice.

I scented the antique moistures when they sharpened
The air of my room, made the rough wood of my bed, (most
  dear),
Standing out like roots in my tall grave.
They slopped in my mouth and entered my plaited blood
Quietened my jolting breath with a soft argument
Of such measured insistence, untied the great knot of my heart.
They spread like whispered conversations
Through all the numbed rippling tissues radiated
Like a tree for thirty years from the still centre
Of my salt ovum. But this calm dissolution
Came after my agreement to the necessity of it;
Where before it was a storm over red fields
Pocked with the rain and the wheat furrowed
With wind, then it was the drifting of smoke
From a fire of the wood, damp with sweat,
Fallen in the storm.

I could say nothing of where I had been,
But I knew the soil in my limbs and the rain-water
In my mouth, knew the ground as a slow sea unstable
Like clouds and tolerating no organisation such as mine
In its throat of my grave. The knotted roots
Would have entered my nostrils and held me
By the armpits, woven a blanket for my cold body
Dead in the smell of wet earth, and raised me to the sky
For the sun in the slow dance of the seasons.
Many gods like me would be laid in the ground
Dissolve and be formed again in this pure night
Among the blessing of birds and the sifting water.

But where was the boatman and his gliding punt?
The judgment and the flames? These happenings
Were much spoken of in my childhood and the legends.
And what judgment tore me to life, uprooted me
Back to my old problems and to the family,
Charged me with unfitness for this holy simplicity?

OLD HOUSE

I lay in an agony of imagination as the wind
Limped up the stairs and puffed on the landings,

Snuffled through floorboards from the foundations,
Tottered, withdrew into flaws, and shook the house.
Peppery dust swarmed through all cracks,
The boiling air blew a dry spume from other mouths,
From other hides and function:
Scale of dead people fountained to the ceiling –
What sort of a house is this to bring children to,

Burn it down, build with new-fired brick;
How many times has this place been wound up
Around the offensive memories of a dead person,
Or a palette of sick colours dry on the body,
Or bare arms through a dank trapdoor to shut off water,
Or windows filmed over the white faces of children:
'This is no place to bring children to'

I cried in a nightmare of more
Creatures shelled in bone-white,
Or dead eyes fronting soft ermine faces,
Or mantled in carnation, dying kings of creation,
Or crimson mouth-skirts flashing as they pass:
What a world to bring new lives into,

Flat on my back in a warm bed as the house around me
Lived in the wind more than the people that built it;
It was bought with all our earned money,
With all the dust I was nearly flying from my body
That whipped in the wind in this normal November,
And outstretched beside her in my silly agony
She turned in her sleep and called for me,
Then taught me what children were to make a home for.

THE BIRD

That bird upon the birch branch stirs my ear
With a long cool pole of sound,
The spiders shift uneasily behind the bearded boards
Piled damp beside the woodshed,
For it underhunts a tatter of curled bark
And when it cannot get a grub it takes a spider
And does not refuse their bodies in its beak
The black-and-suet bodies that I shudder at

Nor their bitter break of juices at the bite,
And flies worms rot-coated to its children,

But so unlike we please each other
Since I put out water from my drinking tap
And summer and winter it stirs the garden
Out of its hot body with a long cool pole of sound.

FLIES

The small wind of a fly's wing stirs my thumb,
And rounds and stops, and bends a dog-eared paper,
And flies away upon a shadow, then pauses on a cloth,
Poses, a shabby, crooked, thin-shanked trumpeter
With comb-and-tissue-paper voice,
Small elephant on wings with dabbing trunk,
Almost a circus animal: think
Of him tamed with spangled side-cloths.
Comic, he keeps the seasons of the refuse-dump,
And clusters round the grimy housemaid as she throws it out,
And in the sun they leap upon each others' backs:
Fawning, predictable, that die in hordes,
Shun the rain, in winter live in caves,
Savage with no weapon but a voice,
Twitching, nervous, short-lived, suspicious,
Spry, lecherous, dirt-mouthed and golden-bodied,
They wash their paws and faces like any sleeking cat,
They fill the air in chase of livelihood,
They snuffle up the smells around dry bone.
I walk in leeward of a mound of dung,
They offer me a bouquet of high-pitched wings,
A tapered whirlwind of dirt and filmy lace.

Fine-grained eyes, hemispherical and dull,
From lakes of sewage bordered by dusty hills
You infect my meal with your self-interest
Steadfast in the light with dabbing trunks,
Infect my tender mouth with what I kiss.
What refuse of whose loves is my career,
Whose diseases must I take upon my back,
What silent lips and nostrils are your food,
Whose film-eyed ending is my start of pain?

THE COLLECTOR

Caught in a fold of living hills he failed,
For, out of his childhood, he had wandered on
An alien soil;
Extending his amiable senses, he found them blind.

The senses still, the reason kept its sway;
Nothing could be of conscious choice but still he chose
Observations made to stir him in default of love.
And thus the beauty and the terror of his life
Moved him mildly. This living landscape where before
He failed, was absorbing, with the horny rocks and the
Mist that glittered like a skin,
And with reasonable curiosity he saw
Crows fall from the sky, lilac tongues
Of death in the square-cut hedge; such omens
Were full of interest.

A busy life it was, watching the people with the
Gay clothes and the lives whipped like tops;
The tongued folk who burned with
The fire that warmed his watching.

At the end, as he would have wished, the Divine
Fingers plucked him from this skin
With much pain for both;
For he was interested in his illness,
And the world, strange to relate, had grown fond of him.

SHEARING GRASS

The long grass searches the wind.
Her rust grit shears snap. She leaves
A broad path behind
Like a barber's matted floor. A squab mouse flees
In a quiver of hair. She's
Fatal. The fumbling beetle on its flower
Cracks its back as the crisp stalk falls.
Yoke-muscles under her tumbling hair
Squeeze shut. Some foot-splaying grass moves on with
   her heels

14

Stuck in its sap. The long tree-polyps snatch
Their birds.
Flowers, spread on their safe beds, watch.
In its bulk a black laurel stills
The air, leaves piled like an audience regard the stage,
Or as the breeze breathes its lines, applauds.
The sun draws rich oils from her hair,
Through her shirt pours in its rage
From the electric softness of her flesh distils
More there that through the warm cloth wind.
Later I take her up the stair;
We stride in the house above the garden where
Two blisters at the third finger-roots left
And paid for a ravaged festering weft.

BEDTIME STORY FOR MY SON

Where did the voice come from? I hunted through the rooms
For that small boy, that high, that head-voice,
The clatter as his heels caught on the door,
A shadow just caught moving through the door
Something like a school-satchel. My wife
Didn't seem afraid, even when it called for food
She smiled and turned her book and said:
'I couldn't go and love the empty air.'

We went to bed. Our dreams seemed full
Of boys in one or another guise, the paper-boy
Skidding along in grubby jeans, a music-lesson
She went out in the early afternoon to fetch a child from.
I pulled up from a pillow damp with heat
And saw her kissing hers, her legs were folded
Far away from mine. A pillow! It seemed
She couldn't love the empty air.

Perhaps, we thought, a child had come to grief
In some room in the old house we kept,
And listened if the noises came from some especial room,
And then we'd take the boards up and discover
A pile of dusty bones like charcoal twigs and give
The tiny-sounding ghost a proper resting-place
So that it need not wander in the empty air.

No blood-stained attic harboured the floating sounds,
We found they came in rooms that we'd warmed with our
    life.
We traced the voice and found where it mostly came
From just underneath both our skins, and not only
In the night-time either, but at the height of noon
And when we sat at meals alone. Plainly, this is how we found
That love pines loudly to go out to where
It need not spend itself on fancy and the empty air.

MEMORIAL

(David Redgrove: 28th December 1937–24th December 1957)

Two photographs stand on the dresser
Joined up the spine. Put away
They fold until they kiss each other,
But put out, they look across the room.
My brother and myself. He is flushed and pouting
With heart, and standing square,
I, already white-browed and balding,
Float there, it seems, and look away.
You could look at us and say I was the one of air,
And he the brother of earth
Who, in Christmas-time, fell to his death.

Fancy, yes; but if you'd seen him in his life
There'd be his bright blond hair, and that flush,
And the mouth always slightly open, and the strength
Of body: those muscles! swelled up with the hard
    hand-springs at night
Certainly, but strong. I, on the other hand
Was remote, cross, and disengaged, a proper
Bastard to my brother, who enjoyed things,
Until he was able to defend himself. It's June;
Everything's come out in flush and white,
In ruff and sun, and tall green shoots
Hard with their sap. He's ashes
Like this cigarette I smoke into grey dryness.
I notice outside my window a tree of blossom,
Cherries, I think, one branch bending heavy
Into the grey road to its no advantage.

The hard stone scrapes the petals off,
And the dust enters the flower into its peak.
It is so heavy with flowers it bruises itself:
It has tripped, you might say, and fallen,
Cannot get up, so heavy with dust.
The air plays with it, and plays small-chess with the dust.

THE ARCHAEOLOGIST

So I take one of those thin plates
And fit it to a knuckled other,
Carefully, for it trembles on the edge of powder,
Restore the jaw and find the fangs their mates.

The thorny tree of which this is the gourd,
Outlasting centuries of grit and water,
Re-engineered by me, stands over there,
Stocky, peeling, crouched and dangling-pawed.

I roll the warm wax within my palm
And to the bone slowly mould a face
Of the jutting-jawed, hang-browed race;
On the brute strength I try to build up a calm,

For it is a woman, by the broad hips;
I give her a smooth skin, and make the mouth mild:
It is aeons since she saw her child
Spinning thin winds of gossamer from his lips.

THE PLAY

(A Buffo Dialogue for reading aloud: Two Old Gentlemen)

A: I don't want to play

B: But we want you

A: I don't want to play

B: You must play too

A: I'm not going to play for you
    You play too rough, I'm not tough enough

17

B: (A red silk mantel with fur below)

A: I'd rather not

B: Why is that so?

A: I need something to do
But I'm not a fool
I don't want to play
No, not today
No, not with you

B: But there's this fur: these red silk gowns
The hat, the beard, and the buskins

A: Will I have a wig: will I have a wig?

B: Oh yes, that too: oh yes, that too

A: And a pink silk handkerchief with thin green squares
To flourish in their faces and clean me ears

B: That too oh dear me yes: you must have that too

A: And pantaloons with cherry-bobbled tops
A big fat pipe and a frilly stock

B: Yes of course you can have that too
You can have these decorations put on you

A: What do I do?

B: You have to die.

A: I have to die?
No, really, surely, that's not a fact.
Do I die too soon or in a late act?

B: In the last act.

A: Is that a fact?

B: You have to die; for most of the play
You just stand around making puffing noises
Waddle on, get lost, or out of the way.

A: Until the last act.

B: Yes, and then in a loud voice
You have to die in a loud voice
Gigantic enough to deafen us
Terrific enough to panic the audience
And bob them and sway them like the cherries dance

A: O that's all right that's all right

B: I want to hear your soul race
In the forefront of that voice

I want it to start with a physical push
And end with a seagulled hush
On the shore of that land where your forefathers are
And I want the whole company to weep when they
    hear

A: I can do that I can do that;
    How do I die then, now tell me that.

B: With a sword, a height,
    A mad dog's bite,
    Poison, razor,
    And you choke on a fruit.

A: That will make a noise, a noise
    To bring the house down

B: It'll bring the house down
    And that'll kill you too
    And you'll shout at that

A: Then there'll be a fire and a rushing wind

B: And that'll kill you too
    And you'll shout at that

A: Then the gas-mains will explode

B: And that'll shout you wide
    And the winds will come again half-solid with snow
    And the firemen'll be unable to get anywhere near you
    For you'll burn in the winds and shout with the snow
    With the gilt and the gore and the toppling gods
    And the plush and the pipes and the pattering plaster
    And the fire and the wind and the wind and the fire
    All shouting
    All shouting
    And the greasy smoke rising higher and higher
    And the arch will crash and kill you again
    And hard fire will come and kill you again
    And the wind sneaping round half-solid with snow
    And the firemen trying to grab at you
    No one could suffer as hard as you do
    No one could last as long as you will
    No one could shout as you would
    And the voice and the voice
    And the voice and the voice
    What do you say, eigh? what do you say?

A: When can I start: give me my part.

B: Here is your part

A: Is that my part? now watch my art
As I die as I scream as I die for my art.

WITHOUT EYES

Today, to begin with, she will do without eyes.

Staring at the speckled ruby eyelids make of the sunny window
Now she tries the world with her eyelids closed;
Pulls the length of her body out of the rasp of sheets
Into her self-made night-time; delicately shuffles her way along
    the hairy carpet
To the cool rim she traces round with a finger.
Heaves the heavy bulging of the water-jug, tilts
And lets it grow lighter,
The tinkling in the bowl wax to a deep water-sound.
Sluices her bunched face with close hands, finds natural grease,
With clinking nails scrabbles for the body of the sprawling
    soap,
Rubs up the fine jumping lather that grips like a mask, floods
    it off,
Solving the dingy tallow.
Bloods and plumps her cheeks in the springy towel, a rolling
    variable darkness
Dimpling the feminine fat-pockets under the deep coombs of
    bone
And the firm sheathed jellies above that make silent lightning
    in their bulbs.

Moves to her clothes – a carpet-edge snatches her toe
Plucking the tacks sharply like flower-stalks from the boards
    but
Leaves her smirking in darkness. Dresses:
Cupped hands grip. The bridge chafes quickly over the thighs
And closes on the saddled groin,
Her silk dress thunders over her head and on to the flounced
    opening
Into quiet

And her eyes clip open on the ardent oblivion of her
    resolution and
The streets and clouds from her high window, swimming and
    dazzled, rush in.

PICKING MUSHROOMS

A: What are you doing?

B: The usual; it's the season; picking mushrooms.

A: Boletus omelette and tummyache this year?

B: Or young white puffball, grilled in butter.

A: Let's see what you've got. Yes, I thought so: boleti.

B: It's a hell of a mess; this one is broken
And this and this; they're more brittle than usual;
And stubbier too; you can't see where they are;
I'm too late on the scene; the caps are sticky;
They get leaf-clotted; like tar and feathers;
You have to hunt them like birds and creep up softly
Not clump hamfooted and squash them down –
Look at your footprints

A: Whoops – I'm sorry.

B: I coveted that clump for my moss-lined basket.

A: Here's one!

B: Lawyer's wig – it drools to an ink.

A: What's that white one, through the trees,
By the big tree, on the leaf-drift?

B: Lepiota! The parasol mushroom –
Shoots three feet up on a warm wet night,
Tabbed with shaggy leather-coloured scales;
They wash off in a torrent of rain;
It stands in the rain like a tiny ghost
Quite white, arms outstretched;
But those are seldom the best.
They're slightly luminous too.
This is a fine one, just three feet high!
If it gets any bigger it's riddled with worms.
Wonderful with cheese in a casserole.
Right sir, I'll have you!

A: Great flabby thing with no roots at all;
It overflows your basket; the cap's cracked across.
Will it last home?

B: Young and fresh it keeps two days.
Tomorrow and Sunday: good as a roast.
Those shallow roots you despise so much
Run back to where I was stooping
Only ankle-deep in leaves, trifling for boleti.
That fuzz, white threads in the stem-crater
Feeds deep in the leaf-mush and wraps tree-roots,
Rests on rocks, riddles the sub-soil.
This is the sex, the parasol,
Just like your own, it has deep roots,
And makes as much seed. Billions of beings
Fly from the cap and may take root
Or again may not. You can't stop them breeding;
Burn down the forest: spores would rise up
And flurry for miles on the first gust of hot air.

A: Give me your stick. Crisp on top,
Sour underneath; they go a long way, like spider-web;
No rustling down here; it thicks up like fog;
Steams a bit too, from the tamped-down layers;
Soaked paper, stuck matwise;

Legs, angled breastplates, eliding from light, glimpsed;
Ringed, pointed, greasy and quick;
Thin red wands, ragged with limbs;
Slithering flow; adorable creatures!
Whew! what a smell; you shouldn't jump like that—
Only a click-back skipping; if you want to be
A mighty fungus-hunter . . . don't look like that

B: Put it back quick. There's a baby there.

A: God no. Stay here, I'll get a doctor—
No, police. Put back the flap. Don't stir;
Don't stir it about. . . I'll be back.

B: Was it the woman or the man
Chose the tenderest, deepest, most shaded from wind
'Lie still here' until I arrived
Licking my chops, eyes licking the ground.
What tiny ribs. A hairpin of a jaw.
Soft in the leaves, shrunk to the bones,
Itch of the wet and leaf-stench sent

The small ghost out for another body,
A monstrous sex which I would have nibbled
For my palate's sake, with red wine and pepper.
'Lie here baby' but he wouldn't stay still:
The bad baby signed to my friend through the trees.
They'll be punished, and I am sick to my stomach;
Sick of abounding life and a flowing palate;
The red beetle kneels, and gobbles my progeny.

III

THE NATURE OF COLD WEATHER
(1961)

FOR NO GOOD REASON

I walk on the waste-ground for no good reason
Except that fallen stones and cracks
Bulging with weed suit my mood
Which is gloomy, irascible, selfish, among the split timbers
Of somebody's home, and the bleached rags of wallpaper.
My trouser-legs pied with water-drops,
I knock a sparkling rain from hemlock-polls,
I crash a puddle up my shin,
Brush a nettle across my hand,
And swear – then sweat from what I said:
Indeed, the sun withdraws as if I stung.

Indeed, she withdrew as if I stung,
And I walk up and down among these canted beams,
    bricks and scraps,
Bitten walls and weed-stuffed gaps
Looking as it would feel now, if I walked back,
Across the carpets of my home, my own home.

GHOSTS

The terrace is said to be haunted.
By whom or what nobody knows; someone
Put away under the vines behind dusty glass
And rusty hinges staining the white-framed door
Like a nosebleed, locked; or a death in the pond
In three feet of water, a courageous breath?
It's haunted anyway, so nobody mends it
And the paving lies loose for the ants to crawl through
Weaving and clutching like animated thorns.
We walk on to it,
Like the bold lovers we are, ten years of marriage,
Tempting the ghosts out with our high spirits,
Footsteps doubled by the silence . . .

. . . and start up like ghosts ourselves
Flawed lank and drawn in the greenhouse glass:
She turns from that, and I sit down,
She tosses the dust with the toe of a shoe,
Sits on the pond's parapet and takes a swift look

At her shaking face in the clogged water,
Weeds in her hair; rises quickly and looks at me.
I shrug, and turn my palms out, begin
To feel the damp in my bones as I lever up
And step toward her with my hints of wrinkles,
Crows-feet and shadows. We leave arm in arm
Not a word said. The terrace is haunted,
Like many places with rough mirrors now,
By estrangement, if the daylight's strong.

THE STRONGHOLD

We had a fine place to come –
Into the keep of the old oak,
The frill of leaves to challenge through,
The tower-room in the old trunk,
The knot-holes, loops and battlements,
And the chinks wedged open with sunlight,
The fine soft shavings of decay
To putter in, run through our toes.
We were the breathing of the wood,
Its tender core, the faces, watchers, guardians,
Bare and bony-cold in winter,
Warm and odorous in summer
And in the autumn rustling in our leaves.
That is all gone now; by haunting
I learn that oak-tree strongholds are out of fashion
And I grow too big to squeeze inside:
The shadow of my head cuts off the light
And I peer into unrelieved and cramping gloom.
The sun breaks in hiding darting shadows outside
And smooth children's faces form among the rough
    tree-barks.

MISTS

They do not need the moon for ghostliness
These mists jostling the boles,
These boy-wraiths and ogre-fumes
That hollow to a breasting walk;

They are harmless enough in all conscience,
Wetting eyelashes and growing moulds,
And do not speak at all, unless their walking flood
Is a kind of languid speech. Like ghosts
Dawn filches them for dews.
They wink at me from grasses pushed aside
And impart a high polish to my shoes
That dry in dullness, milky, sloven leather,
From walking in ghostways where tall mists grope.

TWO POEMS

I SPRING

To pass by a pondbrink
Trodden by horses
Where among the green horsetails
Even the hoofprints
Shiver with tadpoles
Comma'ed with offspring
And moist buds flick awake
On breeze-floundering sallows.

II EPHEMERID

The fly is yellowed by the sun,
Her plating heaves, her wings hum,
Her eyes are cobbled like a road,
Her job is done, her eggs are stowed
No matter in what. The sun
Yellows the hemlock she sits upon;
Her death is near, her job is done,
Paddling in pollen and the sun,
She swings upon the white-flowered weed,
As a last duty, yellow with seed,
She falters round the flower-rim,
Falters around the flower-rim.

I STROLL

My grey-barked trees wave me in
In my stout double-breasted with the buttons winking,
Shirt blue as the thistle-heads, grey-barked stick
To swing great circles on the morning
And eyes glistening green as the pool.
The dog leaves thundering as I glance at him;
I beam back at the sun, my hair is grey as gossamer;
The bird-shadows hunt like rats through the grass.
A cobweb plashes my face
And plucks a frown from my nature, but that will pass.

My trees, grey-barked, waft me in . . .
But the holly, stiff as carving, lashes my hand –
Lèse-majesté – I flick the blood-drop at its roots and listen to it
    wither
Like tissue-paper from my path.

My trees draw back and bristle as I enter the open space,
Dog growls because the couples do not rise,
But I motion silence, and walk among them considering
    offspring,
And the sun hides his face:

They shall have a boy, and those a statesman,
That one will miscarry, and that die in infancy,
A whore for the blond ones, and a centenarian under the hedge,
And no issue for the one that lies on his side and sneers at his
    partner;
I finish, and the sun ducks out of hiding . . .

As I stroll among my human creation
In my park along my walks, disguised,
Waggling my fat caterpillar-eyebrows,
Evening mist-tides hissing past my brogues.

DISGUISE

Coat over arm I step off the moss-silenced stairs
On to thick turf that drains noise
And makes the heaviest walk like shadows; I

Have fat that hangs over me like heavy clothes
In wet sobbing creases, and I dash the sweat away like flies.
What do the people around see besides?
A young head, small and bony, smooth and rosy,
Nipple-pated to the shirt-bright paunch,
As I'm well aware, and people are upset by characters;
I have a body thirty years my senior.

House with grounds . . .
Very well then, I will join the scene,
Join in by subterfuge; the lake's attractive
With the lilies massed like flock beds near
The strutted wooden bridge, an ornament,
That skips to the birdhouse on the marooned island.
I thumb the ground past faster. I will join the scene,
But not before I've bent with kilting paunch
To pry this midge out of the water-drop,
And held it out on pencil-point, clung like a wet feather,
Into the breeze to dry,
Struggling to its lashes, frail diagram.

The lazy bench-beams wheeze to me as I shake off my tie,
Unleash my neck, breath hissing hard, buried heart pounding,
Lean back and watch the shadows sliding through the lake,
And think of it iced, cool sheets and plates,
And see the flame has gripped the chestnuts,
Hear the wind hiss through them, and close my eyes,
Spread a clean handkerchief slowly over my face . . .

And look the part, an old gentleman relaxing
On his accustomed bench in unswept leaves,
Relaxing to the leaf-hiss, braces swooping
Round calm stoutness in the dottle of the year,
Only the margin of the white cloth fluttering –
A gentle snoozing laid beneath a cloth –
Only quick coolnesses from people passing close.

CORPOSANT

A ghost of a mouldy larder is one thing: whiskery bread,
Green threads, jet dots,
Milk scabbed, the bottles choked with wool,

Shrouded cheese, ebony eggs, soft tomatoes
Cascading through their splits,
Whitewashed all around, a chalky smell,
And these parts steam their breath. The other thing
Is that to it comes the woman walking backwards
With her empty lamp playing through the empty house,
Her light sliding through her steaming breath in prayer.

Why exorcise the harmless mouldy ghost
With embodied clergymen and scalding texts?
Because she rises shrieking from the bone-dry bath
With bubbling wrists, a lamp and steaming breath,
Stretching shadows in her rooms till daybreak
The rancid larder glimmering from her corpse
Tall and wreathed like moulds or mists,
Spoiling the market value of the house.

MORE LEAVES FROM MY BESTIARY

I SPIDER

Now, the spires of a privet fork from the hedge
And stretch a web between them;
The spider-nub eases his grip a trifle, twists a thread safe,
And the afternoon is quiet again.

Damp clouds drift above him; a burst of rain
Runs him back along a vane
To a leaf-shed, while it beads his web
And raises weed-smells from below
Of vetch, fumitory, and small mallow.

Hanging there are a dozen or so
Brown shells which tremble.
The curtain is ripped from the sun, and grass again
Leaps into its fumble:

Ants totter with their medicine balls and cabers, stone walls
Pop with their crickets;
A bluefly, furry as a dog, squares up
To the web and takes it with a jump like a hoop

And spider springs round like a man darting
To the fringes of a dogfight;

Tugging like a frantic sailor, buzzing like a jerky sawyer,
Fly finishes in swaddling
Tight as a knot
From the spinnerets' glistening.

And though spider
Hangs a little lower than the sun
Over all their heads, all
Seem ignorant of that passing;
The afternoon, the ebullience increases
Among the low boughs of the weeds
And spider steady, like a lichened glove
Only a little lower than the sun; none
Takes account of that to and fro passing,
Or of the manner of that death in swaddling.

II BASILISK

Rising above the fringe of silvering leaves
A finger, tanned and scaly, gorgeous, decayed,
Points to the shivering clouds, then turns down
Most slowly, towards you. The light catches, cold and hard
Pulls round the polished bone of fingernail
Arrests attention, the prey falls dead.

Bone mirrors have the quickest way to die
The sunlight loses strength and sap drained
Out and lost, distils a beam of purest mortality
Set in the velvet sockets of a fabled bird.
A mandarin of birds, exalted, alone
Sweeping its cold avenue of dying trees
Its restlessness oppressed for new fuel, warm
And busy not to lift its eyes, unrealised sin
Committed out of favour, and it dies.

But when it dies the silks collapse and draw aside.
The idle naturalist to draw this legend to its wisest close,
Pries. The walking-stick at first disturbs a swarm
But no danger from the tawny ground, it lies
As still as where it dropped. Newspaper and a spade
A tin tray in the quietest room; probes,

Licks like an eagle with his sharpest knives.
Fat, flesh, yes, and normal bones
Sincerely documented, the head from behind now
The brain, enlarged, hard and crisp as ice
No poison, the smell of preservatives, the face
At last, nostrils and beak, a wrinkled neck,
The eyelids closed. He pulls these aside,
They rustle, a smell like pungent spice

He catches. How curious, the eyes as dead
And white as buttons, hard, adamantine, he tries
To scratch them with his knife, with no effect,
Revolves the problem in his clouding head.
Then the light catches, and he dies.

MALAGUEÑO

Warming his buttocks on the hot stone at his master's threshold
He flaps his eyelids against the light; from his shoulder
Brushes the dust; the poor in this country are rarely cold.
His trousers stiffen in the heat, as starched, and moulder,
His sweat ferments. He is a simple labourer with a daily wage
Sawing up sewer pipes in the direct sun, or dragging them
Along trenches muddy with man-sweat. There is no cage
He bruises his hands against. His offspring teem
Under a thatch of rushes near the sea-front.

He can mount
Under the guidance of the church until his eyes glow like a
    saint's;
He can have another child; for sixpence he can get drunk
And be a torero, the government, or a saint; he has no taints
On his soul that the church refuses, he is not sunk
Even by adultery, just as in the streets, hot to his rope-soled
    feet,
Tobacco-juice or dung whitens with light like warm milk from
    the pitch-dark teat.

VARIATION ON LORCA

Neither the house nor the rooms
Nor the ants under the stones, nor the horses,
Nor our child nor the misty evenings
Knows you. You are dead.

The headstones, the white satin
Into which you crumble,
My memory of you, know nothing
Of where you are. You are dead.

Autumn will come with its snails creeping,
Apples blushing,
Boughs pushing through the rent bushes but
None of us wants to be with you now;
We are ignorant and frightened;
No one would wish to look into your eyes. You are
    dead.

You are dead, piled with the rest of earth's dead,
The smoked ends of earth's dead;
Nobody knows you from them, or wants to know
The condition into which your body has fallen,
But I sing,
Standing for your posterity, of your restlessness,
Your profile, the purity of your understanding,
Your appetite for hazard and the taste of death,
Of the sorrow in recollection of your gaiety.

I doubt whether we shall soon see another,
So evident a man, so rich in adventure;
I sing in words that moan and raise
A sad breeze among all that knew you.

That last full-stop dries like a bright eye closing.

THE SECRETARY

At work his arms wave like a windmill
Slapping designs on crisp pads with a thick soft pencil,
A girded grin next morning at his desk, but
No cross words once the pencil gets slapping,
Sliving out our luxury. No cross words.

Silk dressing-gowns and wine-dark coverlets,
Grey hair bushing on my shantung lap,
Remorse, and sheep-eyes spinning water,
Remorse, the cord smiles deeply in his girth.
A glass of water then; quick comfortable speech;
We step from silks; the cords hang loose and heavy;
I catch his breath. His teeth stained tawny with tobacco
It is rank and vicious, like menstrual blood.

Buffing his nose with a forefinger,
Sipping tonic-water at breakfast,
Relaxed and special out of the bath,
He twinkles, and I twinkle back,
Pantless, under a slim formal skirt,
Ready for work. He holds my stocking
Like a hoop in two fists as my foot flies in
And lays his palms flat along my thighs
And kisses me. My skirt is creased
And beard-rash twinkles on my thighs
But I sit up and catch the notes
He flings to me grinning,
Fly for files and mend my shoulder-strap.
They send him north occasionally
My beaked fingers pecking meanly at the keys,
And he sends me letters; I'm drawn naked
On wine-dark coverlets on crisp pad-paper
The letter scribbled down my whiteness
With XX at customary halts. Could I cook a meal perhaps?
Or change the coverlets to creamy candlewick –
Anger booms among the giggling dressing-gowns
And I sit beside the bed holding water
Until grey hair bushes on my lap
And a hand collects itself to sweep my buttocks;
He feels really close to me if I forgive him
Constantly; I watch for the rewinding of his spring
And arms begin to whirl like windmills.

Wine, restaurants, dancing, creased skirts, beard-rash,
Pleasure just this side of painful fun, and a look,
A finger laid along his rummaging nose,
That makes me laugh down into my note-book,
Keep us young; a money-spinner
Twenty years my senior with a body
Just the age of mine, for the moment.
The maid dies first, then the young woman,
But the secretary keeps growing all the while
Into perfection and exemplary service,
Sharp-pencilled, clean-typer, indispensably informed,
The memoranda ticking down the page,
Footage filed away, and yellowing miles
Accumulating in the dust-proof cabinets
Signposted in her careful lettering;
I shall have to tout myself elsewhere, trim personnel.
What is sincerity anyway, flat on one's back?
It foams everywhere, and floats out one's best:
Best lover, secretary, and perfect staff.

EXPECTANT FATHER

Final things walk home with me through Chiswick Park,
Too much death, disaster; this year
All the children play at cripples
And cough along with one foot in the gutter.
But now my staircase is a way to bed
And not the weary gulf she sprinted down for doorbells
So far gone on with the child a-thump inside;
A buffet through the air from the kitchen door that sticks
Awakes a thumb-size fly. Butting the rebutting window-pane
It shouts its buzz, so I fling the glass up, let it fly
Remembering as it skims to trees, too late to swat,
That flies are polio-whiskered to the brows
With breeding-muck, and home
On one per cent of everybody's children.

So it is the week when Matron curfews, with her cuffs,
And I draw back. My wife, round as a bell in bed, is white and
    happy.
Left to myself I undress for the night
By the fine bright wires of lamps: hot tips

To burrowing cables, the bloodscheme of the house,
Where flame sleeps. That,
With a shallow on the mattress from last night,
Is enough to set me thinking on fired bones
And body-prints in the charcoal of a house, how
Darkness stands for death, and how afraid of sleep I am;
And fearing thus, thus I fall fast asleep.

But at six o'clock, the phone rings in – success!
The Sister tells me our son came up with the sun:
It's a joke she's pleased to make, and so am I.
I see out of the window it's about a quarter high,
And promises another glorious day.

BEING BEAUTEOUS

A spiderweb stretched between the trunks of the last two forest trees.
The trees were loaded with snow, and the web loaded with the spider,
which was smooth khaki, big as a football, with a black hourglass shaped
across its heavy back, quivering a very little on the taut, almost invisible
strands.

The web must have been spun since the last fall, for it was clean of
snow, and glistening with adhesive as if it had just been extruded.
Neither were there any husks in it, and had I not paused to recover
my breath and admire the sparkling of the sun on the snow-plain
beyond, I should never have seen the gigantic wheel-and-hub shadow
thrust into the wood almost to my feet by the cold sun. I should have
hung there like a cloudy stocking with a full cap of bushy black hair,
before my cries had shaken off their last snow from the far reaches of
the forest.

The spider clutched the very centre of its trap. As I stared, a claw
reached from beneath the speckled haunch and seized as with tortoise-
shell pliers the next coil of the spiral.

With a sudden revulsion, and not wishing to see its face, or have it
bounding across the snow at me on terrier legs, I plucked my revolver
from my pocket and fired. The spider exploded with a soft thud, and
like a firework showered its gold and vermilion contents all over the
wheel.

The sun broke on the shambles of wrinkling tissues; golden juice
lashed away from it. Gobbets of amber gum, rags of crimson flesh, black
plates thickly set with spines and thin brown sheets like mica cascaded
past, frosting and shattering in the cold. Ginger, strawberry and apricot:

it was as though pots of various sorts of jam had been flung across a whitewashed wall. The bony forehead-piece studded with its eight eyes in sets of two, the size of walnuts and clear and unwinking as diamonds, glided over a hump of ruby tissue and sank into the snow. The whole mess started to steam and through the rolling clouds I glimpsed a portion of the copper-coloured jaws still munching.

The web sagged, and then ripped upwards to the highest strands, which broke with a click. The robes swung aside, wrapping themselves round and round the trunks of the two trees, which shuddered and relinquished great slabs and wedges of snow. I picked a way between pits and craters where matter still steamed, but before I had gone half-a-dozen yards disgust shook me, and I flung myself down on the clean snow, throwing my own matter before my face.

When I had finished, I cleaned my face with handfuls of the snow, and as I looked up I felt new air-borne flakes whisping against my open eyes. I knew all would be made good, white and even once more.

But the mind cannot cope properly with disgust, and mine shrank from the horror and thought only of the weaving: madame launching herself from the bare twigs, flinging her bottom from side to side and throwing out threads which hardened and on to which she danced, twisting loose ends together, springing and returning on the long straight rays and even spiral, light, live, and smaller, much smaller.

MR WATERMAN

'Now, we're quite private in here. You can tell me your troubles. The pond, I think you said. . .'

'We never really liked that pond in the garden. At times it was choked with a sort of weed, which, if you pulled one thread, gleefully unravelled until you had an empty basin before you and the whole of the pond in a soaking heap at your side. Then at other times it was as clear as gin, and lay in the grass staring upwards. If you came anywhere near, the gaze shifted sideways, and it was you that was being stared at, not the empty sky. If you were so bold as to come right up to the edge, swaggering and talking loudly to show you were not afraid, it presented you with so perfect a reflection that you stayed there spellbound and nearly missed dinner getting to know yourself. It had hypnotic powers.'

'Very well. Then what happened?'

'Near the pond was a small bell hung on a bracket, which the milkman used to ring as he went out to tell us upstairs in the bedroom that we could go down and make the early-morning tea. This bell was near a little avenue of rose-trees. One morning, very early indeed, it tinged loudly and when I looked out I saw that the empty bottles we had put out the night before were full of bright green pondwater. I had to go down and empty them before the milkman arrived. This was only the beginning. One evening I was astounded to find a brace of starfish coupling on the ornamental stone step of the pool, and, looking up, my cry to my wife to come and look was stifled by the sight of a light peppering of barnacles on the stems of the rose-trees. The vermin had evidently crept there, taking advantage of the thin film of moisture on the ground after the recent very wet weather. I dipped a finger into the pond and tasted it: it was brackish.'

'But it got worse.'

'It got worse: one night of howling wind and tempestuous rain I heard muffled voices outside shouting in rural tones: 'Belay there, you lubbers!' 'Box the foresail capstan!' 'A line! A line! Give me a line there, for Davy Jones' sake!' and a great creaking of timbers. In the morning, there was the garden-seat, which was too big to float, dragged tilting into the pond, half in and half out.'

'But you could put up with all this. How did the change come about?'

'It was getting playful, obviously, and inventive, if ill-informed, and might have got dangerous. I decided to treat it with the consideration and dignity which it would probably later have insisted on, and I invited it in as a lodger, bedding it up in the old bathroom. At first I thought I would have to run canvas troughs up the stairs so it could get to its room without soaking the carpet, and I removed the flap from the letter-box so it would be free to come and go, but it soon learnt to keep its form quite well, and get about in macintosh and goloshes, opening doors with gloved fingers.'

'Until a week ago . . .'

'A week ago it started sitting with us in the lounge (and the electric fire had to be turned off, as the windows kept on steaming up). It had accidentally included a goldfish in its body, and when the goggling dolt swam up the neck into the crystal-clear head, it dipped its hand in and fumbled about with many ripples and grimaces, plucked it out, and offered the fish to my wife, with a polite nod. She was just about to go into the kitchen and cook the supper, but I explained quickly that goldfish were bitter to eat, and he put it back. However, I was going to give him a big plate of ice-cubes, which he would have popped into his head and enjoyed sucking, although his real tipple is distilled water, while we watched television, but he didn't seem to want anything. I suppose he thinks he's big enough already.'

'Free board and lodging, eh?'

'I don't know what rent to charge him. I thought I might ask him to join the river for a spell and bring us back some of the money that abounds there: purses lost overboard from pleasure-steamers, rotting away in the mud, and so forth. But he has grown very intolerant of dirt, and might find it difficult to get clean again. Even worse, he might not be able to free himself from his rough dirty cousins, and come roaring back as an impossible green seething giant, tall as the river upended, buckling into the sky, and swamp us and the whole village as well. I shudder to think what would happen if he got as far as the sea, his spiritual home: the country would be in danger. I am at my wits' end, for he is idle, and lounges about all day.'

'Well, that's harmless enough . . .'

'If he's not lounging, he toys with his shape, restlessly. Stripping off his waterproof, he is a charming dolls'-house of glass, with doors and windows opening and shutting; a tree that thrusts up and fills the room; a terrifying shark-shape that darts about between the legs of the furniture, or lurks in the shadows of the room, gleaming in the light of the television-tube; a fountain that blooms without spilling a drop; or, and this image constantly recurs, a very small man with a very large head and streaming eyes, who gazes mournfully up at my wife (she takes no notice), and collapses suddenly into his tears with a sob and a gulp. Domestic, pastoral-phallic, maritime-ghastly, stately-gracious or grotesque-pathetic: he rings the changes on a gamut of moods, showing off, while I have to sit aside slumped in my armchair unable to compete, reflecting what feats he may be able to accomplish in due course with his body, what titillating shapes impose, what exaggerated parts deploy, under his macintosh. I dread the time (for it will come) when I shall arrive home unexpectedly early, and hear a sudden scuffle-away in the waste-pipes, and find my wife ('just out of the shower, dear') with that moist look in her eyes, drying her hair: and then to hear him swaggering in from the garden drains, talking loudly about his day's excursion, as if nothing at all had been going on. For he learns greater charm each day, this Mr Waterman, and can be as stubborn as winter and gentle as the warm rains of spring.'

'*I should say that you have a real problem there, but it's too early for a solution yet, until I know you better. Go away, take a week off from the office, spend your time with your wife, relax, eat plenty of nourishing meals, plenty of sex and sleep. Then come and see me again. Good afternoon.*

'*The next patient, nurse. Ah, Mr Waterman. Sit down, please. Does the gas fire trouble you? No? I can turn it off if you wish. Well now, we're quite private in here. You can tell me your troubles. A married, air-breathing woman, I think you said . . .*'

IV

AT THE WHITE MONUMENT
(1963)

A SILENT MAN

I love the cold; it agrees with me,
I am minded like its petrifaction,
Or do I mean perfection? My heart
Is cold and loves to stroll through cold,
And seems to see a better speech
Rolling in fat clouds of breath.
I keep talk for my walks, silent clouds
That flow in ample, mouthing white
Along the paths. At home
Where I've closeted my wife
And instituted children in the warm
I keep my silence, lest
Those I love, regard, catch cold from me
As though I strolled through mould, and breathing,
Puffed white clouds to spore more fur.
I never take them on my long cold walks alone,
I save them for a warmer time, some kind of spring;
Saved up in me like frozen seeds among
Crisp-flaring turf, stiff marsh, gagged stream,
Paths the skidding ferrule will not prick;
Where floes creak and yearn at floes
To fuse and bind the Thames for walking on.

This narrowing path punctuated with my stick,
This fuming field where in galoshes
I can watch winter tinkle in the stream

    And clap its ice across the water-voice
    Where it buttocks through the marsh,

    And throttle birds, or shoo them south,
    Crazing its flat glum sky with trees . . .

    And leaves waggled till they snap and drop,
    The robin crouching on his back

    Fur-legged amid the bristling white,
    Horned twig, fence fanged, whetted blades . . .

    Fur them of its own even colour
    To cling and blur and sheet,

These are my walks;
Where winter acts and silences,

Where all is firming underfoot,
Where I can watch the cold flat water

Fizz into my prints
Till I can shatter crusts; my walks.

FANTASIA

My parents went down to the river to drink.

And why go there when they had taps
Full of great crystal staves to drive in their mouths
When the river is slow and green and thick as soup
And motes dance in it that meet and breed?
One might have been a murderer
And the other the natural murder-ee
Persuaded to drink from a cold natural syrup
Was manly and good for the bowels.
Then as her body sank
The other might be persuaded to think
That what he wiped from his brows was blood.
                                        No, I cannot say
That two went down and one came back
For I saw them return conversing quietly,
(One of a series to lull suspicion?)
And I cannot ask them twelve years ago
If they went down to the river to drink
For hatred of cisterns and constant questioners;
Or apologize for mishearing them speaking so low,
Going down to the river to talk and think.

A SCARECROW

A scarecrow, enlaced in bridals,
Staring across blank meadows with cold pebbles;
Mice crouch in his head, in the warm straw centre;
A scamper dies across snow, slower, slower;

Then the sun breaks out and drowns the world,
Fry skip in the ponds, birds
Fill the steady pressing wind miles-high,
And in the wood, sliding like wet felt to the foot,
In the shadows, eyes cry lookout for the teeth;

And after the summer with the flowers and the sun
Glaring at each other and after the winged ants
Have mounted and broken like pottery,
Slathering the heel with oils and membranes
On the hot pavement;

The birds beat south in a steady blanket
Whisking their shadows over dusty hard-fruiting grasses,
Baffled by winter in a land of brown marshes,
And the sky shivers and lets the night in;

And the land swells with snow over the sticks and
    membranes,
While another spring calls close, appallingly different,
Mothered out of nature, the enemy of persons.

IN COMPANY TIME

He's been somewhere far away for ten minutes,
Not in this office at the sharp steel desk
Barking his lap. The phrase holds:
'An ecology of anger'. He's been at home
With new young so-and-so, in reverie,
Six weeks old in a reach-me-down suit of fat.
It was the rose awoke him, since it's pouring,
Flashing at the corner of his eye,
A white rose like a teacup on the bush, he thinks,
Beside the tennis-courts, that brims and bends and dips,
Dashing its contents in a roughed-up puddle, rip!
It's kept him looking all this rainy weather,
Thrashing with pauses; it has a something,
What, he can't tell. In company time
Now he's going to write his father what's
Been happening this last six or seven weeks.

First that blister-belly, thumping day and night
With a rabbit-warren life, broke water; she,
Before they sent him off, still bell-round in bed,
Soothed white and sleepy. There's plenty left in her, she
    says,
If it's another little grapefruit-head with blond crew-cut,
Blinking on his back, trying out his eyelids. Flash!
Another roseful, pealing it off like a churchbell.

They've been changed, they think.
Since the hurt, she looks inwards more.
His brother's death at Christmas sobered both lives:
Just grown up; blond as the new one is.
Father's reduced, and likes his new job,
Takes up his pen, 'an ecology . . .' and notes:

'It has been said that if the whole world save only the bacteria of it
was suddenly brought to judgment and dissolved utterly, its misty outlines
would endure by reason of their presence, right down to the last egg-stain
on each ghostly waistcoat-button, and the lash on each phantasmal eye.
The antibiotics are a clear triumph over the randomness of decay and
decomposition: raising by a power one factor in the reversible equilibrium
between high organization and simple death, and pushing it back in our
favour and our children's.'

Too flowery for a drug-firm's pamphlet,
But he's triumphing over randomness himself
With hybrids, and increase, while obese household paper,
Squashy piles of disorderly abundance not answered
Is under auspices of lists of what to do;
Tossing out his wastestuff he consumes disorder
But flash! the rose does it in far better style,
It brims and bends and dips,
It jerks its skinny wrist, small castaway bailing
All the rustling, wastepaper-coloured waterlands with a teacup:
It's gained a slice of blue above
And the pavement's running with wild combings now.

They've never had the cash before; this firm pays well;
Is nice besides, has roses for the staff, and tennis-courts;
And breeding seems to suit them splendidly,
So different from that death, the dirty death which now they
    both know,
That detestable undertaker's headfrill round the wound

He never saw and can't forget;
The party-tidied hair and purple marks;
And, forever, four days off twenty, to oblige a friend.
'I'd say two sons are not enough, if one
Can smash a strong voice like it did your own.'
The rain falls down; its freshness fills the room.

It started with the bursting of the dews
That this father learnt to gossip, bustling speech;
The rag-man, first unwilling partner, fidgeting in the rain,
Bewildered, by his rusty cluttered cart,
And the milkman, parted with their views on circumcision,
As he talked on and her sobbing filled his ears
And baby sparred his way out, crumpled up,
Pink and sticky like a bud before its time
At this same office – where a rose sets out to save them
    drowning.

'But she doesn't chat so much; milk leaps sharp-white in beams
As Rubens painted bountiful Venus; our baby's mouth
    approaches
And claps tight. Knobbly from my slimming,
Like an opera-cane poked round the door at six-fifteen,
I catch him lopside on the knee, practising hiccups,
Finger-grabbing, and such useful skills.
Baby laps up what he knows of life; Mother
Is thick and cream, motion wafts him back
To sprawl on fat as on a sofa, negligent;
Curds droop heavy from his lips.'

The rose hesitates, and gives out once more.
Of course she's closed to him for two weeks still;
Her blister-scarf is soft as anything he loved; his
Boneless skull is pulsating to her teat, but father's
Grown-up kisses soaked her nightdress-front with milk.
'They meet each other's eyes and gaze right through
From one straight neck, one greengrained and wobbly . . .'
Something is there suddenly with its silence.
It's his rose has broken on its stalk –
The crumpled firmament proves too much for it, as anyone.

Heavy and many-folded, drenching out, filling again,
Flopping sideways on its strings at last. A petal skitters.
It looks like clearing up – and so must he;
It's nearly five. On this machine
He has gushing fingers, torrential fatherhood, and ends:

'Sorry to go on so. But, Dad,
We must have grandsons,
Death is such a risk. When you lift them up,
Be sure to guard the head with your outstretched fingers;
And take care of Mother, in your preoccupations.'

V

THE FORCE
(1966)

THE FORCE

At Mrs Tyson's farmhouse, the electricity is pumped
Off her beck-borne wooden wheel outside.
Greased, steady, it spins within
A white torrent, that stretches up the rocks.
At night its force bounds down
And shakes the lighted rooms, shakes the light;
The mountain's force comes towering down to us.

High near its summit the brink is hitched
To an overflowing squally tarn.
It trembles with stored storms
That pulse across the rim to us, as light.

On a gusty day like this the force
Lashes its tail, the sky abounds
With wind-stuffed rinds of cloud that sprout
Clear force, throbbing in squalls off the sea
Where the sun stands poring down at itself
And makes the air grow tall in spurts
Whose crests turn over in the night-wind, foaming. We
    spin
Like a loose wheel, and throbbing shakes our light
Into winter, and torrents dangle. Sun
Pulls up the air in fountains, green shoots, forests
Flinching up at it in spray of branches,
Sends down clear water and the loosened torrent
Down into Mrs Tyson's farmhouse backyard,
That pumps white beams off its crest,
In a stiff breeze lashes its tail down the rocks.

I SEE

I see a man and that man is myself
Standing in the trees in a downpour cloudy with rush
Who penetrates the soft swarming element with his senses alive.

He is aware of the wet apples,
They snag like a rosy mist in their orchards;
He is aware of the spray of the rain running like sharp white
    mist
Across running white mist, which is the spray of the grasses
    seeding;
He watches the crows stepping within a white bubble of
    watershed, a dome,
How they fletch the sopping mud deeply as they step forward,
    which closes again;
(The look of them sounds of wet grain creaking deep in
    crammed bowels;)
He stoops easily and notices a bug embracing a grass-bole:
It peers through the green gloss at the heavy sap-veins stiff
    with their flow,
He sees its mouth-awls working with excitement for the
    plunge,
And he sees it fuss back again stout with its eggs; (a water-load
    shatters nearby and the green mother starts to stillness;)

Now I feel manly and that man is myself
Digesting his dinner in his study after dinner
Digesting my drinking and my senses are confirmable and shut
With purple wine-drapes more magnificent than the rags at my
    window,
And I have the small hard globe of dinner warm under my
    clasped hands
And I ask myself without impatience (for impatience is an
    outdoor thing)
Who is that man who can stand in the rain and get his feet
    wet
And spit a cherrystone out into a weed-clump believing it will
    spring
Of his mouth, having warmed it and started the small germ
    moving,
And who is that man I ask no who is that boy who is he
A good dinner hurt nobody and drink is nutritious and wears
    off,
And I resolve to begin my exercises again after breakfast
As those tight-bellied crows are all fluttering underground
And in my belly tug and flutter as though picked to and fro by
    the wheat-roots.

THE HOUSE IN THE ACORN

Ah, I thought just as he opened the door
That we all turned, for an instant, and looked away,
Checked ourselves suddenly, then he spoke:
'You're very good to come,' then,
Just for a moment his air thickened,
And he could not breathe, just for the moment.
'My son would have been glad that you came,'
He extended his thick hand, 'Here, all together –'
We are not ourselves or at our ease,
I thought, as we raised our glasses, sipped;
'Help yourselves, please. Please . . .'

'If anyone would care . . .' He stood by the table
Rapping his heavy nails in its polished glare,
'My son is upstairs, at the back of the house,
The nursery, if anyone . . .' I studied
Stocky hair-avenues along my hand-backs,
Wandered through grained plots dappled and sunlit;
'My son . . . sometimes I think they glimpse
Perhaps for a while through sealed lids a few faces
Bending in friendship before it all fades . . .' I nodded,
Slipped out, face averted,

And entered oak aisles; oaken treads
Mounted me up along oaken shafts, lifting me past
Tall silent room upon tall silent room:
Grained centuries of sunlight toppled to twilight
By chopping and fitting: time turned to timber
And the last oak enclosure with claws of bent oak
Where his white wisp cradled, instantaneous,
Hardly held by his home in its polished housetops.
A breath would have blown him; I held my breath
As I dipped to kiss . . .

Now the instant of this house rolls in my palm
And the company spins in its polished globe
And the drawing-room reels and the house recedes
(Pattering dome-grained out of the oak)
While, ah, as I open the door I hear their close laughter,
Cool earrings swing to the gliding whisper,
More apple-cup chugs from the stouted ewer.

THE FERNS

The ferns, they dip and spread their fronds
With moisture easy through the stems,
Green moisture, that interior wash
Of living sugars. Spores dehisce.

Under the baking sun, they breathe
In currents, swirls and soundless gasps
Though you below here, standing idle,
Perceive no influence. Sun rifts the clouds,
Ferns die and breathe, arch and curl,
Breathe and remake their forms above,
Are clouds, that spread and dip their fronds,
Unravel fingers and moisture-banks
Of filigree bracken. All's water.
All stoops and curls with water, gathers, droops

And doles the ferns their green moisture
Five miles down there on the baking earth,
And dunks the ferns in green moisture.
Spores dehisce. The ferns are breathing.
Then frost descends, like thronging ferns.

THE CONTENTMENT OF AN OLD
WHITE MAN

The sky is dead. The sky is dead. The sky is dead.
I'm an old white man, if that is your opinion I'm content.
The fat white clouds roll in the old dead sky
They do me good, for all you say they're dead.
They pat my brow. They sweat me a little wet, perchance.
Just as my dazzling beard parades my cheeks, they give me
Ornament. I'm an old white man as well . . .
Dead indeed! You're a sack of wet yourself.
Step on them? Can *you* support the stroll of a razor?
They loll over my brow and childer my thoughts,
Or think I think them, so fond I am – not water-curds,
Thoughts! and correspondence! Dead skins and scurfs
And water-curds . . . but see how fatherly the sunset looks.
They rain, they pass into the ground, you piss,

You pass into the ground, I do, I know my kin,
My great kin, as a microbe is my lesser. Oh,
Lower a little shower and feel some roots, I say,
You've not slept in a bed at my age till you've wet it.
They pass and snort and snow, I'll catch my death
Squatting under a rainshower and pass away
At 105° all rubicund like a sunset. We're all kind,
All water, they're a little quicker, which means
Cleverer, sometimes, don't it? Oh and ah
The graceful fruity woods, cabby! of the clouds,
Snow running on snow and bending as it deepens.
I see I coach among them, my breath sends out;
These woods on mountains, we send up shapes together
Ridge upon ridge, offering them, these clouds,
The only things large enough for God to watch
And judge from, we'd better get there fast. I'm halfway
Being an old white man and here the tree-heads straighten
Slowly and slowly leaf again as
Flickers of white drop off them and
Slowly straighten heads hurting with spring
As their white dreams leave them. Cabby! the clouds rise
Because the sun wants them. Each cloud is unique.

THE HEIR

Now here I am, drinking in the tall old house, alone,
The wide brown river squandering itself outside,
And there's a fine smell of cane chairs and conservatory dust
    here,
With the mature thick orchards thriving outside,
And I am drinking, which is a mixture of dreaming and
    feeding,
Watching how the stone walls admit all their square glad
    answers
To the sun that is alive and thriving outside,
And rests folded in a full pot of beer brimming before me
    now.
Or it could have been cider, agreed, because of our thriving
    orchards,
But it is beer, because of the brewery just down the way
Sipping at the wide brown river all the year round.
So I am a feeder and dreamer both

Of firm thriving apples and of the wide river outside
And of the sun that arrives and rests gladly, folded in my
  food.

And I agreed to that, and to the passing of the days,
With winged lips of the mist streaming at night, and in the
  morning
Thick mists grinding themselves thin, and grinding themselves
  to nothing,
For mothers murther us by having us, naturally, and I am glad
  to be alive,
Drinking, with the beer squandering itself inside,
Sun folded in upon me and cider thriving among the trees,
And as I am a living man, Mother, I bear you no kind of a
  grudge,
Not to you, nor to the good kind cider or beer
Killing me and having me, for you agreed to die, and bear
  me no grudge
For being alive and dying, and dying much as you did . . .

So I'm glad to sit dreaming and feeding at the wide cane
  table set
For a solid meal that never comes, glad to be spending myself
As the river spends, and the sun pours out, and the ripe fruit
  splits,
Smiling juice sweetly to the hacking wasps, and you did as
  you agreed
Which was to give me life, and I agree to that too
For the beer agrees with me as I said, and I undertake
To go on agreeing so long as there's passage in my throat.

DIRECTIVE

Attend to the outer world.
See the calm delicate spray of the branches,
Watch the cool grey spurs of the sky
Sliding volumes the one over the other,
Listen, not inwardly to that gravel-crunch
(Yourself strolling over your nature,) but
Listen and wait, for,
Falling over the springy testing boughs,
The sliding volumes of the clouds and roads,

Out of the light clear rain shed,
Out of the open hot throat
The world attends you
Like a friendship, in three clear notes
Out of a bird's open throat.

THE ROOM IN THE TREES

The scent in pulses blowing off her beds,
The children birds cackling on their seeds;
The thirsty bee slaps my polished boot
Its horny snout humming with perception –
I love his black and honey-swinging club.
Great swashing heaps of birds struggle over rubbish.
Like shuffling footsteps now
The rain breaks, throbbing down the posts.
Then, through windows from the beds
And swerving back, the sound,
A weeping voice that rushes through the room,
Rains full into the glass and passes through,
Dashing droplets, and flashing shows the tasks
Born with me, into my very soul. It drops
And swings, and sinks into the wood
As into green foam and spray,
Dwindles, hooks up to a bush,
Cool waxy horn of yellow masses,
And that one flower's whiteness draws me through the
    wood.
All moves past slowly as it drives me in
Through lurching timber, toothy weeds: it stares
Full into my eye, my eye poised in that bush.
My flowering jowls tug heavily at my sight,
And here I come, head of blossom, swollen, nodding,
Rain-lensed, frilled and pulpy, flower-betongued,
It seeks its way for me through my thickening scent.
I stoop and sink, my mane matting with the mud.
I lift my dews to what I shall become, and there
Before me trees stand glories, feeding, feeding,
Upon convulsive shifting of the sun
In palpable thick stalks set with shadow-lawn,
And on the muddy, lily-laden lake
Reeking of raisins – green wood all around

That sweats out spring in milky drops and blossom.
I'm only the wood then. You think you
Fancy faces in the trees, my rooms;
I think I only fancy rooms, crowded with faces,
But I pass through, taking mouths of treetops,
Jackets of vine, boots of water-topping stones,
Drubbing long grass like flames to flit my hearths
Of chimneys in their stout and hollow trunks,
I wander through my tables of the hawthorn
Thick-set with seeding food in empty rooms,
Gust them once again with tugging mouths
Thick-leaved and parting as I wish, and I lodge
In bearded boulders, berried heads of moss
Of mouths cracked wide with flowers from wishing
    hard.

SUNDAY AFTERNOONS

I want a dew-keen scythe –
Peering or prodding into the puddles
Outlook reflections or shadows
I want a power-mower –
Banging about in all breezes
Shaggy thick heads without repose
Lolling about in the rain, doddering in it
I want shears –
Joyous colours for suffering in
And those wet red blooms like sliced tomatoes –
I want to get in there with a thick insulting stick.

NOISE

Suddenly in this dream I was printer's ink
Poured through the presses, patterned in every man's
    mind,
Ideas lodged in his farthest recesses were mine,
Had taken in my angular black, the engrams
Of my pain under the presses.

Now I revenge, for when one dies
I let him see it all clearly, all that he's learned
Now in its entirety for the first time known,
Laid in front of his soul's eye, painfully learned . . .

Then lightly, laughingly, carelessly I withdraw my spirit.

Letters, sentences, paragraphs shudder and mingle, a
    little black smear
Replaces each most delicate printed utterance,
A little ragged black snigger like a smudge

That bites like a scorched hole, spreading,
And each book blackens with thick noise
Full of the cries of the words lost in it.
And the libraries! They haemorrhage from their stacks.

So you would do well never again to read books
Nor to build up your children's brains on foundations
    of books
For it is a bookless pain and it lacks pictures
And it is an ocean of night-pain and noise.

REQUIRED OF YOU THIS NIGHT

A smoky sunset. I dab my eyes.
It stinks into the black wick of the wood.

Sparks wriggle, cut. I turn my back.
And night is at my frosty back.

I turn again. All stars!
It's bedtime.

There's no sky in my dreams, I dream none.
I work for sky, I work by sprinting up,
Breathing, sprinting up, and one star appears.

I chase it. It enlarges and I wake.
Dawn climbs into the sky like black smoke with white
    nails.

It's compact with the day's sharpness.
I'll dry my sopping pillow in it.
How long'll that take? I guess till sunset.

And then it sinks
All befrogged into that white glare.
The night is at my back instantly,
Draughty, and no star at all.
I weep again. I weep again frankly.
Sleep is nothing when you do it,
And nothing but a prim smile,
Except you're fighting to pull the sun down
That may not come unless you fight
Not for you anyway, Peter.

THE ARTIST TO HIS BLIND LOVE

Slut, her muddy fingers leave a track
She buckles to her waist.
She stoops. She feels
With fingers in the turf.
She touches coarsened snow and gets
Cool fingers. It almost runs away
On freshet-fingers scuttling from the sides.
Watch the excrement!
Slut, her muddy fingers leave a track
She buckles to her waist.

Foodspots patter down her front. I haven't the heart.
Her hair swells close around her head.
It's not clean. She smiles,
She scrolled her own mouth this morning, I can see;
Air lies like thick soil on both eyes, sunbeams
Fall on top of that like warm twigs.
I haven't the heart. Foodspots patter down her front.

Your eyes have their nightside uppermost,
Beauty, soiled with blindness, brave one.
The redness of those berries reaches for my eyes
And plucks them to the bushes, to and fro.
Every eye has a black target, yours empty,
Tumbling, twinkling away like berries.

Which of us is the eyes' slattern?
We bath at night, and go to bed. I'd not have heart
To love without the light;
You live with night-time uppermost.

SWEAT

I sit in the hot room and I sweat,
I see the cool pane bedew with me,
My skin breathes out and pearls the windowpane,
Likes it and clings to it. She comes in,
She loves me and she loves our children too,
And still the sweat is trickling down the pane,
The breath of life makes cooling streaks
And wobbles down the pane. We breathe and burn,
We burn, all together in a hot room,
Our sweat is smoking down the windowpane,
Marks time. I smoke, I stir, and there I write
PR, BR, a streaming heart.
The sun strikes at it down a wide hollow shaft;
Birds swing on the beams, boil off the grass.

ON THE SCREAMING OF GULLS

The wet wings of birds into the air
Making off from our roofs in the rain
Clapped hard to the drenched flank
In a spray of feather-wet
Must sting the sleek body as they clap.
The muscle-yoke across the back
Stings and spurs the armless animals
And spurs them until they scream
As they do, as they do all night
Whizzing into the mist like chain-shot
That howls where it strikes.
They are ridden upon by their wings,
By their ability for flight,
The wings enjoy the use of them,
Clapped tight around the panting heart.
Brute muscle is the brain, and the brain

In the slippery bright eyes
Mere watcher and recorder
Of muscles on the go, always,
Forcing screams from stung panting sides,
For fish, more fish, fish
Sustaining their spurts across the estuary,
For use, to enjoy the flight
Tight along their screaming mounts.
The gull is delighted in by others,
Ridden by other passengers, parcel of jockey-owners;
The sex jaunts from ground to breeding-ground,
The oval, perfect sex, the thinking egg
Skilled to spin them, bank, and keep their trim
In tight mating flocks
As though furnace were gyroscope,
Compass and owners' orders in one packet;
Compassionate more than the wings,
Mapping no ground, it gives, though the way is lost
Good company in payment.
The weary bird launches its neck
Over the grey rollers.

Cherry-seed, nematode, spore
Of bacilli without number, fern-, alga-spore
Ride too, rafted
To claw, feather, beak
Of this airship
Whose furnace-draught is screams,
Or grow folded into the grey bowel, bilge
And breeder too of the gull's own rotting
Just as it falls, log
Scattered, fluttered
Into unbound leafy bones
Or feathery bones suspended in rut,
Worked to the last instant, thin plans
Surviving pursy passengers.

THE ABSOLUTE GHOST

Well, in good time you came and gave it, God,
Rest of a kind in the mansions
That lapped at my feet like a watery hound,
And friendship feigned – that's dangerous!
At my feet the fissure yawned,
Long, low and cold the lake invited
Visitors to its mists, and I, in my draperies
Dressed like mist came, while the reeds
Parted like opening arms for me to go in.
Like opening arras. In dungarees next
They came to drag, the colour of mud;
In draperies I floated, the colour of ghosts
My substance licking every corner of where I was
To know it as I was known – then I was legion
There in the glades of the great lake
Whose lightest lilt of current, consent,
Moved us into a mansion. No breath
But the breathing of the current in which we were
     riven.
We passed, we passed, I did my job as matter
As I tried my mental, but not enough;
See, this slime-slide opening under her heel
Is where I ended, is me,
Spat out by some fish,
Among the crowds of small evils.

THE WIDOWER

Yawning, yawning with grief all the time.
The live ones are often alive in fragments
And some of us scream as the weather changes.
Or I raise a frequent steak to my pluming nostrils,
Starving, or yawning, so hungry for air,
Gasping for life. And a snowflake was her friend.
And the sky of clouds hurrying and struggling
Beyond the skylight, were her friends.
She was daytime to the mind,
A light room of trees, spray of water, high flowers
Over a cloudscape, and I brought her
Twelve-hour lyings down for fear of this world,

Head buried in pillows for perfect darkness,
And into this she walked with nothing but advice
And what I called her spells for company.

Ah well, no doubt such happens to many.
Now I myself am alive only in fragments,
A piece of uncertain, of filthy tattered weather.
Pull the clothing to shreds; huddle the tatters together,
Wild and horrible! easily in my rags.

But you said, take another look!
Watch the mixtures, the things moving with one another,
Water running across running water, wind woven on it,
A sudden bleat of black birds marking across the marshes,
Beating wind across water, rooms built of glimmer and
    mist there.
I don't say it wouldn't have worked in time,
But my brow knitting it was lighted up my brain,
Mere strain over a surface,
And I just couldn't believe anything, anything at all.
Now look at me!

There's always something there, you said; now let me try
(That leaden waterspout searching so thick and tall
Over the mincing sunny water is no good to anyone)
Some vista of life, some mentality, so let me try now,
Something to watch always, and it's called your spell,
So what do I notice now in my nice quiet room
With the mullions and the college table and the books?
Why, look, there's that exciting queasiness
That queasy vividness of dark windows before thunder:
So I cross over quickly and there I am!
Up among them, the bad clouds over the bright blue,
Adjusting my black pieces over the innocent cricketers
Who tremble like white splinters in the deep gulfs
    beneath me,
Through the rifting thick platforms . . . I quite enjoyed
    that −
But it wasn't true, was it?

All lies, and here the lies come again,
The dead, and the inventions of the dead,
The night, and what the night contains,
The great quivering jelly of resemblances,

The spreading, the too-great majority,
Whose heads hang from memories and nausea,
Who stroll about vomiting, shaking and gaping with it,
Who goggle in terror of their condition, who retire at
    dawn
To almost inaudible thin quarrels up and down the
    graveyard strata
Who lurk with invisible thin whines like gnats in daytime
But who billow through the deep lanes at dusk
Like a mist of bleached portraits, who do not exist,
Who walk like a shivering laundry of shifted humanity
And who stink . . .

Not true! But thank God the day's come again,
A sunny warm day, a good morning, a morning to
    recline,
To wear shirts, to look simple and true,
To run hands with definite pleasure
Over the shorn bristly lawn full of mentality,
To plunge conjecture
Easily in a bold search for truth through the lawn's
    surface,
To consider the small kin, and their place in nature,
The spires and sinews of the worm, how excellent!
Dragging the long cold chain of life for itself,
And the cold speed of its terror,
And the drops of itself massaging into the corridor.
How it spreads under the harrow with no cry!
How it breaks into the bird's beak!
And what sublime sleep, oh marvellous fortitude,
Ever could breed these quiet pallid delving fancies?

And it was joy, one tells me, joy to die,
Moaning and tugging in terror of her condition,
With a thin grip around my ankle out of the turf,
Sinking into the majority, wobbling reminiscences,
And here they come again! because it's the nighttime,
Gelatinous bundles nozzled with portraits
Unconvincing and terrifying, but how many lie there!

You never actually saw one, do you think it's true?
Look for the truth in the lawn, one said, and I don't
    doubt she's found it.

Now somebody melts . . . but thinking of death got them
    this way
That's what you're saying, in these environs,
These parts of the mind, any mind, these fancies,
Thinking of horrors created them horrors.
Love frightens them, so let's frighten them.
It frightens them because it's so mysterious.
It frightens me. You are a shapely white.
Oh, I droop with admiration. No, no, I spring!
That kills them . . . and are you really there?
Yes, especially there. What happens then?
It makes them so thin. They are gone from themselves.
Did I frighten you then? Everyone fears.
Two is a round reality. Dead is a nonsense.
But a real one. And one of us is dead.

DECREATOR

Grown-up idiot, see the slow-motion of him,
And that slow-motion sludge of a tongue
Coiling along its stream of happenings,
Head lolling and tongue lolling,
Sudden brightenings, lurches. He was brisk,
Carried his headpiece like a haughty dish,
Suddenly his brain churned thick
And with a dull chime his brain turned over
A clucking and he sat down suddenly.
His poll curdled with a dull clack,
Cocked listening, a crooked cork of the neck,
A lid flipped. Not a spatter of larks
Rising, cheerily callous and irresponsible, nor
    melodramatic
Red entrails labouring, living brain split
All over, like a hairnet, bolting out of the ears –
Though the red mouth chewed, clack,
And the raw eyes soaked suddenly –
But a dull cluck and a dull kind of clay twisted
And skeined into a surprise and twirled up to
And round and round a wide stare.

Thereafter he was to wander
With a hesitation at either elbow
And a little free-wheeling spittle
Through a kind of pastoral, in the parks of patrons,
By their dusty greenhouses, bubbling glassy streams,
Springing up in odd corners, by snivelly taps,
Serious avenues. Their doves
Would babble off their lawns at him, their crones
Croon to him over the spinning,
Their tapping blind pensioners fall nodding as he came
    up to them
Leaky-lipped, faulty, and no part of it at all.
For one ordinary Sunday strolling
He looked down himself as with a dull crash
His brain fell several floors and stopped
And he sat down suddenly. It was a glance
From the sinewy confident husband and the rolling pram
Hooded like a whelk and pearly, started it, its scrap
Of white meat and fluff lodged in recesses and the
    woman
Fluffed on the man's arm
Like a floss of him, and he an elbow of her,
And the face-bone with its marrow of eyes,
Stare-marrow, and the lurking look in the whelk,
The same look, and all six with the one stare,
One flesh with six eyes, one person
In three stares, and the creation all rolled of it,
And he looked down himself and the creation trundled
Uphill at him and he looked
Down at himself and he sat down
Suddenly and his brain dropped several storeys
Burst the front door and pitched away downhill.

THE SERMON

Minister: Dearly beloved. I should say, Friends!

Coming events! God will roast the globe like a goose on a spinning spit, the tiny mites of men will lie enfolded and faceless in the crackling of its crust, he will come with his hot knives and trumpets and carve the steaming tender flesh of its rocks and lick them up with smacking lips of fire, the savoury crisp much praised in his mouth, and his coming, so great he is, will seem like the dripping upon us of galaxies before the fire takes us all. Repent! Repent!

Congregation: But you told us before that God suffered for us, that his face was webbed with tears for our loss.

Minister: I was coming to that.

Ah, brethren. In the fear and terror I struck you all with just then, in the gracious sweat I drew from under your hairlines like cool and pure spring water that leaps from a tap in clean arched crystal staves, in the shivers I clothed you with like sackcloth, it was but the fear of death I gave you to give you back again the appetite for life.

Appetite for life, friends . . . in all your pantings, your teemings, your pantings, the green roofs of your fields, the juices of the laid grasses, the soft beds of feathery hay in the sun and of haymaking feathers in the night-time, in all of these you may sometimes meet God – in the city's symphony of bedsprings on spring nights under the peppery sky twirling with stars, in the white soft babies waited on hand and foot, in the bedrooms and in the bedsprings . . .

Congregation: We don't understand at all. Didn't he make us? Isn't he above and beyond us? Doesn't he live in heaven, out there? If he's infinite how does he get into our houses? How does he know what goes on down here?

Minister: I was coming to that. Yes indeed, he is above and beyond us all. But how does he get to us, how does he know what goes on? Why, he feels the hydrogen bomb like a little prick in his foot; he knows it all through that little shard of awareness, of god-power, of *soul*, he put in each one of us – rather like the barb and bud of a nerve-ending to him. It is a bright crystal and splinter of understanding in each of us that he could not and would not destroy any more than he would pluck out one of his own all-working fingers.

Congregation: But then tell us why he came to earth, if he's within us each from birth.

Minister: I was coming to that.

If you poked your finger in an ants'-nest could *you* get a good idea of their lives, how they live? Would you suddenly become a sav-ant? No, you'd get bitten, and the teeming sooty little creatures would scuttle all up your wrist and down your shirt-collar and you'd have a hell of a picnic. In us, God is blistered and bitten by the ants'-nest of nature, its hissing acid teeth and lies, its dirt and greenery, its love and venery, its steaming hay-quilts and its uncovered and dangerous well-shafts. Every suicide is a nasty shock to him, every motor-smash a new tooth-mark, every rocket into the sky a little dart in his side.

We then are God's littlest fingertip, our world is formed and built up around him, our ploughed fields are his looped thumb-prints, so are our ridged and whorled streets, our roundabouts, our sweating neon circuses.

But – he visited all this, he visited it with his eyes, and left the heavens empty as concentration upon the pages of a book dims the stars. He held up, you see, the tips of his working fingers, they were smarting, they stung, he came to heal them, not to finger in the dark any more, but to see what he was doing for a moment – and may he not have been a little surprised by what he found on his fingers? It was as though he were riding a bicycle – look! no hands – and in his visitation had suddenly gripped the handlebars. And it's a *good* ride – look at our tools, our machines, our skyscrapers, our friends of the American continent, our technical economy . . .

Congregation: How lovely! Now tell us again about the day of judgment. You tell it all so gloriously.

Minister: I was coming to that. And I will tell you what I see in my dreams.

It is the valley of dry bones. A dry, long valley. Heaped bones, like an ancient massacre. A dust-coloured sky, burning hot, coppery. Then, at the tip of the valley, a shaft of real sunlight, sunshine. It begins to cross the splintery ground towards me. A small white figure seems to carry it; it swings with him, like a caber. It is a naked child, a toddler, struggling over the burning rock. He picks his way over the scattered bones, and, in his wake, they stir, twitch, flip on their ends, and fly together like filings in a magnet's field, bone to bone. Sinews spread over them, flesh creeps upwards, eyelids blink on the flayed flaces, and skin whitens and flexes there like hot milk. A host of them stands, and where they stand the young grass begins pricking through the rocky soil, so that soon they throng, and breathe, in a great green moist meadow, a mighty host of men and animals. Ezekiel 37.

Then the fleecy clouds in the new, blue, summery sky gather, and pile up and up into a great white chasm, and the naked child behind whom these hosts have sprung to life begins to climb up and up the bolstered clouds. Angels appear, with their staring golden eyes, nodding like sunflowers large as planets. The child totters up to eternity, past the steeps of the sky, past the hills of angels, and his eyes blaze with authority. Up and over (say) poor Mr Jackson, on his newly-assembled knees and wearing them out already. The infant is a boy, and strides higher, over the toad that has popped its thin white wits into their sockets to hear the angels sing, and has jumped back into its sloppy-throated skin. The boy is a youth who strides higher and higher, over our drowned dapper friend Pincher Martin, his bones rolled here by the sea, who shoves on the red-lined gloves of his hands, adjusts his heavy casque of bones and brains, and strolls out to kneel to the tiers of madrigalists, the Shining Ones piled over the sky with throats of power, that sing dead pigeons spurting out of the turf . . . and above all their heads the youth becomes a man, beard flickering at the lips, and the man strides up and beyond the limits of sight, up the white-hot rock-hard funnel of witnesses, to fetch his father . . .

Something is coming with a deep note . . .

Closing all eyes as it comes . . . both men and angels burst with praise as the father nears, nothing but sealed eyes and adoration in the fire of him, with the eschewment of flesh, and the basting of tears . . .

Congregation: This is good comfort. We tremble and glow. But what of comfort down here – below?

Minister: I was coming to that precisely, to give you real and immediate comfort. Of such is the kingdom of heaven. Mark 10. And here is his special dispensation and mercy, the Secret, the innermost heart of the forest.

You think you're going to age, fall apart, get dusty and grey, smell, plunge into a wallow of decrepitude, a slough of incontinence, annoy little girls with rattling sweetiebags, wet your pants at the flash of a white skirt and the rumble of a baby-carriage with longing for the starchy lap of a young plump nursemaid, lose your tongue in your teeth mumbling old sockets for gamey meat-shreds and sit speechless, death's worst, winding-sheets, and tumbling to decay – but it's not so.

You see, *we live backwards*!

Haven't you noticed? We start as angels, spirits, pure souls – little children. When we grow up – maybe not so good. And in some of us the orient and immortal wheat gets ground exceeding small. But we've got the memory of it. So isn't it best and wisest to have the reward first, so nothing can spoil it? To live first and pay later? I know you all must have many things at home you've bought without paying for. That television set? The mortgage? The very clothes you stand up in? Feel the nap of the cloth. It's somebody else's. You're paying for it now. But nobody can take your childhood away from you. Your reward is safe. You've had it! For I dare hazard a guess that there is nobody here who has not at some time, it may be in the distant past, it may be yesterday or last week, nobody who has not been a child of some sort or another. You may not quite make it when you're grown up, but never mind. Little angels.

Congregation: All this is a great comfort. But tell us, reconcile us to that bomb. It hovers over our heads like a spiteful thumb.

Minister: I was coming to that.

O, my dear, dear brethren and friends, let me once again appeal to you, let me try. Do not worry what happens to your flesh, your mere bodies. Go back to your lives, deliver your babies into their reward, it is God's work. Shift the lead out of your pants. What happens to your flesh, your tissues, can only a little rust the bright white metal of your souls, a little dust it, obfuscate, occlude, corrode, but only a little, constipate, tie it in knots, it cannot *kill* it, not even in the great blaze of pain, the sheet of lightning, the great sheet of agony, and remember it is God's pain, our blazing agony multiplied by our millions, for him. You have seen the dry burnt corpses of that agony with their poor cindered fists caught up like a boxer's. But God cannot die, and by the same token no more can we! Remember that whatever happens cannot hurt us, because we *are* God − not hurt us permanently, anyway. Brothers − and I am speaking to God − do not sit about wailing here for God's second-coming-before-it-is-too-late − he is already here, and We will be There, each of us a shard of him, a ward of him, a bright, piercing, secure, razor-sharp splinter of him, and heaven . . . where no moth nor rust . . . Matthew 6 . . . We are already Here . . . and More of Me arrives every day!

Congregation: We've had enough. This is blasphemy. You are Antichrist. You are the Devil. God is not mocked! In his own house too! And I saw a beast rise up out of the sea, having seven heads and ten horns, and upon his heads the name of blasphemy; and there was given unto him a mouth speaking great things and blasphemies. Revelation 13. You can't carry on like this in our church! You can't carry on like this in our church!

Minister: But I was coming to that—

What I am asking you to do, friends, IS to carry on before it is too late, before we are all snatched back to God from whom we came, and who frightens us so; before we're all snapped back like elastic, blown up back to God whom we will not understand, any more than the clippings understand the toenail; snatched back away from life as we know it − I am asking you, all of you, whoever you are, cutthroats, croupiers, cripples, blacksmiths, wordsmiths, birdsmiths, birdbathmakers, billiard-markers, in-patients, waiters, head-waiters, hairdressers, hairy or hairless, bright or stupid, good-headed or beheaded, I am asking you, friends, whatever it all means, whoever is right, whatever explanation we use − to − carry on, so *some* good can come of it, to carry on, to experiment, as I am doing, good my dear sweet world, to carry on, to carry on . . .

THE CASE

for Roy Hart

'Man . . . is an experiment and a transition. He is nothing else
than the narrow and perilous bridge between nature and spirit.
His innermost destiny drives him on to the spirit and to God.
His innermost longing draws him back to nature, the mother.
Between the two forces his life hangs tremulous and irresolute.'

Hermann Hesse, *Steppenwolf*

I am a gardener,
A maker of trials, flowers, hypotheses.
I water the earth.
I raise perfumes there.
Mother told me to stand, and I did so,
Stepping towards the window in which she sat.
'Now, did you find him, your other half?
And mine,' she said, and I shook my head:
'No, my time is so short and I'll take no oath.'
'You've just taken one, by standing,
My dear one,' she said, and she told me how the stars
Had said as much, and I concurred and saw
How the crystalware of the polished table,
The cabinets of glass things walling the room,
The tall roses beyond the glass, the gloss of the table,
Had said as much in sunshine from my first tottering.
So she lifted my hand and kissed it and said I was to be
    celibate,
And this was great good fortune and I was a good child
For I had a quest and few had as much.
The roses nodded.

So I became a gardener,
A maker of prayers, flowers, hypotheses.
A gardener 'washed in my fertile sweat',
My hair of an opulent brown 'like the Lord's,
That makes you think of fertile fields'.
And among the flowers, in the walled garden, 'This is life!'
    she cried,
'What a shame, oh what a shame,' she said,
'What a shame we have to die,' she cried, all
The flowers pumping and pumping their natures into her,
Into her nostrils, winged wide, she leaning,

Leaning back, breathing deeply, blushing deeply,
Face shining and deep breath and tall brick
Holding the air still and the heat high in a tall room.

And I swam in the thunderstorm in the river of blood, oil
     and cider,
And I saw the blue of my recovery open around me in the
     water,
Blood, cider, rainbow, and the apples still warm after sunset
Dashed in the cold downpour, and so this mother-world
Opened around me and I lay in the perfumes after rain out
     of the river
Tugging the wet grass, eyes squeezed, straining to the glory,
The burst of white glory like the whitest clouds rising to
     the sun

And it was like a door opening in the sky, it was like a
     door opening in the water,
It was like the high mansion of the sky, and water poured
     from the tall french windows.
It was like a sudden smell of fur among the flowers, it was
     like a face at dusk
It was like a rough trouser on a smooth leg. Oh, shame,
It was the mother-world wet with perfume. It was
     something about God.
And she stood there and I wanted to tell her something
     and she was gone.
It was something about God. She stood smiling on the wet
     verge
And she waited for me to tell her but she was gone.
And three gusts of hot dry air came almost without sound
Through the bushes, and she went. Through the bushes
Of blown and bruised roses. And she went. And the bushes
     were blown
And the gusts were hot, dry air, nearly black with perfume,
Alive with perfume. Oh shame. It was like an
     announcement,
Like an invitation, an introduction, an invitation, a quick
     smile in the dusk.
It was like a door opening on a door of flowers that
     opened on flowers that were opening.
It was like the twist of a rosy fish among lily-pads that
     were twisting on their deep stems.

The rosy goldfish were there in the dusky pond, but she
was gone.
It was something about God. My hand made a wet door in
the water
And I thought of something I knew about God. My
mother
Stared at me from the pool over my shoulder and when I
turned she was gone.
Then the wind blew three hot dry gusts to me through the
broken rose-bushes
And she came to me dusky with perfume and I walked
toward her
And through her, groping for her hand. And it was
something about God.
And I searched in my head for it with my eyes closed. But
it was gone.

And I became a gardener, a hypothesiser, one who would
consult his sensations,
For 'we live in sensations and where there are none there is
no life',
One with the birds that are blue-egged because they love
the sky!
With the flocks of giraffes craning towards the heavens!
With the peacocks dressed in their love for the high sun
And in their spectra of the drifting rains, one
With the great oaks in my keeping that stretched up to
touch God!
And one who could look up gladly and meet God's gaze,
His wide blue gaze, through my blood, as I think;
And God was silent and invisible and I loved him for it,
I loved him for his silent invisibility, for his virile restraint,
And I was one with my peacocks that sent out their wild
cry
Sounding like shrill 'help!' and meaning no such thing,
While my flocks of deer wrote love in their free legs
Their high springy haunches and bounding turf. And they
would pause
And look upwards, and breathe through wide nostrils, and
all day
It was wide and firm and in God's gaze and open: tussock
and turf, long lake,
Reed-sigh, silence and space, pathway and flower furnace
Banked up and breathing.

And the people. And the causeway into the walled garden.
And the people walking in so slowly, on their toes
Through the wide doorway, into the cube of still air,
Into the perspective of flowers, following each other in
  groups,
Gazing around, 'Oh, what shame, to die!' and the great
  doorway
And ourselves, smiling, and standing back, and they
  changed,
Concentrated, concentrating, at the edges of the body, the
  rims
Tighter, clearer, by the sensations of their bodies, solidified,
  bound,
Like the angels, the bodies' knowledge of the flowers
  inbound
Into its tightening and warming at the heart of flowers, the
  fire called
'Then-shall-ye-see-and-your-heart-shall-rejoice-
And-your-bones-shall-sprout-as-the-blade. . . .'

And she was gone. And she lay down like the earth after
  rain.
It was love-talk in every grain. And something about God.
The brick walls creaked in the wind, grain to grain.
And judgment came as the father comes, and she is gone.
Clouds swoop under the turf into the pond, the peacock
  cries
'Help!' strutting in its aurora, love talks
Grain to grain, gossiping about judgment, his coming.
  Ranges
Tumble to boulders that rattle to shingles that ease to wide
  beaches
That flurry to dust that puffs to new dusts that dust
To dusting dust, all talking, all
Gossiping of glory, and there are people
In the gardens, in white shirts, drifting,
Gossiping of shame through the gardens, 'Oh glory!'

Through the gardens. . . . Well, father, is that how you
  come?
Come then.
Whose breath is it that flares through the shrubberies?
Whose breath that returns? Look at the people

All ageing to judgment, all
Agreeing to judgment. Look at that woman
Still snuffing up the flowers. My mother!
Look at her. She bends backwards to the tall flowers, falls.
Her flower-laden breath returns to the skies.
I think this garden is a prayer,
Shall I burn it as an offering?
And I think these people are a prayer,
I think they are a message.
Shall I burn them for their syllable?
There is a fire crying 'shame!' here already!
It mixes dying with flowering.
I think we husk our uttering. I think
We tip it out. Our perfect syllable,
Tripped out over the death-bed, a one,
Round, perfectly-falling silence.
Look how they seek the glory over these flowers!
I wanted to say something about God,
My syllable about God. I think
We are a prayer. I think
He wants his breath back, unhusked
Of all the people, our dying silences.
Our great involuntary promise
Unhusked, flying out into the rain, over the battlefields,
Switching through shrubberies, into the sky. . . .

You press, oh God!
You press on me as I press on an eyeball,
You press sunsets and autumns and dying flowers,
You press lank ageing people in gardens 'Oh shame
To die,' you feather roses and matchflames like wisps of
    your fingers,
Your great sun cuffs age at us. I will bring,
I will bring you in, father, through the bounds of my
    senses,
Face to face, father, through the sockets of my head,
Haul you in, father, through my eyes with my fingers,
Into my head through my eyes, father, my eyes, oh
    my eyes. . . .

To live in the blind sockets, the glorious blunt passages,
Tended by gardeners, nostril, eye, mouth,
Bruised face in a white shirt ageing,
To be called 'Father' and to hear call high

'Oh shame, what a shame, to die' as they see the great
flowers,
To hear the peacock 'help!' that means no such thing,
And to live unseeing, not watching, without judging, called
'Father'.

VI

WORK IN PROGRESS
(1969)

THE OLD WHITE MAN

adapted from a Chinese T'ang Dynasty story

Having immured his new bride
In an inner room without doors or windows
Sunk into the earth, dry but cobwebby,
Through a trapdoor on which he sat guards
Of many years' experience and unlined faces
Save for the two furrows of fighting concentration
As if the prongs of the face stood at midnight, he
Felt he could rest in the open bedroom
With the balcony and straw matting
That plucked the hairline starbeams as it swung.

At three a.m. something blocked the stars
And with a swishing noise of breath
Started up a high breeze which rolled
Him over once, who was so tired.
The guards' alert eyelids flickered.

Suddenly he sprang out of bed,
The guards sprang up, it was a fright
With no cause, why should they wake?
They made sure of that looking for her
And flung up the trap in the wooden floor
With a cruel slap to any sleeper —
But there was none by shouts, nor by lights,
By taking lanterns and peering for escape,
She'd gone, not even a mousehole:
A city gate for mists. Outside
(They made intent to follow) all men were helpless,
A thick fog wadded up the night —
It was the great god had turned his back
And his shadow shone around them in the dawn.
It stayed awhile, then broke up
In pieces with the sun, and flew away.
He swore to stay till she was found.
A military commander after all
He'd use the expedition,
Station here and send out patrols.
A month later they found an embroidered shoe
On a bush some thirty miles off
Quite sopping with the rain, half-rotted.

He moved his camp right up to it,
Let the relic swing in its centre.
The hills were to be scoured by all personnel
And he at their head not flopped in grief
But map-making busily.

In rings they spread out, in bands of thirty,
He working like the rest. All rock.
All rock and ridge and high bare cliff
With torrents bounding on the rock
Flexing like basketwork to stones.
The cliffs it seemed had shaken out their ridges,
The ridges had shuddered off their stones like houses
And anything rubbed finer than house-size
Hurled away quick by water or wind-torrent.
So nothing grew, like a beach of pebbles
And they nits on a mouseskin. Seventy miles
Of this from the camp they reached a peak
Where they could see a green tree-clad mountain
Higher and more thunderous than the rest
With jungle at its roots and temperate pine
In broad bands up its flanks
And scudding misty snowland at its crown,
The peak missing in the sky.
The jungle was cleft in gorges full of water
Rushing along like busy traffic
The trees seemed full of people in bright colours
Chattering and laughing among the man-sized leaves,
The boles marched away among the undergrowth of
    bushes
Linked to the tree-tops with swinging vines
And there seemed a flow of shapes just out of sight
Where the beasts slunk or the sunlight scattered,
They couldn't tell. They had to build bridges
And toiled easily being men of war
With faces set at midnight, up, till it was cooler
To the temperate terraces, and the tang of pine.
There by a cliff and a new swinging bridge
They set camp for a day and rested
Having been a week up on these slopes
And glad to have high level ground beneath them.

And rested, and yet could not rest,
Not for worry of their commander's bride
Untouched except by pleasant jests
But for something just out of hearing
A sort of pipe like bats or twitter in the ears
A tinkling like hanging shapes of glass
And to straining eyes a flutter through the trees,
A waterfall perhaps on a gusty ledge,
A broad, spasmodic waterfall, or a plantation
Of flowering bushes, maybe, whose colours
Turned over, appeared or disappeared in wind,
In the soft wind through the warm pines,
And, yes, just at the edge of scent too
Perhaps, just, a new perfume?
It tickled at their senses all that night
As though they saw and heard and smelt
Through a deep silver bowl of reflections
And just at the rim something moved
Glimpsed stretching, hinting and – teasing?
But being the men they were all obeyed
And got a good night's sleep among the needles
With the portable shrine set up among them
And the veiled god watching over their prayers
And watching through the night of – tickling?

Night and their dreams and long soldierly celibacy
Gave them the answer by guessing long before
The wooden fretted houses and broad walks
Of avenues trained in shade; the second guess too
Of flowering bushes had been correct but
In such profusion and piled high
In banks and cloudworks of perfume
And many flowers to their amazed
And eye-rubbing senses had detached
And glided in shapes between their bushes,
Thronged avenues with their scent and with
Their high flower-speech talked. They sang
And laughed too; this took all their surprise
From them as well for none showed through
When the band of men went up to a dawdling group
That had stopped to stare and explained their
    business.

'Your wife has been here over a month,'
The first words, and no surprise,
'Just now resting in bed for the child
Is strong and tires her with his jumping,
But you can go and look at her.'
He had lost his anger with surprise,
His senses were so full perhaps
And let himself be led across a courtyard
And through a stone door and through wooden gates
Through an enclosure open to the pine-patterned sky
Where flowers in banks and flower-patterned couches
Vied in profusion with all their colours.

Their air was heavy with all their colours
And the cries of rejoicing of the bees
And among them all in that enclosure
One white flower raised her head eating
And smiled over creamy plums and gourds
And signed for him to leave.

The first woman said:
'Some of us have been here ten years already,
While your wife has only just arrived.
This is where our master lives. He is a match
Face to face for a hundred armed men even.
We must go behind his back, where his shadow is.
Slip away before he comes back but let us have
Forty gallons of strong wine, several dozen
Catties of hemp, and ten dogs
For him to eat. That will hold him.
Come at noon, no earlier, ten days from now.
Now leave quickly.'

Back to their camp on the lowest terrace
To be over-rested and tormented,
Tinklings and flashes through the trees,
Thoughts at night how they might send down a party
Of flowered silken night-visitors,
And thunder growling from the summit
And the nature of the god keeping them back.

At last ten days had moved along the pine-needle floor
In sunblades, and quiet-walking they returned
With strong liquor, dogs and skeins of hemp.

The woman said:
'Our master is very wise and godlike
And a great drinker and likes
To try out stupidity by drinking.
He loves to test his strength when he is silly
And gets us, laughing at us, to tie him down
To his couch with silks all twisted
Then he frees himself with a leap.
But once we bound him
In silks twisted in threes together
And it took him two leaps to get up.
His body is like iron, but he protects his groin.
We think hemp within the silk will keep him down.'
She pointed to a gorge: 'Hide there – it is the food-
    store.
Be patient and quiet. Put the wine by the flowers
And tether all ten dogs
At the fringes of the forest-walk.'
They crouched under cheeses, salted joints and bales,
And did not like the salted joints, nor waiting
Like food among food. Late that afternoon
A something like a streamer of white silk
That seemed painted across with black letters
Fluttered from a distant peak
Straight to a cave just there on the hillside.

After a pause a fine old man
Six foot with a long white beard
Emerged all dressed in white robes
With a peeled staff in his hand
Walking firmly and with dignity
And attended by the women.
At the sight of the dogs he gave a great start
Then leapt on one tearing it limb from limb
Amid the squealing barks and bounding pack
Tethers cracking like whips but holding
Stuffing his mouth full of slippery flesh
Spitting the fur out stuffing the pink
Dog after dog until they'd gone
Then rounded on the women grinning
Patting a new paunch, laughing.
The smiling women offered him wine from jade cups
And sighing he lay back on the grass all caked with
    blood

Beard black as a young man's with it
Clotted to the sleeves, and the women
Gathered around and sat down with the wine-jugs
Joking and laughing as they must have done
At many feasts of this kind. When in the sun
He'd drunk several pints of wine, they helped
Him in, the women, deep into the cave
And sounds of merriment and laughter
Singing and the gong-sound
Of the master's voice wound out. He seemed
To speak like a chorus of clear frosty deep voices,
Like a chime of gongs. He laughed to split their ears,
A boulder fell and bounded off down the mountain,
The women chimed and tinkled, against his,
It seemed, very far away and faint.
The cave-mouth like a pool of ink.

The cave-mouth like a pool of ink, and soon
Shadows and lights gathered in it
And round the corner torch-bearing women
Their shadows bending like leathern shapes
Appeared, beckoning them in.
They drew swords and walked cautiously
Through the rock, shadows flexing over its wall.
Around the turn the tunnel fattened suddenly
And was a blaze of light and warm air
And here were flowers in banks too, cut flowers
Withering a little in the heat, and on a flowered couch
Tied by silk garments caught in stout knots
Tied by the corded arms by cords as thick
Cords of flowers that bulged and strained
Glaring, an ape, a white-skinned ape.
Or looked like an ape. In his prime
At the height of his powers whatever it was
Presented to their senses stiff with their limits
A hale old man, and now, declining, an ape
With white lips spread thin on its great jaws
And sparkling teeth, and the beard that rolled to its
    chest
Abundant fur, now entwined with flowers
Crushed by his heavy straining.

The soldiers fell on it with their blades driving
Their brows set at blackest midnight
But the blades rebounded as though they had
Attacked boulders – one laid his own shoulder open
With clanging and ringing. Alas
They remembered as the ape strained like the
　　mountainside
Itself in its basketwork of torrents
And he, the husband, sighted along his blade
And plunged it to the roots in the only softness
Through the groin, deep into the bone.
The gentle blood spurted and fell with a patter
On the flowered silk of the bed.

The ape gave a long sigh and said to the husband
'The will of heaven, the will of heaven –
Otherwise I am immortal. Your wife, your wife
Is pregnant, don't kill the child, he is
Mine, will be great,' and died.

That was that. The great body lay like a rock
Ready to crumble to soil, and stiffened fast.
They heaved it outside and down the hill
It rolled faster and faster like a great peeled tree-trunk
Bounded off a cliff into the river
Was whirled away. His caves were full
Of treasure and perfume, weapons and silks,
His women all beauties who feted the men,
And helped them carry the Ape's goods down the
　　mountain,
A hundred women, all beauties, enough for a small
　　army.

The village was left to rot in the flowers,
The flowers to fruit and reseed and fight the small
　　pines,
The white strong talons sliding from the husk,
And the tinkling of women passed down the mountain,
And left the houses silent and empty.

He had had them all to himself. He wore white silk.
He would not sleep but took his women
Night after night over and over

Bouncing and dashing between the beds. There was but
   one child,
From the most recent.
The only fruiting, by it he knew
He was to die. He read from a scroll
That went under a stone.
On a clear day he would practice sword-play,
Encircling himself like flashes of fire,
Then a moon-halo. He loved the rich blood of dogs.
He would fly up in the hot noon
As far as the snow-crests, and circle there.
When autumn showed in the flowers, the child leapt,
He knew it was the end. Lightning struck the stone
   step
And singed his fingers and burnt the scroll.
He looked down at the bride and shed tears a while.
The mountain was his and men had never been there,
The beasts in the jungle had kept them away,
The deep gorges and torrents,
But the beasts were all scared and the men could build
   bridges,
And this must be the will of heaven.

HUSH! THE SUN

A warm tawny street. Houses buried in trees,
Broad hollow sunshafts, leaves plump as fruit,
Bright russet walls. Hush burns from the heat,
You can see it, it spreads,
Great cars draw away, like threads in silk.

Up through our window, hung on this hush,
The silences rise, and we fall quiet.
Green mowers spray a deep whitening hay-hush,
Boys play in the street, skip and call out.
One trips in a knee a knock down to the quick;
It lets red silence fall like an idling flag.

He is strung on his cry, tongue high in the mouth
Stretched like a mast; his mouth at full gasp
Brimmed with the hush. The air is too thick,
The summer too broad, too easy, too sweet,

It coils down his throat, he hangs crook'd in its honey,
It glints at his lids, he is strung on its flow
Too golden and sunny, too rolling and hazy
For mere blood to shake, too heavy, too lazy.

Great cars draw away, like threads in silk.

QUASIMODO'S MANY BEDS

My teeth are very bad, but I am not to be blamed for
    that.
I dreamed darkness until I raised my head
And saw the river flowing away from my mouth.
Dearest, your dress seems to be yellow in this sunshine.
I take the ashes of our bonfire and scoop them
Carefully into letters that say this. You run,
And your skirt, swirling, disturbs the script.
How bad are my teeth? Only as evil as an autumn forest.
Should I have them pulled, and gain gums
Pink as a baby's, mouth appropriately searching?
The rain rinses my ashes into the turf and
We have a muddy grey paddock. The rain it is
Consecrates a muddy grey bed, I want you to wear grey
    and ashes.
You stand there still in astonishment
And thus your dress is no longer yellow in the sunshine
But translucent with the rain over the light of your body.
Your great straw hat droops so! Fling it away,
Let's see you snaky, with the rain hissing.

You are in grey, your hands, your head, are ashy.
I caper in front of you over the sodden sheets
With a banana in my mouth. I am a grey bird, with a
    yellow beak, whistling.
I offer you my bill, which you decline with white teeth
In an ashen face. You look crippled.
So I pull my beak in imitation down to its creamy flesh.
It is so easy to look crippled. Here is couched black mud
In rich satin cushions. It is washable disfigurement.
We are all mire, and we are all clean, and this is a
    Quasimodo's bed.
Great things, like you, or water or sun, mire or ashes,

Or any little thing, pull my heart out of shape
Which is no deformity. I sit, enthroned in mud
Like an opulent person watching. Lounge through your
    wardrobe.
And come, never fear. I like you far better in black than
    red.

VII

DR FAUST'S SEA-SPIRAL SPIRIT

(1972)

CHRISTIANA

for Barbara

That day in the Interpreter's house, in one of his Significant
 Rooms,
There was naught but an ugly spider hanging by her hands on
 the wall,
And it was a spacious room, the best in all the house.
'Is there but one spider in all this spacious room?'
And then the water stood in my eyes
And I thought how like an ugly creature I looked
In what fine room soever I was,
And my heart crept like a spider.

And my heart crept like a spider into the centre of my web
And I sat bell-tongued there and my sound
Was the silvery look of my rounds and radii,
And I bent and sucked some blood, but I did it
With care and elegance like a crane unloading vessels;
I set myself on damask linen and I was lost to sight there,
And I hugged my legs astride it, wrapping the pearl-bunch
 round;
I skated on the water with legs of glass, and with candystriped
 legs
Ran through the dew like green racks of glass cannonball;
And I saw myself hanging with trustful hands
In any room in every house, hanging on by faith
Like wolfhounds that were dwarfs, or stout shaggy oats,
And I wept to have found so much of myself ugly
In the trustful beasts that are jewel-eyed and full of clean
 machinery,
And thought that many a spacious heart was ugly
And empty without its tip-toe surprise of spiders
Running like cracks in the universe of a smooth white ceiling,
And how a seamless heart is like a stone.
And the Interpreter saw
The stillness of the water standing in her eyes,
And said,
Now you must work on Beelzebub's black flies for Me.

95

MINERALS OF CORNWALL, STONES OF CORNWALL

A case of samples

Splinters of information, stones of information,
Drab stones in a drab box, specimens of a distant place,
Granite, galena, talc, lava, kaolin, quartz,
Landscape in a box, under the dull sky of Leeds –
One morning was awake, in Cornwall, by the estuary,
In the tangy pearl-light, tangy tin-light,
And the stones were awake, these ounce-chips,
Had begun to think, in the place they came out of.

Tissues of the earth, in their proper place,
Quartz tinged with the rose, the deep quick,
Scrap of tissue of the slow heart of the earth,
Throbbing the light I look at it with,
Pumps slowly, most slowly, the deep organ of the earth;
And galena too, snow-silvery, its chipped sample
Shines like sun on peaks, it plays and thinks with the mineral
    light,
It sends back its good conclusions, it is exposed,
It sends back the light silked and silvered,
And talc, and kaolin, why they are purged, laundered,
As I see the white sand of some seamless beaches here
Is laundered and purged like the whole world's mud
Quite cleansed to its very crystal; talc a white matt,
Kaolin, the white wife of Cornwall
Glistening with inclusions, clearly its conclusions
Considered and laid down, the stone-look
Of its thoughts and opinions of flowers
And turf riding and seeding above it in the wind,
Thoughts gathered for millennia as they blossomed in millions
Above its then kaolin-station within the moor,
The place of foaming white streams and smoking blanched
    mountains.
Asbestos had found this bright morning
Its linear plan of fibres, its simple style,
Lay there, declaring, like the others;
Granite, the great rock, the rock of rocks,
At home now, flecked green, heavily contented in its box,
Riding with me high above its general body,

The great massif, while its fellows, the hills of it
Rise high around us; nor was lava silent
Now it remembered by glistening in this light
Boiling, and was swart with great content

Having seen God walking over the burning marl, having seen
A Someone thrusting his finger into the mountainside
To make it boil – here is the issue of this divine intrusion,
I am the issue of this divine intrusion,
My heart beats deep and fast, my teeth
Glisten over the swiftness of my breath,
My thoughts hurry like lightning, my voice
Is a squeak buried among the rending of mountains,
I am a mist passing through the crevices of these great seniors
Enclosed by me in a box, now free of the light, conversing
Of all the issue this homecoming has awakened in the stone
    mind
The mines like frozen bolts of black lightning deep in the
    land
Saying, and the edge of their imaginings cuts across my mind:
We are where we were taken from, and so we show ourselves
Ringing with changes and calls of fellowship
That call to us ton to ounce across Cornish valleys.

The valleys throng with the ghosts of stone so I may scarcely
    pass,
Their loving might crush, they cry out at their clumsiness,
Move away, death-dealing hardnesses, in love.
The house is full of a sound of running water,
The night is a black honey, crystals wink at the brim,
A wind blows through the clock, the black mud outside
Lies curled up in haunches like a sleeping cat.

SHADOW-SILK

Rapid brothy whispers in the bed.
It was like silk splitting in me.
The house is full of the sound of running water.
A wind blows through the clock.
It is like a frail leaf-skeleton
Shivering in a casket.
We are heels over ears in love.

The window-frame blackens.
Below, the trees flood darkly,
The wind butts in the curtain
A doddering forehead.
We have a one candle.
Your hair is like a weir,
Or fields of posture,
In terrace upon terrace
Rising forest murmur,
And across the garden
Frothily flows the ghost.
The night is black honey,
Presses hard on the glass.
A sudden set! The stars are out.
This is too much; adventuring nectars
Wink with packed crystals
That hang depth upon depth
Age clotting the frame.
I must close this picture-book.
I must wade through these shadows.
Black springs from the corners
Brim the quartz-crystals
Engorge the ewers
Flood from the cupboards
Soaking the dresses
Pile under the bed
In black satin cushions.
That candle is unsnuffable!
We are afloat!
But the ring on your finger
Spins without stirring,
I pad through the undertow
Reach out and close
That heavenly almanac.
Our wonder still lingers
Over the covers
As within the pages
All the stars glitter.
A wind blows through the clock
And across the garden
Frothily flows the ghost.

THE MOON DISPOSES

Perranporth Beach

The mountainous sand-dunes with their gulls
Are all the same wind's moveables,
The wind's legs climb, recline,
Sit up gigantic, we wade
Such slithering pockets our legs are half the size,
There is an entrance pinched, a plain laid out,
An overshadowing of pleated forts.
We cannot see the sea, the sea-wind stings with sand,
We cannot see the moon that swims the wind,
The setting wave that started on the wind, pulls back.

Another slithering rim, we tumble whirling
A flying step to bed, better than harmless,
Here is someone's hoofprint on her hills
A broken ring with sheltering sides
She printed in the sand. A broken ring. We peer from
   play.

Hours late we walk among the strewn dead
Of this tide's sacrifice. There are strangled mussels:
The moon pulls back the lid, the wind unhinges them,
They choke on fans, they are bunched blue, black band.
The dead are beautiful, and give us life.
The setting wave recoils
In flocculence of blood-in-crystal,
It is medusa parched to hoofprints, broken bands,
Which are beautiful, and give us life.
The moon has stranded and the moon's air strangled
And the beauty of her dead dunes sent us up there
Which gave us life. Out at sea
Waves flee up the face of a far sea-rock, it is a pure
   white door
Flashing in the cliff-face opposite,
Great door, opening, closing, rumbling open, moonlike
Flying open on its close.

INTIMATE SUPPER

He switched on the electric light and laughed,
He let light shine in the firmament of his ceiling,
He saw the great light shine around and it was good,
The great light that rilled through its crystalline pendentives,
And marvelled at its round collection in a cheval glass,
And twirled the scattered crystal rays in his champagne glass.
He spun the great winds through his new hoover
And let light be in the kitchen and that was good too
For he raised up the lid of the stock-pot
And dipped a deep spoon in the savours that were rich
And swarming, and felt the flavours live in his mouth
Astream with waters. He danced to the fire and raked it and
    created red heat
And skipped to the bathroom and spun the shining taps
Dividing air from the deep, and the water, good creature,
Gave clouds to his firmament for he had raked the bowels
Of the seamy coal that came from the deep earth.
And he created him Leviathan and wallowed there,
Rose, and made his own image in the steamy mirrors
Having brooded over them, wiping them free
Again from steamy chaos and the mist that rose from the deep,
But the good sight faded
For there was no help, no help meet for him at all,
And he set his table with two stars pointed on wax
And with many stars in the cutlery and clear crystal
And he set thereon fruits of the earth, and thin clean bowls
For the clear waters of the creatures of earth that love to be
    cooked,
And until the time came that he had appointed
Walked in his garden in the cool of the evening, waited.

YOUNG WOMEN WITH THE HAIR
OF WITCHES AND NO MODESTY

'I loved Ophelia!'

I have always loved water, and praised it.
I have often wished water would hold still.
Changes and glints bemuse a man terribly:

There is champagne and glimmer of mists;
Torrents, the distaffs of themselves, exalted, confused;
And snow splintering silently, skilfully, indifferently.
I have often wished water would hold still.
Now it does so, or ripples so, skilfully
In cross and doublecross, surcross and countercross.
A person lives in the darkness of it, watching gravely;

I used to see her straight and cool, considering the
    pond,
And as I approached she would turn gracefully
In her hair, its waves betraying her origin.
I told her that her thoughts issued in hair like
    consideration of water,
And if she laughed, that they would rain like spasms
    of weeping,
Or if she wept, then solemnly they held still,
And in the rain, the perfumes of it, and the blowing
    of it,
Confused, like hosts of people all shouting.
In such a world the bride walks through dressed as a
    waterfall,
And ripe grapes fall and splash smooth snow with
    jagged purple,
Young girls grow brown as acorns in their rainy
    climb towards oakhood,
And brown moths settle low down among ivories
    wet with love.
But she loosened her hair in a sudden tangle of
    contradictions,
In cross and doublecross, surcross and countercross,
And I was a shadow in the twilight of her late
    displeasure
I asked water to stand still, now nothing else holds.

A SMALL DEATH

My friend was gone. The sob wouldn't come.
They blow as they please. I owed her a sob.
It sank back into ashes. I tried again
It sank parching in vain. My friend was gone.
She wouldn't end. I couldn't begin.

I sealed my eyes shut. There photos awoke
Where she nodded and talked along a green walk,
Eloquent bee-hives, my rose pinned to her dress,
A shadowy face under a wide straw hat,
A sundial of sandstone warm with its time-telling.
The sob began, I fostered, obeyed it,
It reamed in my throat as she nodded and talked
Then turned under me gasping.

Seed brawled in my groin as she turned to me gasping;
My groin stung alight; the filament faded.
I woke from this stillness into a stillness,
Aching godseed of stars, a vase of black flowers, an
    empty armchair,
A night-laden window. I was emptied, quite emptied
Of a small distress. I looked down: one tear
Hung on a lash. It stretched to my cheek,
Snapped, sparkled and sank.
The sob wouldn't come. I owed her a sob.
My friend was gone. But she wouldn't end
I couldn't begin

THE YOUTHFUL SCIENTIST
REMEMBERS

After a day's clay my shoes drag like a snail's skirt
And hurt as much on gravel. You have mud on your jersey,
This pleases me, I cannot say why. Summer-yolk
Hangs heavy in the sky, ready to rupture in slow swirls,
Immense custard: like the curious wobbly heart
Struggling inside my pink shirt. Spring is pink, predominately,
And frothy, thriving, the glorious forgotten sound of healing,
And cheering, all shouting and cheering. With what inwardness
The shadows of autumn open, brown and mobile as cognac,
And the whole of my beer comes reeling up to me in one
    great amber rafter
Like a beam of the purest sun, well-aged; as it travels the grass
The dead smile an immense toothy underground, kindly.
I cannot explain why. You pointed out that the lily
Was somebody's red tail inside their white nightie
                                        So much so

That I am still sober and amazed at the starlight glittering in
   the mud,
I am amazed at the stars, and the greatest wonder of them all
Is that their black is as full as their white, the black
Impends with the white, packing between the white,
And under the hives of silence there are swarms of light,
And padded between black comb, struggling white.

I cannot explain this, with the black as full as the bright,
The mud as full as the sunlight. I had envisaged
Some library of chemistry and music
With lean lithe scores padding the long pine shelves,
Plumage of crystal vials clothing strong deal tables;
Had thought that the stars would only tug at me slightly,
Or sprinkle thin clear visions about me for study –
Instead you point at that flower, your dress fits like a clove.

THE IDEA OF ENTROPY AT
MAENPORTH BEACH

'C'est elle! Noire et pourtant lumineuse.'

To John Layard

A boggy wood as full of springs as trees.
Slowly she slipped into the muck.
It was a white dress, she said, and that was not right.
Leathery polished mud, that stank as it split.
It is a smooth white body, she said, and that is not right,
Not quite right; I'll have a smoother,
Slicker body, and my golden hair
Will sprinkle rich goodness everywhere.
So slowly she backed into the mud.

If it were a white dress, she said, with some little black,
Dressed with a little flaw, a smut, some swart
Twinge of ancestry, or if it were all black
Since I am white, but – it's my mistake.
So slowly she slunk, all pleated, into the muck.

The mud spatters with rich seed and ranging pollens.
Black darts up the pleats, black pleats
Lance along the white ones, and she stops
Swaying, cut in half. Is it right, she sobs
As the fat, juicy, incredibly tart muck rises
Round her throat and dims the diamond there?
It is right, so she stretches her white neck back
And takes a deep breath once and a one step back.
Some golden strands afloat pull after her.

The mud recoils, lies heavy, queasy, swart.
But then this soft blubber stirs, and quickly she comes
    up
Dressed like a mound of lickerish earth,
Swiftly ascending in a streaming pat
That grows tall, smooths brimming hips, and steps out
On flowing pillars, darkly draped.
And then the blackness breaks open with blue eyes
Of this black Venus rising helmeted in night
Who as she glides grins brilliantly, and drops
Swatches superb as molasses on her path.

Who is that negress running on the beach
Laughing excitedly with teeth as white
As the white waves kneeling, dazzled, to the sands?
Clapping excitedly the black rooks rise,
Running delightedly in slapping rags
She sprinkles substance, and the small life flies!

She laughs aloud, and bares her teeth again, and cries:
Now that I am all black, and running in my richness
And knowing it a little, I have learnt
It is quite wrong to be all white always;
And knowing it a little, I shall take great care
To keep a little black about me somewhere.
A snotty nostril, a mourning nail will do.
Mud is a good dress, but not the best.
Ah, watch, she runs into the sea. She walks
In streaky white on dazzling sands that stretch
Like the whole world's pursy mud quite purged.
The black rooks coo like doves, new suns beam
From every droplet of the shattering waves,
From every crystal of the shattered rock.
Drenched in the mud, pure white rejoiced,

From this collision were new colours born,
And in their slithering passage to the sea
The shrugged-up riches of deep darkness sang.

THE HOUSE OF TAPS

To P.D.S.

In the house of the Reverend Earth and Dr Waters
Moonlight strikes from the taps.
In the daytime, it is sunlight, full clear beams of it!
When they give water, these faucets, it is holy water,
Or river water, with green shadows of great ship-hulls
    gliding in it.
There are some also that bundle out exceptional ripe golden
    cornsheaves
And blackberries also, and pineapples and nightshade and
    innumerable other kinds of berries.
There is a large curved one like morning glory full of strong
    birdsong
And the smell of woodsmoke mixed with wet nettles.
Others I would not turn on again, not if you paid me, there
    are some
That throw out glittering lead, or rushes of fire,
And these are all made of wood, so that they smoke and
    scorch as they run,
And if they char too far they can never be turned off again.
There is another which is the faucet of pouring darkness, my
    eyes dim,
I grope, can I ever find it again to stop the darkness coming?
And there is yet another and this is the worst that seems to
    give out nothing
But when you look round there are certain articles missing.
But mostly they give out good things, sunshine and earth,
Or milk, or fine silky stuffs that glide out rustling,
The sleepy evening sounds of a town on the edge of the
    country
With rooks cawing as they settle, the clank of a pail, a snatch
    of radio music,
(Though I remember another that turned on a soft and
    continuous cursing
And from it extruded a pallid foul-mouthed person

Whose mouth foamed as I turned him off at the chest . . .)
But so many of them turn out good things, there is no
  majority
Of flowing blood or raw gobbets of flesh, it is mostly
Womansong, a stream of laughter or of salmon or bright
  blue pebbles –
And the lion-headed spigot that gushes mead and mead-hall
  laughter –
There are so many giving moonlight and in the day bright
  sunlight, rich dark barley-wine, and dew . . .
In this house of personages that prefer tenants to use the taps
  and sample the waters
And best of all to install faucets running with their own
  personal tastes and choices,
In the great house of the Reverend Mrs Earth and Doctor Waters

THE HAUNTED ARMCHAIR

'. . . and hid his lord's money . . .' (Matthew 25)

I want it not it not to go wrong. I want nothing to go wrong.
I shall guard and hedge and clip to the end of my days
So that nothing goes wrong. This body, this perfect body
That came from my mother's womb undiseased, wholesome,
No, nothing must go wrong. It is not I. It is not I.
No, it is not I. I is lodged in its head's centre,
Its turret, a little towards its eyes; it is not I, it is not I but it is
  mine
And an over-ranking shame to disease it, to let it disease.
I wash my hands, I wash my hands, I wash my hands once,
  twice, thrice,
I rinse my eyes with the sterile saline; I close, I pull the thick
  curtain,
I close the door and lock it, once, twice, thrice, I sit, I lie, I
  sleep in the great armchair,
And I sleep. Sleep, sleep is the preservative, cultivate sleep, it
  keeps me perfect.
No, no, it is not I; I lives only in the turret;
It is the body, it is the body, it is the body is the loved thing,
It is from my mother, it is my mother's
It came from my mother, it is an organ of the body of my
  mother

And I shall keep it with no rough touch upon it
No rough disease to ramp up and down in it. The world?
And the world? That is the mind's. In the turret. And now I
    will sleep.
I will sleep now, for my body exists. That is enough.
Something wakes me. Is it the fire?
It crackles like a speech. The buffet of winds, the cracks
Of the beams, the taste of the sun, the swimming shark of the
    moon?
No, I think, no, I think, I think I hear time flowing,
No, I think I hear time eroding, the cinder withering in the
    grate,
The grate withering with the time, my hands raised to my eyes
Where my eyes are withering, I look close at my withering
    hands. How long?
How much time have I seen withering? Did I come here
    today?
Suddenly everything grants me withering. Shall I sit here again?
The body is gone. I sit here alone. A nothing, a virgin memory.
A grease-spot. A dirty chair-back.

FRANKENSTEIN IN THE FOREST

'I am afraid for the meat
Of my illegitimate son
In the warm autumn.
When will the lightning come?'
Much wisdom had congregated there
In the open-air laboratory which is a cemetery
Under the great oaks
In the litter of acorns:
Mute parcels of impending forests.
There are grim-mouthed toads
Flocked round a boulder of quartz
Deep, complex and prodigious
That gloams in its depths
And twitches there as with a flutter of lightning.
On a portable radio
The size of a hymn-book
A harpsichord plays Scarlatti,
It suffers an attack of amnesia
As the lightning steers near.

The darkness has eaten everything except his face
The alert wise face
Backed by a view of tossing trees,
The bones of his skull
Are as loose as the leaves of the forest,
'I will send lightning through him
It will live under his skin
It will heal his mouldering
Undead bric-à-brac of other men.
There are so many bibles
Without a crack of light;
Mine has pages of slate
With fossils clearly inscribed,
Leather from racehorses
And crocodiles,
Thin frying leaves of electricity
That lies obediently in its place,
Man-skin, oak-bark and quartz. . . .'
The marble grave-stones
Are covered with equations
In the master's quick black analytick crayon,
Their stone books open at only one page;
'It is my great lightning son
Dressed in metal and bark
And the limbs of departed men,
Lightning peers out of his eyes;
He will heal their mouldering.
It is time
To raise him on the sizzling platform.'
The lightning makes a blue cave of the forest,
It strikes violently at a hawthorn tree,
A sweet smell fills the air,
It has blossomed heavily.
Now the bright blue
Thistling sparks have stuck to his poles,
His crystal machine
Fills with spangled golden oil.
His golden beehives' buzz rises to a wail
And the monster ascends on its winches,
The clouds draw up their heavy black pews
The rain falls
And the lightning services.

The storm clears.

Cloud-men are digging
Deep blue graves in the sky.
Out of the machine steps
The man, mute, complex and prodigious,
His clothes flickering with electricity,
His first murder not due until tomorrow.

THE HALF-SCISSORS

Humming water holds the high stars.
Meteors fall through the great fat icicles.
Spiders at rest from skinny leg-work
Lean heads forward on shaggy head-laces
All glittering from an askew moon in the sky:
One hinge snapped; a white door dislocated.
The night leans forward on this thin window;
Next door, tattered glass,
Wind twittering on jagged edges.
Doors beat like wings wishing to rise.
I lean forward to this thin fire.
A woman leaves – even the flames grow cool –
She is a one hinge snapped, I am a half-scissors.

DR FAUST'S SEA-SPIRAL SPIRIT

For Julie Kendrick

I am frightened. It makes velvet feel too tall.
Its crest peers in at the library window and I cannot open
    the books,
They hug themselves shut like limpets months after it has
    gone.
The roses have learnt to thunder,
They spread petals like peals of red thunder echoing,
The sky looks like blue boxes of white powder being
    smashed by grey fists.
God is an angel in an angel, and a stone in a stone,
But everything enters this, and is gone.
That cry makes everything look afraid
And how small a whisper do we hear of him

Merely the brushing of his outer garment.

It passes pallidly over the meadow
And suddenly it is brilliant with pollen
It will now seek out female fields of flowers
It cannot help that, they will draw him.
It will pass through a field of bulls
And every hair will be stripped
And every bone broken
But the seed will spin on
A column of translucent horn pulled to the cows
Its seething tip.
It will so use a city
For the sake of one woman.

It destroyed an archipelago.
It was selecting human organs and a dhoti.
It reverses direction and is a person
For I have spoken to him, and he inhales deeply
And thinks deeply, and he speaks and he ceases speaking
Then there is an unforgettable perfume on the air
The woman to fit which I will seek for ever,
And an unforgettable tune for her to walk to.

That cry makes everything look afraid.
The bones float up to the ceiling and the iron bar bends.
It strips a whale for its immense bones
And stands the empty meat on its tail.
The rapid alteration of perfumes in it
Will kill with alternation of memories.
It is a shop of carpets furling and unfurling.
The plain pinafores alert themselves
And are a hive of angry spots.
It is a house of wineglasses and towering butter and cabbages
And its scream is the cry of wool under torment
Or a silk scream, and it is constructed like buttons
And I cannot hear what he is saying
For the wool-and-bone
Screaming at me of his buttons.
Yet the practised shaman
Drums until it appears,
Runs up its sides and travels the whole earth over,
Pees over its crown, a magical act
It is his glass ladder to heaven, his magical cannon

That can be fired once only, what nonsense!
Master Alice descended it, inspecting the good things
Arrayed on its shelves, it may also be summoned
By wounding the air upwards
With a rifle, or by burning Dresden
(There it was seen spinning between
Ranks of buildings gustily burning,
Casting light from winged chevrons), or
By laying the Tarot in an anti-clockwise pattern.
I suspect it and its wife are responsible for Moses' head
And the ten great transmissions whose echoes never stop
Piped along the pair of them hurt my head too
Among all the others.
It will also let down as on a four-cornered cloth
Ancient gifts and treasures, such as
A whole slum of Ambergris like a
Giant's pock-marked skull in curly earwax.

God was found with his head poxed to the bone
He had walked through a hungry cloud of it
It is everywhere it is one and many
It is ships of the desert-seas that sail fleets of it
It stands in linked chains on a calm among icebergs
It is playing its enormous chess and takes a berg with one of
    itself
Crashing a boom, and it takes each other
With a twang like a bridge breaking,
At Christmas dinner I have cracked it
Out of the brown dust of a walnut and as the bathwater
    runs out
It tickles my toes, it is manifold behind the iron doors
Of the neglected casemate, swinging
And breathing in restless thickets,
They say space is sewn of it and I have seen it pouring
    through the telescope
There it is at the north pole shining with the moon
And with the midnight sun, go to the south pole you will
    find it there too,
And between them they keep us all spinning
Growing so tall their crests freeze and throw off
Ice-circlets sparkling, flying diadem upon diadem
Called UFO by the observers, scrutinizing our latitudes.
And yet I have known it
Stand still at my right hand long enough

I have opened the little cupboard in its flank
And plucked out the small brown monkey who lives there
Who became my friend and stayed with me a good while.
It wrenched itself from the head, and the head listened with
    its lack,
It wrenched itself from the rock, and the snail crept in its
    wake.
To Red Indians it always carries a dead spider gently in its
    buzzing jaws
As the refugee mother carries her dead baby many miles in
    the dusk.
The anatomist tells me I have a pair of small idols of it set
    in my head
That are the kernel of hearing: the tone-deaf apparition
Is a river on tiptoe, rhythmically digesting its own bed.
But it is also a band of eyes and a solid wall of God
Seeking embrace, and it is the great one from the North
That opens like theatre-curtains and there are four beasts
    marching
With a man on a throne inside, but I know too
That it sets with a click and leaves skimming on the waves
The great pearly nautilus that lets out its sails and scuds
    gently off
Its inhabitant glowing dimly through the thin shell walls
A coil of luminous foam by night and a swimming red bone
    by day.
Thus it seems to me. To itself
It is trees, with high leafy galleries
And scrolls of steel, equation-shaped; a man, bearded,
Strolls up its staircase, a bird
Alights on its branches. With our spiral stairs
We have built it homage, it mounts itself in homage
To its own perfected double helix; that crucifix
Dangling between your breasts is a long-section of it.

Like the unicorn's horn it is male and female at once
And emits waves of all lengths from intense internal friction,
It will make a white sound on your transistor
Though a few notes of church organ might fly together:
Chance will have it so among all the other sounds;
And the electricity that branches through its lacquered walls
Is of a purer fine than armature-power, that whining sham;
You can time a great clock on its global pulse.
It is the pouring tower of pebbles

That walks the coast glittering in the cool evening,
It is trees among trees that are trees
Until it decides to leave the forest by revolution.

But men have pinned the giant down in clocks and churches
I watch its face wounded hour after hour
Behind the glass of my bedside clock,
Hacked into numbers, plucked
By enumerating metal
Welded inside a castle:
Within its fortress-windows rounded axes
Powered by its replica in metal
Chink like milled money
Fiscal time
But I would love to go to the church
And be served by its priest
In whirling petticoats
Where the Host
Greasy with electricities
Flies into our mouths
Like flocks of roasted pigeons.
It changes places
With Job continually.
It carries seven directions in itself
And five elements,
Music, and thunder,
And small gods laughing with patient happiness.

Slice it low down and find a fish
Lower still, granite and chrysoprase
Fairly high, the embryo babe in water
Higher still, his wail winds out of the wound
He travels at youth-speeds
In the slimmer reaches
Moves zodiac-slow with beards
Through the greater girths.
I take a sip
From the cup chained to its waist.
Faust shunted himself.
Indeed he tamed it
Peered through the sea in it
Inspected the mountain for gems.
I saw him bounding over the Carpathians
Like a child on a pogo-stick.

To cheat the devil he was interred in it four hundred years.
Its grip over the land has eased.
Warm summer breezes
Flow from its palm
Faust strolls happily
Through its flowering palms.
At the bow, the atom; at the stern, the zodiac.

The atomic bomb is a bad picture of it, clumsy and without
    versatility,
It discriminates not at all, and there are too many bad things
    to say about it,
I will not spend time on that figment of the thing I am
    talking about.
It hums like a top and its voice smashes volcanoes,
Yet it will burrow and from the riflings of Etna
Speed skyward, hurtling pillar of red rock.
The mouth is not necessarily a one-way trip
Though you should take plenty of room.
It has shaggy lips, a necklace of pines.
It electrifies Perranporth sand-dunes
Every grain crackles and hums
In flickering organ-notes under
My blue slippered prints.
It is a great traveller and sometimes slips
Up its own back-passage to assuage its terrible wander lusts.
When men and women embrace
They impersonate it
They are a cone of power
An unbuilt beehive
We two are a brace of them behaving as one
We invaginate, evaginate,
Time stops inside us.

In it the ticking
Of innumerable stolen clocks
Welds to an organ-note.

It is sometimes made of lightning
And at others nothing but magnetism.
It is a kind of knot
Too intricate to undo
Too virile to pull tight.
Untied, a world explodes,

Tied, it winks out.
Or it hovers
Too restless
To untie the human knot.
It is the last trumpet
And the first trumpet.
It fashioned Glastonbury Tor
With helical fingermarks.
The burglar by night bears
Ten small tough patterns of it
Through the polished house,
Each one speaks his name.
It is a kind of walking cliff
And a walking well.
The fossil shell and the empty penis
Alike await this wakener.
The Master comes!
He shuts his blue snuff-box
And the wind stops.
He knows how to wind it
With a certain key
That makes the whole home disappear
Inside-out up the chimney;
Knee-deep knee-deep beware
Croaks the frog far inside it.
Its vomited bees float
Coiling down the hillside.
It has much in common
With the round-dance and cyclotron;
It will hover
Over the winding dance on the sand-beach
It will suddenly reverse
The people vanish and all that is left is a shell.
The Master says, learn from this power,
It is strapped to your wrist like an oyster
And allow it to descend into your mouth
And suck you dry
And let it pluck out your eyes
So they can ride on the storm.
Is the shaft weary?
If this shaft is not tired
There is no tiredness anywhere;
If this shaft is tired
Wait for the new world.

Subdue it if you dare.
My master did.
The long thin one enters
The open lid of his cranium,
Screws down his spine,
Sets with a click.
My master wakes,
Gets up and laughs suddenly,
Totters widdershins picking things up
Favouring his left hand
Since this is the northern hemisphere.
And it whirls directly over his head –
Do not look up, it is his hypnotist!
And the sun, that squints through its sun-spots.

It is the best of rainstorms
Since it so mightily collects
And so mightily lets fall.
It has subdued the great sea-worm
Who hangs upright, frothing in its embrace.
Throw a knife into it
You will wound the heel of a grey witch
Who will not bleed, she is made of cobwebs.
It is the spirit of the sealed boulder
It was born of a beach-pebble, and left by a pock,
It is the spirit of the oil-gusher, the black that yellow burns.
It touches the rock, that rock
Speeds up and is petrol for motor-cars:
A spark of its friction catches
The rock is no more in a shuddering flap! But mostly
It buries this rock-spirit until it is needed.
I will call it a magical name in the Linnean system
Vortex macromphalos and I carry on my watchchain
A silky cocoon reminding me of its quiet moments
Of its transformation and presence anywhere:
In the gnat-swarm with smoky feet,
Faltering in spirals; in the tons
Of aching black-water-muscle poised over the campus
Peering in through the long library-windows;
In four winds bound round in one breast and breeze.

Dr Faust's receipt for THE NAILS
Seek out its unfreighted apparition
It will be a shimmer between oaks at evening

Celebrated glancingly by gnats
In broken spirals, falling and rising.
Anoint with the lizard. It will turn horn-white.
Now take nails of sweet-tasting iron
Drive your nails into the floating bone
Strike it as it returns each time
Draw sparks with your blows, keep it
Spinning, persist. The Whirlwind
Will shrink, measuring gradually
Its substance into the nail
That falls to the grass heavily.
You may use this nail for many benefits.
Drive it into rock and the hill will be glass,
You may peruse its secrets.
Drive it into a table of dry wood
It will bloom like a bridefeast.
Drive it into the skull of a blind man
He will see men like trees walking.

VIII

THE HERMAPHRODITE ALBUM

(1973)

THE SNOW-SHIRT

There is a door opening on
A vision of health after long illness.
There is a lighted staircase,
There are the deep levels of her blouse,
White cats struggling among roses.
My chest is proffering
Two rosy bouquets,
They prickle my shirt.

There is a cold green square
Among houses,
Crackling the air
There are black trees,
There is a wood-fire
Belling with shadows
And a father leaning against
The heavy mantleshelf:
He is most elegant
In a shirt of deep frills,
The shirt is very white,
His hair very black.

The child of me toddles
Across the warm carpet,
Now my father's shirt-frills
Settle over the square
In flakes heavy and soft as winter,
The fire warms us,
We blush like roses.

SIX ODES

I TABLE-LADY

I sent her into the wine-glass to listen.
I prodded her into the apple-burrow; I told her to take out her
    pin-dagger as soon as she heard the maggot chewing.
I gave her a bath in a walnut-shell.
She made a salt-necklace, piercing the crystals together.
I was frightened when she fell into the mustard, but I rolled
    her clean on a piece of bread.

I told her to sit in the cruet like an information kiosk and
    answer some questions.
I compiled a savoury blanc-mange for her studded with
    angelica; it was a gobbet of my fish-sauce.
But she ran from the reek of my steak, the evisceration of an
    elephant; I gave her a cress-leaf fan.
She got drunk in a grape. I found her snoring like a scarlet fly
    on her back in the skin like a flabby canoe.
It was after I had eaten the blood-orange that I missed her.

II WATER-LADY

He asked her to go into the wood and tell him what she saw
    there.
She walked between the trees and the first thing she liked was
    the pond.
She knelt down and stripped off the thin film of reflections, rolled
    it up and put it into her pocket to show she had been there.
The water's new skin reflected with more brilliance and better
    colour.
So she knelt down and took this new skin and put it into her
    pocket, throwing the other skin away.
But the colours of the newest skin were without equal so she
    took this instead.
In due time she emptied the pond in this manner.
All that was left was a slippery hole, a sloppy quag with a few
    fish skipping.
She felt sorry for the fish so she went down into the quag and
    captured them in her skirt and climbed out.
Then she looked for where the torn scraps of reflection had
    settled among the undergrowth and she slid a fish into each
    one.
After she had done this she went back to him. 'What are those
    stains on your skirt?' were his first words . . .
But his suspicions were drowned in amazement as she unrolled
    the tapestry of reflections for him.

III HOWDAH-LADY

A little bloodstained clockwork in a puddle of blood.
She picked it up sighing, wiped it on her skirt.
Look, she said, it's all that's left of Peter, I wonder what could
    have done it?
I shrugged my heavy shoulders.

I don't know, she said, whether one can give a piece of
    machinery a proper burial. Might it not be better, she
    sniggered, to fasten it in a memorial clock, so that one
    always thought of poor Peter as one looked at the time?
My eye itched, I rubbed it with my ear.
I suppose he was thrown from his elephant, she said, placing
    one tiny foot in the crook of my trunk, and when they
    dragged him away this piece remained.
I hoisted her to my back.
But I don't want the beastly thing, she cried from the howdah,
    and she flung the clockwork into the swamp.
As we left, I saw it turn into a golden beetle that buzzed off
    into a belt of wild nasturtiums.

IV WARDROBE-LADY

She wears the long series of wonder-awakening dresses,
She wears the fishskin cloak,
She wears the gown of pearl with the constellations slashed
    into its dark lining,
She undresses out of the night sky, each night of the year a
    different sky,
She wears altitude dresses and vertigo dresses,
She plucks open the long staircase at the neck with the big
    buttons of bird-skulls in the white dress of sow-thistle.
She has leather britches known to be chimp-skin,
She has combed star-rays into a shaggy night-dress,
She has a bodice of bone-flounces, a turbinal blouse through
    which the air pours.
There is a gown she has that shimmers without slit or seam
    like the wall of an aquarium:
A starfish moves slowly on its pumps across her bosom,
A shark glides, a turtle rows silently between her knees,
And she adopts in turn the long dress of sewn louse-skin,
The romper suit of purple jam packed with tiny oval seeds,
The foggy grey dress, and lapping between its folds
Echo bird-cries and meteor-noises and declarations of love,
The ballgown of ticker-tape,
The evening dress of flexible swirling clockwork running
    against time,
The cocktail dress of bloody smoke and bullet-torn bandages,
And the little black dress of grave-soil that rends and seals as
    she turns.
Often she sits up all night in the philosopher's library

Sewing strong patches from his wardrobes of thought
Into her wounded dresses.

V LEARNING–LADY

I sprained my wrist taking her skirt off; it was moving too fast
    in a contrary direction.
I grasp the difficult mathematics of topology because I know
    her saddle-shapes.
I know conic sections also from the fall of her skirt.
Transcendental numbers are not difficult since inside she is
    much bigger than she is out.
As for theology, she always gives me good answers to my short
    god.

VI COMING–LADY

She comes like a seashell without a skin,
She comes like warm mud that moves in sections.
She comes with long legs like a tree-frog clambering
Towards some great fruit, niddip, niddip.
A small acrobat lives inside her flower;
The canopy blooms.
She has an underground belfry tolling the bushes
Which shakes the ground,
It is full of shivering bats that fly out and return.
Her blouse comes off like the clean paging of new books,
There is a smell of fresh bread and a clean active
Strong-teated animal inside.
Her knickers come off like opening party invitations,
And between her legs pigeons are laying eggs without shells.
I have lost dread there longer than a man reasonably may,
I believe I know there white lids sledding over mossy wells,
Shearing prisms and silk splitting for me to walk
Into the red room in order to inspect the ancient portraits
In warm loose oils that are always repainting themselves.

EROSION

Darkness is a power. She haunts with power.
I begin to fear the pebble and its outpourings, I fear
The blood of the nearby hills, the outpourings
Of the rock. She makes endless soil

And ponderous thick earth earth wanders through,
Presiding from her hills, reflecting herself
In her wet estuaries. She reclines at ease
In emerald flanks and winding satin clefts,
And wanders through herself. Mire gloats everywhere.
The lurching packs of birds
Bear mire-stings in their tails,
They eat her fruit and make more mud.
I admire
The clean acid scut-bite of the enormous wasp.
She was rock, now she is endlessly deep
And too soft for thought:
Too much dark and power to stifle in. Her rocks
Rot the clear rain. Sometimes I see the clouds above the
   shored-up mud
Tugged open as if by the hymns of mud mud sings,
Hymns to the sky out of her low dank softness.
Each night from hedgerows
Huge glossy slugs skim out, hour-long transparencies
With mire-cud inset deep that melts
To individual flesh and back again,
Not like those hills that spend themselves completely,
Leave place slowly in their thick green dresses
To bathe their heads and sink in ever-mud.

BRAINWALL CORNGHOST
HORSESTORM

They are not sheep on our hills, but rain-bringers,
They are thunder, lightning, and the like,
And the name of the flock is Peter.
One of its names. I will tell you the other one soon.
How the thunder bangs! Look, look, up above,
There is a mask of God still bellowing, and drifting slightly.
Who is that in the shrubbery, in a wet evening gown?
I know one of her names. She arrived recently.
I notice the bees are swarming by night, iced white by the
   moon.
The name of the flock is Artaud, or one of its names.
Your job is to polish the sweet jars in the upper room,
One of your jobs; the low broad room lined with dusty bottles.

There are motes in the late sun dancing like voices
All saying their names, which are Joe Dust
And one other, which I am forbidden to tell you
As yet, until you have changed into dry clothes.
The stars are bony tonight, and the river bright like a worm;
It is never the same river twice, so I cannot tell you its name.
Our hens are laying soft-skinned eggs now, for the stars
Take all their calcium, despite our prayers. There is also
A granular stench in the refectory, and I fear
Scab hardens somewhere, like precious stones
Perfecting themselves in the earth, chalcedony or bezel,
And the great gate rots on its posts. Moths called Eliza flutter
Against the puttyless panes rattling in the tall windows, the
   chanting
Of words called English seeps through the birdsong stables
And horses are there for the riding, called Kindness,
Gaiety, Intuition and Poetry, despite our fears.

SOME BOOKS, SOME AUTHORS, SOME READERS

There is dead wood in this author; open his book and certain pages crumble like rotten wood between covers of bark. Out of so much else scramble boot-shiny beetles, very compact and intent, like the readers it inspires, like the sincere readers of difficult dead books.

This one sloughs off his dead faces. They are the pages of his books. The old gentleman! – meet him now as pink and sweetly-smelling as a freshly-washed baby. A new book gathers in his face as we talk. He adjusts the shade of the club-room lamp so that it shines away from the darkness gathering in his face.

This one specialises in pages that become water as their white crests turn. Thus you can only read on, but there is a sea there containing many curious fish, and whales that move in schools together among their scented milt.

This one travels over sunlit waters in a shiny tin boat. He is very tanned, almost black, and sails with one hand grasping the white mast, but he cannot look down, the water is so bright.

This one writes books you do not read because they read aloud to you. Immersed in the writing, you lounge up to your neck in the talking water, your collar of water high around your neck, your river-robe fast-flowing.

The books of this one are like biting seaside rock. The same word runs straight through to the end.

This one makes books of stinking quicksilver. It is your own face you regard as you read, but the smell is the author's.

Opening the covers of this one's book is like opening a stove that has not been lighted for centuries. But its clinker is thousands of pearls.

How can I evaluate or describe to you the plots of any of these books, or the information they contain! For I am a lover of books, and this is my misfortune; to tell their worth is beyond me.

FOR DAVID

She has six-dimensional laughter.
Her face closes placidly on twelve intersecting horizons at right
    angles.
She dresses in colours that taste of wells.
She stands on pebbled beaches and I think of the skulls of foes.
She stands on sandy beaches and I think of a billion years.
She builds a sandcastle with bucket and spade and I think of
    the children I want.
She paddles, and the tide inches up her legs.
I am the sea immediately, and I contain seaweed and ink.
My brine wets her skirt with a quick splash and I travel
    through her vesture.
She wades slowly along my shore.
My surface shines with a straight path that reaches as far as the
    setting sun, a far-retching pang.

IX

SONS OF MY SKIN

(1975)

THE AGNOSTIC VISITOR

for Roy and Agnes

Dawn, his first day.

Slowly the mountain fills the window.
They are off to the church. They offer him coffee.
Gently enquire how he'll pass his first morning.
'Finish my coffee, browse in a book, take a short stroll.'
They hear him out mildly, carry plates from the kitchen,
Lay him knife and fork quietly, with an indwelling look,
God-takers, inlooking, take none for themselves,
Lay him fork and knife quietly, a white folded napkin,
Carry plates to the kitchen. God-partakers
Touch his hand mildly, bid him goodbye.

And on that walk the visitor paused
Looked head up around me snuffing the hill air;
The hill-face opposite across the valley-steep:
Slate racked and slotted like shelves of great books
Leaning tall folios, and the hills bent-shouldered
Like great slow readers crowded around
With their indwelling look, sides trodden by god-lovers
With their indwelling look. And I pulled at the roadside
Tugged down a small slate.

                                      Into the rock bed
Clear water gathered, water spilled over
From inside the mountain, long cool water
Threading the mountain within the soft turf
Under the hard rock, falling presence of water
Reaching from peaks, downward and cool,
Moist stone aflow, thick turf-springing.
I plucked my stone down, the socket a freshet,
Dabbled a hand, raised my palm to my lips,
Sipped indwelling water. With an indwelling look
Trod on down the cutting, reading my brief slate,
The mountains following.

FROM THE QUESTIONS TO MARY

The Virgin Mary gave birth to Dionysus, who said:
When I have grown my horns I shall begin listening to
    them.
Meanwhile, Mother, why do you yet give me that blissful
    milk
While I can give you nothing back but these turds
Which we throw among the straw?

No, says Mary calmly, there is no blame.
Make me a turd, my son.

And Dionysus makes Mary a warm little turd scented with
    his body
She holds her white palm out and Dionysus lays his
Egg of earth in the palm of her hand
And she takes the turd and she digs a little hole
In the soft earth of the garden and she lays
The turd therein and she takes a nutmeg
And lays it on top of the turd.

Look, she says, we shall water this spot for a year.

That was March, Dionysus three months old.
By April, a slick green spear through the soil.
May gives it white flowers in foamy tufts,
In the summer bees come with their eternity drone,
By the autumn the tree is Dionysus' height,
It bears fruits of gold and others of silver.

Mary says, did I ever make you feel you had stolen milk?
Her son replies: I used to wonder, before this tree,
What I could ever give that was half so good as what you
    gave me.

THE ORACLE

'You shall be my partner in fainting'
(Puppet-magician in my 11-year-old son's play)

He is very impressive. I am very impressed by him.
His hair escapes from his collar like white steam boiling from
   a pot.
I don't care if he remembers nothing. I don't care if he is
   deaf.
He is helping me he has agreed to go the whole way with
   me.

Depression is withheld knowledge is his theme
Go into the dark bravely

He leaves me in the garden
Into the dark bravely
I am in the seat by the sundial, I am waiting for a beam
Time illuminated in a shaft
A tall-beam, brimming with health-days
It comes
            a precise shadow on the stone clock
I rise and look at the time VII on a sunny winter evening
It is a time that reaches into the past and this clock never
   stops
It resembles time written with fast ink on parchment
It is horoscope time it gives me hope

Behind me the shadows are assembling
I am their hustings and they are holding an election
They are the shadow-party in opposition
The sun's platform has fallen vacant they are unopposed
The shadow-ministers propose an increase in taxes
I remove my jacket and throw it into the shadows
They impose an additional surcharge
I give them my tie
There are further concealed duties and taxes
Where I am going there is no need for shirt and trousers
I shall walk like Adam through the pinewoods until it is time
   to die
And the dew fall on me and the dew fall on me
I sigh and turn away from the sunny hours
Away from the garden sundial along the shadowy path

The shadow cabinet is waiting for me
With opening doors with open arms
They bear me away I burn in the dark I go bravely
Like a wisp of black hair a white cinder
A voice bravely

Part of the dark offers me a black book I had better not say
    no
His dark eyes flash like rains falling expecting dark pages I
    open the book
I am right the pages are black but the writing is moonlike
The moon is writing on wavelets, the endless nibs busy
I am on the cold black sand reclothed I am cold
I peer over the water trying to read the moon's script
Downy bones in the mist can that be me? If the wind blows
My bones fall to the sand, my bones rise as the water elects
Wavelet flesh of slow water, a gathering-place for mists

                              The dark story of the child
The blood-tides and your mother rides with all womankind . . .
The moon writes a sudden picture of a woman in a silver
    boat
A silver woman and the blood sea is ceaseless pulsing

The sundial in the seagarden shows me a moontime V
I look back over the black book of the waves
I have read some of its writing

I know how to faint how to wake how to be written on a
    little.

A PHILOSOPHY IN WELSHESE

The summer before last I saw my vision
Driving back from the cinema along the Pwllheli road
Having consumed no more than a quarter of Welsh whiskey
Glancing out of my driver's window to the right

There was the vision walking over the sea
In a cloud of fire like raw tissues of flesh
Like an emperor bleeding at every pore because he is so alive.
On my left the sun westered behind the mountains

Which were dark and packed with too much scree,
Too many pebbles in slopes like millions of people

But on my right hand you walked over the sea in your single
scarlet garment!

I searched in my head for what you were called and I shouted
silently
OSIRIS or some such name and you wheeled slowly
Bowing to acknowledge my cry then as the road turned
inland
The mountain got up slowly and laid along the crisp shore
Its pattern of farmers' fields that fitted each other endlessly.

Once there was this Chinese philosopher driving his horse
and cart
Through the mountain passes and he was not thinking exactly
of philosophy
His one thought was fuck the slut as he drove carefully along
the road towards her
Which concept alerted a nearby cloud that was coloured
exquisitely
Like blood washing away on a cool stream. The same cloud
Had been appearing nightly at this spot for six million years
Pondering over the pass in the ancient mountains without
hearing philosophy
Expressed with quite such concision and determination before.

Brother! Old Friend! Colleague! I shouted to China.

This cloud rolled down the mountain like an immense
glowing dog
Followed him home and all night wrapped his house
As all night he fucked the slut and every night
People of the area observed that the sunset descended
To attend this holy man whom the gods kept safe.
He never understood why his reputation grew but he kept
hard at it
Preaching that if you wish to be loved by men of discernment
Find a slut and fuck her deep as she will go into her yin
Indulging your manifold perversions which you must woo as a
fair person
Which is what the Welsh whiskey showed me and I wonder
whether it's true

On the road to Pwllheli driving back from the cinema at
    Bangor
Through the great mountains on no more than a quarter
    bottle taken
With Dante Alighieri, Charles Lutwidge Dodgson and Albert
    Einstein in the back of the car.

THIS CORNISH PASSAGE

The stone church whitewashed for navigation.
These terrible seas. The tall church trees
Spurting rooks like fountains of the dead,
The gorge leaning towards the shore and the boulders
Great as giants' heads, great as their bolsters,
Great as their white beds, towards the sailing vessels.

This mouth, with a white church in it.
The yarrows bend, and weave themselves into odours.
The beetles' furniture of fretted lichen.
Dove-grey tombs, a soft wind.
These dead wrecked in their churchyard, all around.

The gossamer like breathing ladders of glass.

SAM'S CALL

for Derek Toyne

My uncle Sam Lines always seemed
an enlightened person to me, but then I
was a child. I never went
to chapel where he preached, though people told me
he was a marvellous preacher. I asked him what he said:
he told me he never could remember.

He saw his double in the garden. Came in to my aunt:
I just saw a funny chap, an old un under the trees,
    he said.
All right, said my aunt. Went up to him
to take a closer look and it was me.

He had a lovely death. My aunt told me.
Almost gone, then up he sat, bolt upright and cried:
Meg lass, get me a clean shirt, I'll not be seen
dead in this one. They got him one,
struggled him into it, he never spoke again.

That was when I was guided, the one and only time.
Sam was laid out and waiting for his funeral.
I felt suddenly curious about an old box in the barn
Meg had said was full of old writings, now I must see
    them.
I went out quietly because of the death in the house
and the blinds down into the barn-smell
of chicken-shit and damp feed. Inside the box I found
one old piece of paper with green writing
'To be buried with Sam Lines', folded,
a red mark and something stuck round and crinkled,
like an ancient condom, then the tears
spurted into my hand, I understood
it was his caul he had been born with.

He could tell the time without looking at his watch.
He'd sleep in his chair by the range; after supper
we kids'd creep up, whisper in his ear,
(head back and closed eyes fixed on the ceiling)
'Sam, what's the time?' His big oakapple hand
crept into his waistcoat head still asleep,
He took his turnip watch out and said the time
from his sleeping mouth. He was always right
you could check him from the watch his big hand
would close and tuck away into its pocket again.

X

FROM EVERY CHINK OF THE ARK

(1977)

DOG PROSPECTUS

The dog must see your corpse. The last thing that you feel
Must be the dog's warm-tufa licking of your hand,
Its clear gaze on your trembling lips, then
Snapping at flies, catches the last breath in its teeth,
And trots off with you quickly to the Judge,
Your advocate and friend. The corpse a dog has not seen
Pollutes a thousand men; the Bishop's hound
Tucked like a cushion at his tombstone feet
Once through the door carries a helix staff
And looks like Hermes on that side, the Bishop tumbling
On the puppy-paws of death . . .

                              as a temporary Professor
   at this U
I practise, when the campus swarms with them,
Focusing out the students, so the place
Is amply empty, except for a few dogs.
They should study here, the U enrol them
And take more fees, at agreed standards teaching
Elementary Urinology, and Advanced
Arboreal Urinology: The Seasons and their Smells;
Freshman Osteology: The Selection and Concealment
Of Bones; Janissology: The Budding Watchdog, with
Fawning, a two-semester course. Lunar Vocalisation,
Or Baying at the Moon; the 'lame-dog bid for sympathy
With big sad eyes and hanging tongue,' which is
Cosmetic Opthalmology with Intermittent Claudication
In the Rhetorical Physiognomy Gym. Shit and Its Meaning;
Coprology: the Dog-Turd and Modern Legislation; The
Eating of Jezebel, or Abreactive Phantasising; The Black
   Dog,
Or Studies in Melancholy; The Age of Worry
An Era Favourable to Dogs . . .

                              How to Beg:
A Long-Term Economic Good; with How to Fuck,
Or Staggering in Six-Legged Joy; Fleas,
A Useful Oracle and in this same last year
The Dedicated Castrate or God's Eunuch,
The Canine Celibate as Almost-Man;
And finally how, if uncastrated,
To change places and become Master-Dog,
The Palindromic Homocane and Goddog-Doggod,
Wise Hermes of the Intelligent Nose

Leading to the Degree of Master of Hounds.

The campus throngs with hounds, this degree
Is very popular, alas,
I focus them out: in ample emptiness
A few humans hurry to their deep study
Without prospectus, without University.
This one is desirous of becoming a perfect scribe:
He knows vigilance, ferocity, and how to bark;
This one studies gazing as the dogs used to
On the images of the gods, as prophets should.
What gods, what images?

Those glorious trees, trilling with birds, cicadas,
Pillars of the sky, our books and ancestors;
I piss my tribute here, I cannot help it;
The few humans left, noble as dogs once were,
Piss on this university.

TAPESTRY MOTHS

for Vicky Allen

I know a curious moth, that haunts old buildings,
A tapestry moth, I saw it at Hardwick Hall,
'More glass than wall' full of great tapestries laddering
And bleaching in the white light from long windows.
I saw this moth when inspecting one of the cloth pictures
Of a man offering a basket of fresh fruit through a portal
To a ghost with other baskets of lobsters and pheasants nearby
When I was amazed to see some plumage of one of the birds
Suddenly quiver and fly out of the basket
Leaving a bald patch on the tapestry, breaking up as it flew
    away.
A claw shifted. The ghost's nose escaped. I realised

It was the tapestry moths that ate the colours like the light
Limping over the hangings, voracious cameras,
And reproduced across their wings the great scenes they
    consumed
Carrying the conceptions of artists away to hang in the woods

Or carried off never to be joined again or packed into
    microscopic eggs
Or to flutter like fragments of old arguments through the
    unused kitchens
Settling on pans and wishing they could eat the glowing
    copper

The lamb-faced moth with shining amber wool dust-dabbing
    the pane
Flocks of them shirted with tiny fleece and picture wings
The same humble mask flaming in the candle or on the glass
    bulb
Scorched unwinking, dust-puff, disassembled; a sudden flash
    among the hangings
Like a window catching the sun, it is a flock of moths golden
    from eating
The gold braid of the dress uniforms, it is the rank of the
    family's admirals
Taking wing, they rise
Out of horny amphorae, pliable maggots, wingless they champ
The meadows of fresh salad, the green glowing pilasters
Set with flowing pipes and lines like circuits in green jelly
Later they set in blind moulds all whelked and horny
While the moth-soup inside makes itself lamb-faced in
The inner theatre with its fringed curtains, the long-dressed
Moth with new blank wings struggling over tapestry, drenched
    with its own birth juices

Tapestry enters the owls, the pipistrelles, winged tapestry
That flies from the Hall in the night to the street lamps,
The great unpicturing wings of the nightfeeders on moths
Mute their white cinders . . . and a man,
Selecting a melon from his mellow garden under a far hill, eats,
Wakes in the night to a dream of one offering fresh fruit,
Lobsters and pheasants through a green fluted portal to a ghost.

THE STAINS

The woman in the besmutched dress
It was I who was afraid and the Indians rising
The powder from those muskets   the puffs
Of smoke from our own cannon were harmless

But the smoke stained my sleeves   thus I drifted
Like an off-white truce   a half-hearted white flag
In my stained blouse with the high neck
And bosom-tucks and little fringes, my
Satin skirt with the waterfall back
My long stained skirt that made me glide
Stained with the muddy ground and gunsmoke
This orderly was helping me escape
My husband was busy with the war
I went in a besmutched dress across the frontier
Like a butcher's wife between the staining cannon
Between the groaning men   I saw my husband
In his red uniform lacquered in its colour
I saw his head shatter in a plume
Of coloured smoke that stained me
I cradled it, in my spattered skirt
I crossed the frontier into night and safety
There was a smoking train whose smoke stained
I sat besmattered with the train
Besmattered with the cattle-leavings in the train
A dog sniffed at my dress
As though it were a map of battles and escape
My history written for him in my dress
The dog sniffed at my dress like my child
His thorny pads tick-tocked away from me
The train lurched, new firing began to spatter me.

THE HALF-HOUSE

A dry brown bush feathered with mosquitoes.
A ruined room with a river running through the end of it.
Tablecloths trailing into the fast water.
A silver tureen rolling and clanging among the river pebbles.

A billiard table's drenched green meadow
On which the mushrooms have set out an ivory game,
Their scent of salt meat mingles with the nettles';
Ant-scented nettles; the door swings on blackness
Of a white refrigerator like snow among the brambles
That have stopped the clock with yellow fire
On the marble mantlepiece, next to the crucifix
That has budded, its figure missing, like a white shadow.

That rustling in the bushes, is it a thrush
Or the small brown Christ sprinting among the pine-needles,
In the other half of the house, the little Jesus
Tanned and hard like Robinson Crusoe, shooting
For food rabbits and mice with a string of horsehair
And a gull-feather bow, the hand-wounds
Almost healed in the hard hunter's hands.
He has got into the library, lights
Cooking-fires from the ruined books, tries to pick
Pictures of Mary off the printed pages
(Though, in a fix, he can rip the scabs off
And light a fire with the blood in his veins,
Or scare night-animals by waving his thundering hands.)

He smells like a field-Christ.
Like a fertile field the Lord has blessed.

SERIOUS READERS

All the flies are reading microscopic books;
They hold themselves quite tense and silent
With shoulders hunched, legs splayed out
On the white formica table-top, reading.
With my book I slide into the diner-booth;
They rise and circle and settle again, reading
With hunched corselets. They do not attempt to taste
Before me my fat hamburger-plate, but wait,
Like courteous readers until I put it to one side,
Then taste briefly and resume their tomes
Like reading-stands with horny specs. I
Read as I eat, one fly
Alights on my book, the size of print;
I let it be. Read and let read.

THE DOCTRINE OF THE WINDOW

There are windows, little sliding traps
Of white wood people push exhausted money through
Summoned by bill. There are clear squares
Summating landscapes with the help of chattering highballs;

There are dark high windows, behind which
Great novels are written by young persons
Lacking the price of candles; there are low-down bays
For grim-jawed women in buns of sandy hair
Whose knitting has overgrown them like trellises;
There are waterfalls, whose ever-roar
Reminds visiting hermits of distant hermitages,
Through whose speeding glass the black mountain looks
    back at you;

And there is this doctor in spectacles
Sitting behind his desk like his own high windows,
No he is a clear door, you saw your reflection first
Then you climbed out of him twenty-seven floors up into
    weather
Of city streets that darken as gazes dive,
Office windows flashing with eyes that plunge;
The cops arrive in cars screaming like suicides.

But if you prefer to remain in-windows, this
Glass of water is Eve with her straight face
And clear depths; if Adam saw water
Standing up on its own like this, not flowing
And not falling, neither living nor dead water
He'd run a mile to his psychiatrist out of the Garden
Frantically knocking at his french-window
Where like a reflection the doctor prepares him for the fall.

A TWELVEMONTH

    In the month called Bride
    there is pale spectral honey
    and in-laws made of chain-mail and whiskers.

    In the month called Hue-and-Cry
    green blood falls with a patter
    and the pilchard-shoal flinches.

    The month called Houseboat
    is for conversing by perfume
    and raising beer-steins:
    great stone-and-foam masks.

In the month called Treasurechest
snails open jalousies onto their vitals:
pinecones, pollen-packed.

In the month called Brickbat
the sea is gorgeous with carpets
of orange jelly-fish squads:
and the people ride.

The month called Meatforest
is for flowers in the abattoirs,
catafalques for the steers.

In the month known as William
we watch the deer grazing on seaweed;
police open the strongroom of Christ.

In the month called Clocks
the poets decide
whether they shall draw salary,

And in the month called Horsewhip
they pluck their secret insurance
from the rotting rafters.

In the Mollycoddle month
barbers put up bearded mirrors
and no-one is allowed to die.

In the month called Yellow Maze
all the teddy-bears
celebrate their thousandth birthday.

In the month called Sleep-with-your-wife
the sea makes a living
along this quiet shore, somehow.

TRASHABET

A is for ash, which is primary trash. With it I can make bash, cash, dash, fash, gash, hash, lash, mash, pash, rash, sash but not wash.

B is for buttons, which are a cross between numbers and persons. Snip a button from Joey's shirt, and it is Joey. Snip six buttons, and you have spots to arrange in an equilibrated pattern of Joey. I possess buttons stolen from everybody I have ever known; they are as good as photographs. I have filled four large grocery boxes with the buttons, and I recognise each one personally.

C is for cat's fur. If I rub this old plastic haberdasher's hand with cat's fur, it will pick up light buttons by electricity.

D is for dead wood. Sawdust, and lathe-shavings. I have my great beetle stroll over the yellow sawdust in a black dish. He leaves marks that I can interpret, I read them off as stories or drawings. Lathe-shavings may be dyed, and made into wigs.

E is for egg-shells. Glueing dust-bin eggshells together is good sport for a poor man, but there is always one piece left over.

F is for dead flies. I have one wall in my shack studded like tacks with flies' heads dried and glued to the matchboard, as other men have halls of trophies.

G is for grit. It flies everywhere in the summer, when the wind blows off the dunes. I think sometimes of my house and its treasures riding a tidal sea of shifting grit.

H is for happenings. When I recognise a button, when I complete an egg-shell, when I sell a wood-shaving dog dyed black-and-white, when I triumph over a muscular bluebottle with a rolled-up paper marked 'clubhouse', these are happenings.

I is for myself. I am Midas, but not greedy. There is nothing which does not interest me, providing it costs no money.

J is for jamjars. I use these as a sorcerer uses his glassware. A dead mouse in a carefully-sewn shroud rests on seven layers of grit; the particles are graded by size and colour. The shroud is the silk lining of part of my overcoat, it has a hood. The claws are crossed on the tiny chest, the jar is sealed with a page of the bible tied with waxed string. With this machine, that brims with invisible stench like evil prayers; with this corpse, that threads with silvery maggots like new guesses, that, when the maggots have pupated and risen again, buzzes with tiny voices like a church of the resurrected; with this life-machine I curse rich monks and church commissioners.

K is for Kraft paper that prolongs the life of shoes, that screens the shadow-theatre of my windows. When I wish fresh air, I punch a hole with my fist.

L is for Livingstone Waterstone, which is paraffin wax. When I have a candle, the shadows flow through my boxes and rags and the air feels good like crackling water, and my house is a river of rags of light. On other occasions I never see the night, since I wake at dawn and bed at sunset. Livingstone also crackles and whispers to me. From his scratches in the air, I read off pictures and tales as well.

M is for mousetrap, that provides me with corpses. Another wall is crammed with the bright-eyed, sharp-nosed trophy heads. I used coal-chips for the eyes.

N is for the near-miss I had when I caught cold from fishing in the quarry. I lay on fire, like a horizontal Livingstone burning flames of sweat. Then all my poverty was living vivacity, without any effort of invention at all on my part, and I burned in a world that had never heard of money. This was a near-miss. I near-missed being a holy fool, I near-missed losing all my pride. There was nothing to fight.

O is for objects of no significance and great interest that have survived millions of years. In the quarry I find the fossil of a wave-ripple, the fossil of the common five-winged button-urchin, the petrified crater of a rain-drop in mud.

P is for urine, and for my staff of life, my living waterstone, that, gripped in my hands and radiating its sunny beams, reflects: I am a fruit, I am a stem; as its nitrogen sinks into the soil.

Q is for queer, which I was, and hetero, which I was, and solitary, which I am, and I preserve the best features of both. I live with myself, who am a member of my own sex; and I live with the moneyless ghost, who is a ragged girl, and who enters into more beings than a human woman can. She is the buttons and the urine, and the drenched shirt, and the livingstone and the near-miss.

R is for arse, which she enters when she is in my fingers, and which she leaves as stable-gas. If you do not understand this, I cannot explain it any further to you.

S is for shit, which no, I do not make trophies of, nor are they my babies. I dry it for fires and I spread it for manures, and I shall use it for hairtonic or salad dressing if I please without asking permission.

T is for the architecture of my bed-sitting space. There is a pillar, which supports a roof. The pillar is of wood, and the roof is of iron, which is corrugated for strength and to shed the rain. The cross-piece runs north and south, the pillar penetrates the earth, which is the past and the future, and rises into the present. During my near-miss it was wreathed with vines and nests of grapes in which golden birds chattered.

U is for my uvula when I sing and my upraised arms when I dance around my tent-pole, my mouth full of white buttons.

V is for the forked twig in which I light my livingstone.

W is for the three weathers of the moon, I grow with her, I stand still in her light, my thought decays, and in the decay flash new silvery guesses; and for *W*riting this alphabet, which is taking me to *X* the cross-roads I am approaching for *Y* should I remain poor when *Z* the silvery flash-guess strikes the world to how a child is all-interested and his body made of breathing jewels, but this

> Takes me round the circle to *A*
> Which is for ambition and ashes.

DOLL-WEDDING

Bride and doll.
The hanged woman's portrait, ultimate vexation,
The death-necklace and the curse on the passer-by.
The smell pours from her like a ripped bag.
She dries to stringy toffee, the smell goes into autumn

The smell goes on the wind like an immense
Hanged woman's shadow cast across the world
She enters your lungs and hangs there
The autumn leaf cuts free
She hangs still in her icicle

By the time Spring comes we have forgotten her
She has however filled all the winds
Getting together with all the other dead people
Who share death out equally
With each breath, generously.

ALL THE SKULLS

The skull formed in bliss, judging by its grin,
True heaven packed with skulls, their ecstatic grinning,
So many skulls, like a snowstorm, all pure angels,
The blizzard of blessed fixity, with crystal teeth,
The great clouds white with their smiles, all
Light as white leaves, blown off the skull-tree,
What happiness to be light as a skull, and blown
By God's wind everywhere that blows a tune on you,
And shines a light in all of you, ranged over the sunset,
Singing; and the three-master singing as she sails,
The wind blowing through her tree-bones, and the light
Dazzling her canvas, which is flax-flower bones,
And the mountain singing from a larynx of slate and
        waterfalls,
And every little bubble in the mountain stream
A fragile skull of glass opening its mouth
To sing, and disappearing. The great moon
Floods over, like a birthday skull, shining

THREE AQUARIUM PORTRAITS

(Penzance)

I

The lobster leans, and taps on the glass.
Among the fiery hands of light and ripple
It has a face like a barbershop of scissors
Shaving drowned men in a lambent steely light;
It has a face and shell
Of blue holly-leaves in a beating-gently breeze:
These details cleaning themselves always
Scissors through combs, and leaf rescrubbing leaf.

It walks like three headless armoured dancers
Of a machinetooled Masque of Industry
Who set their precision clawsteps down
With computered watery stilts on feathery ooze
That sends up gunpuffs. It sees
But it sees through sucked black stones on skinny
     telescopes.
Its swept-back aerials are the only red instruments.

It is *loppestre,* or spidery creature, but I dub it
Lob's Man, as a teamster gathers up his reins
Lobster has spikes and studs for harnessing to some evil,
Must be the jigsaw piece for some horn-hoof pattern
Being like a witch that marshlight blue
Carrying its hell's radio in those crimson aerials.
There! I can eat it with good conscience
Being our Lob-Star, the colour of Sirius,
Clanking on its platter, alive-boiled and buttered:
We shall eat the evil and make it our very own,
Cracking his male-claws with our silver pincers.

II

This is one picture along the dark corridor
Of windows like a train under the sea.
Instead of scenery streaming, flocks of birds,
We have the fishes who swim their little masks
Of innocence with big dark eyes in silver faces,
Of pouting generalship, decorated fins,
And nibble at her fingers, through the glass.

With ripples, dusky lights, these frames
Seem full, as the passage is, with fiery hands
That push out with other portraits, as
CUTTLEFISH AMONG GLASS-SHRIMPS.

III

The boots have golden eyes, like cats or sheep,
Slashed with a wavery iris, rippling welts.
They blush dark as fruitcake with a chewing beak
Deep in the centre of a flower of tendrils.
There is a creamy wand set in the moccasin
And when they slip upstairs as they like to do
Aiming this waterhose at their launching-pad
They are something between a pussy and a carnival-nose

Something between a fruitcake and a boot
A cross between a miniskirt and a pasty
Float water-gently like a gold-eyed turd
Of inscrutable wisdom among their glassy shrimps
High-stepping like lean assistants who are
Mainly spectacles and the joints of spectacles
Being entirely of glass with a few guts
But shining like a neon sign at every joint
Like ladders who are greenhouses and jobbing gardeners
Who are bees returning also, joints pollen-packed,
Easing their silver slivers like encased decisions
Of see-through steel whose clickering chimes
Bright-sparkle in water-sound, deafened by glass.

IV

Among the always-twitching hands of fire
The creatures watch us, lobster
Ripped spiky from its pattern of imagined evil,
Precision prawns, those workers in glass,
And the biscuit-coloured, jet-propelled
And boot-faced cuttlefish.
They lean and tap the glass, and shiver
As we scratch back. To them
We are as they are, sea-creatures that float
With no support along the fiery corridors.
Through the glass
They wish to eat us, and turn us to themselves,
We lean back at them, our watery mouths

153

Like smashed aquaria with jagged fangs,
We return each others' looks among fiery hands.

PICTURES FROM A JAPANESE PRINTMAKER

(Exeter Museum, August 1974)

I

Actor robed for a bravura role
Caught in the rain. He lifts a fist,
He threatens the thundercloud
With slices of his sword. Lightning strikes
Like gongs. He discards his sword,
It lands in a puddle. He walks away from his damp
    clothes,
We are dwarfed by his erection.

II

Actor in the role of a ghost-lady
Displaying a scroll. His high black
Eyebrows blocked on the white face
Hold, equilibrated like justice,
Sweetly questioning, 'Do you
Understand now, my dear?' before
She puts the scroll away
Tucking it into a sleeve
And rolls herself up.

III

Women being carried across a river
On the backs of husky watermen;
Foaming robes, foaming water;
One woman glances down at the man's head
Stuck between her legs, taps the face
With her fan. The men are naked to the river
But for breech-cloths and head-bandages,
Their muscles tumesce against the dark brown water.
The ladies are particularly heavy, as they are dressed
In their own rivers of colour

Heavy with rain, heavy with river:
Each of the watermen shoulders his individual river.

Two girls on a country walk. One is a floating head.
She wears a robe of the exact greenness
Of the froggy pond they are passing, so her body goes,
Not even outlined, and her head is turned
Coiffured in oily valances secured with pigmy daggers
Like an armed head appearing above the pond,
Prophesying to her friend in blue.
One instant more:
The girlish friends resume their harmless stroll.

V

A cave-shrine by the sea for communion
With the oysters the visitors sip from the shells
Fetched by naked priests who plunge from pumice rocks
Buoyant as waves-with-faces into the brine,
Pull themselves sitting on to the rocks,
Loosen the sinews of plucked oysters with their knives,
And pass them back up to the visitors for communion
With the sea and each other, for the silked
Visitors are drenched, all holy, all wet,
In the tang of oysters, holy salt water, and any pearls.

VI

Samurai who gets his ki'ai shout
From mating cats, proceeds to contemplating
Frogs in order to improve his
Fighting stance, and his
Fighting expression, and his
Sudden leaps. Foreground
A trinity of frogs enjoy mud-experience
In a sickly cart-track. The Samurai
Is not yet ready for such dingy skills
Of camouflage, he is a
Clean fighter, in young fresh robes.

The story of the solitary house,
A gruesome episode, the pregnant girl

Hoist from the rafters by an ankle-rope
Over a small fire whose smoke rends to reveal
Her hopeless frowning face, while an old woman
Whets a knife, crouched by a block of black stone
    beneath.
The belly bulbed with baby lolls
So hard and fully-round on the chest
The breathing stops. We await
The amateur caesarian and the child leaping
Upright through the waterfall of blood
Straight to the withered tits and the haggard chest
That will cave to darkness in the monstrous lad's suck.
Out of this he will leap to beget himself
On the lady who hangs on her rope from the sky
Waiting for pain, the belly pulled round and tight
And taut and full and shining through the cloud-race.

VIII

Beauties crossing by white steamer; the parakeets
Hackle-plunged in foaming cherry-flower; a Buddhist
    priest
Enraptured by butterflies that swoop in and out
Of his incense smoke, caresses like velvet cloth
The close-springing stubble of his vow-shaven head.

IX

A hero in a faceless helmet, so fierce
His armour bristles with hero-light at every joint,
Confronts his enemy, a gigantic porcupine
Like a black sunburst prickly as he is
Whose face however has informed itself
With bright blue eyes, cat-slotted, and white teeth.
He confounds the beast by leaping on his sword
Balancing on its mirror edge to guide himself
Like twins of fire between the bestial prickles.

X

Two women watch a thunderstorm
By the slid-open paper window, on the sill
A child pulls the pussy's tail, the women
Have a warm brazier of coals with bamboo handles
But the great cat of thunder strikes with lightning claws

And electricity pours from the mountains,
The dry light twitches inside the women. On a ledge
    above
Really enjoying the storm, in the pouring rain,
A liberated girl as fairy mandarin
Stands in the midst of flowers created,
Co-operating with electricity, by her feet
That walk surely among precipices
Storms and waterfalls no deeper than she is.

XI

A ferry-boat's thirty-foot poles for punting
Across the deep river are gripped
Like martial instruments by naked boatmen
For samurai who ride the raft and fiercely gaze
Like wigged sunbursts everywhere. Most people
Avoid that gaze, as do the women
Hurrying across the bridge who tilt
Their great hats as to downpour and hide their faces
That way, with the brims. One, however,
Carries a hatless child who gazes frankly
Down from the trailing bridge deep into the fierce
    water-faces.

WINTER OAT-FLIES

(Hamilton: Upstate New York)

Generations of black snowflakes, frail and durable,
Nothing to them, husk begat husk on husk,
A few jointed vestments put aside of a scorched colour,
Or walked by a dab of moisture:
Just bash the air near them,
That ruptures their skinny heart.
They fly with a soft hum, a low scream
And that sound is all they are
In a suit of dry fingernail, a life
Of tissue-paper and sliver, a lick of sun
Brings them out, or a fart, their instant
Resurrections almost hairless after so many returns
Like tan grapes or banded like oats. Winter sunshine

Shows labouring gizzards like X-ray shadows.
Lycosid spiders patrolling the picture-rails
Spare their leaps, it would be squeezing dry oranges.

I wish they had somewhere better
To hang their toy eggs like sallow bananas,
And unzip their coffins to a better life,
Some oak-grove for little Draculas . . .

The snow through the window has more strength than
    they:
Generations of whitefly-swarms rivetingly six-legged,
Glassy as myriads of cod-pieced gloss-suited astronauts
No bigger than these oat-flies
But pulsing down and settling in white cities
Like the million hands of the slow winter watches.

ON LOSING ONE'S BLACK DOG

(an expression meaning 'to reach the menopause')

I

Thigh-deep in black ringlets,
Like a shepherdess at a black sheepshearing;
Like a carpentress in a very dark wood
Sawdust black as spent thunderstorms;
Like a miller's wife of black wheat
The stones choked with soot;
Like a fisherwoman trawling black water
Black shoals in the fiddling moonlight
Squaring with black nets the rounded water;
Like an accountant, knee-deep in black figures,
A good fat black bank balance in credit with
    grandchildren!
Tadpole of the moon, sculptress of the moon
Chipping the darkness off the white
Sliving the whiteness off the night

Throw down the full gouges and night-stained chisels!

Coughing black
Coughing black
Coughing black

The stained lazy smile of a virgin gathering blackberries.

II

We opened the bungalow.
The sea-sound was stronger in the rooms than on the
    beach.
Sand had quiffed through the seams of the veranda-
    windows.
The stars were sewn thicker than salt through the
    window
Cracked with one black star. A map of Ireland
Had dripped through the roof on to the counterpane
But it was dry. There was no tea in the tin caddy,
Quite bright and heartless with odorous specks.
There was a great hawk-moth in the lavatory pan.
Our bed was the gondola for black maths, and our
Breakfast-table never had brighter marmalade nor
    browner toast.
Two ladies in a seaside bungalow, our dresses
Thundered round us in the manless sea-wind.
Her day-dress: the throat sonata in the rainbow pavilion.
We kiss like hawk-moths.

III EPHEBE

The beating of his heart
There was no translation

Eyes so round
The lad looked at me milkily

I had his confidence
In the dry street
Out came his secret

'The Battleship,' he said,
'We're going to see the Battleship'

As though a flower told me
Opened its deep pollens to me

159

He had teeth perfect and little as
Shirtbuttons, fresh and shining

He was about eight
Like a flower grown in milk

'The Battleship!' he said
So lively   supernatural
His soft thumbprint
Creeping among the canines

IV CRY JELLIES AND WINE

Preparing jellies and wines in autumn
Sad wife alone
The rooms golden with late pollen

The neat beds turned down
The children smiling round corners
Sweet-toothed, sweet-headed
Her fruit, her blueberries on canes

The sad wife who would not listen
Boiling jellies, filtering wines in autumn
What shall she tell the children

They will not listen
They love jellies, russet jams

The sad wife in autumn
Her jellies and wines stolen
Stolen by love, stolen by children

The rooms golden with pollen

V A VIBRANT WASP

A wasp hanging among the rose-bines:
Footballer wandering in an antique market;
Damask and ebony, mahogany thorns, greenglass rafters,
    veined parquets.

Again he struck the wasp with the sheets of paper and
Believes he kills it; the wasp

Clinging to the tendon of his ankle looked very sporting
    and official
In black and gold clinging by the tail the high-pitched
    pain
Was yellow streaked with black oaths

He could not find the wasp-body it had been sucked
Along his nerves
                        after the rage
There is a sore pain turning to lust

That afternoon a plucky infant was conceived
Full of an infant's rage and juices
He struck once, and conceived

He struck at the wasp once, his child
Ran in out of the garden, bawling like a plucky infant
Teased beyond endurance in a striped football jersey
    among gigantic cronies.

VI THE STATUE OF HER REVERED BROTHER-IN-THE-BOAT

She catches the bloodless statue of her
Revered boatman-brother a ringing blow with
A mallet; the pure note vibrating
Through the gouged stone sustains
For three hours of morning reverie
During which time at this pitch
(Om) her petitions come to pass
Beyond her expectations, or anybody's:
                                    gardens, walks,
Silvery lads and encounters among the knotgardens,
Clavichords humming to the shrill-chanting beds
In the manor dark as horn. Too soon
The singing stone falls silent and it is not yet time
To strike the next blow. Now that she has seen everything
It is time to strike the last blow, now that she has
Nothing further to ask, it is time to plead
That the rigid statue may grant its greatest boon and walk
As her living and immortal brother among
All the beds and garden beds and wives and grandchildren
Proved by the magic of her singing jewel; but first
Before he can so walk she must strike some blow,

The ultimate blow, the blow to end all blows
To finish things one way or the other, that will either
Reduce the great icon to bloodless rubble or
Free her brother to return
                              rowing in
From the further shore: either
Make the wishing-stone alive in granting
The goal of bliss, or
                        shatter felicity, all.
                                        (This blow
Is struck only by the lunatic when the moon is
Full and directly overhead and the stony particles
Aligned like the cells of a yearning throat
Ready to sing, the birth-passage of man-song
Through a woman-throat)

In the beginning it was violence only and the shedding
    of blood
That started the gods singing.

VII AT THE PEAK

The tables laid with snow
Spotless cold napery

Tense white snowmen
Seated on snowthrones
Knives of sharp water
Icepuddle platters

Iceflowers

Carving the snowgoose
Slices whiter than pages

The sun rises
The self-drinkers
Swoon under the table,

Glitter the mountain.
The rivers foam like beer-drinkers

Devising real flowers
And meat you can eat.

My anointing
Gathers him
I draw the shapes of him
He has yet to learn
Over his skin
He recognises them

Flowing from feet to head
Baptism

He is a stony river, he swims with his head on the river
The brown body

I draw wings in the oil along his back
He is a youthful messenger

I anoint his chest
He is one of the facetious learned folk
Silky
It is my learning

I tweak his nipple
The county thunders
White oil
Displaces my
Black mirror.

THE TERRIBLE JESUS

It is the terrible Jesus
He walks on water because he hates its touch
He hates his body to touch everything as water does
(As Orpheus sang from the river of his body)
The ulcers close as he passes by
This is because he rejects ulcers
Anything raw and open, anything underskin
He rejects it or covers it with a white robe
He fasted forty days as long as he could because he hated food
And hated those who gave him food
And put worlds of feeling into his mouth

Lucifer came and tempted him out of natural concern
For this grand fellow starving in the desert
But would he pass the world through him
Like anyone else? Not at all.
He came back from the tomb because death
Looked like hell to him which is another thing
He won't do, die, not like everyone else.
Nor sleep with the smooth ladies.
Instead he goes up to heaven and hopes
For less participation there in those empty spaces
But from there he calls down to us
And I know those cries are calls of agony since there
All the sweet astrology-stars pierce his skin
It is worse than earth-death that destiny starlight for those
That won't join in, hedgehog of light.
This is the terrible Jesus. There is another,
And none will give him a name. He takes care.
He lives all around. I breathe him. He breathes.
Like the air we breathe, he is free to us.

THE SKIN

for Mike Smith

A floating green palace: the public park;
Bolts of silk by day: by night bolts of lightning;
And the river easing its way.

The lament of the river-bed, the valances of the candle.

Shadows live in the sunshine, not at night!
The stars are enough for me, and the spring,
There was always a spring in the night cavern,
The clothes come off with a rustle of static,
She is in bed, and asleep

I stroke her wet

The perfume winds out of her

The sun rises and all the animals greet it
With their perfume

In the sunlit fields
A horse gently rests
His great nose on my shoulder
Contented by my silk suit.

SOMEBODY

Somebody rolls a great window open
There is a spatter of rain
A beetle parades the shiny stone
A jagged leaf scrapes a sigh
The swimming-pool brims with leaves
It should have a net
But the leaf falls and the ice darts
The drowned puppy appears to me
In a dream of sopping leaves
He brings in his mouth a green branch
The stars roll overhead
They draw an immense woman-figure
Her hands splayed out to steady the globe
She watches and glitters. Her breath is icy
I see her in all the waters, which veil themselves.

TREE OF SWORDS

A shower of swords from the sword tree
        in autumn
Touch it and it divests itself
        like a falling army
You are cut to pieces
        chrysanthemums of the severed flesh
Or across the lake you see the flashing falls
        the copse of sword-trees
The swinging doors of a fencing-academy
        echoing from cliffs
Where they practise in breathing silence
        but for their sword-notes –
The unwary friend cut to pieces in blood
        the scream, the chiming clatter.

Never in restful graveyards
          but on old fields of battle
Never in quiet mortuary enclosures
          but hard by motorways
Feeding on the splash of collisions
          on the old blood, on the old arrows
The swords rising through the soil
          cleaning themselves
The blood's iron running in the sap
          and the blades clean as peeled roots
Flashing high on the tree
          playing with air and light
Mincing the rash forester
          in a glittering rush
Back to the rusty soil.
          The rain drips bloody from these leaves
And all the leaves make one note
          in the calm breeze:
Rough serpent-chime
          irrefragable hiss.

IN THE VERMILION CATHEDRAL

Your moon ties a dark
funnel of tides,
roads into the sea,
the fishponds heave
the sea bobs in, bobs out;

your doing.

I wish you would step out of the sea;
some signs about you, not too terrifying;
a kelp girdle, a spiracle in your chest;
walk arm in arm with me through the flooded highstreet.

Instead there are vibrations merely,
guest appearances,
a spiral corridor in the soapy water,
the great moon walking far out at sea.

I sit in church, it is abbreviated discourse.
Thou, He, Jesus Christ and the Choirboys,
The true presence, and a little cake like a moon,
The curtseying priest in his frock keeping you out.

Be the miracle that you are!
When I say 'grapes' the wineglasses fill
Goodblood and I drink to remember you
The sabbath apples choir as I walk by,
I sleep it off in the battling rams' field,
The grass is long, the rams tranquil.

If you know all my names and my lusts,
My monthly ransackings and my private games,
I assume you reject me, or you are in the wine:
Visit me in the wine, and visit everyone who drinks,
We lift our glasses and you come to us,
Millions of us and millions of you.

I want you to speak to me alone, please step out of the sea.
Crush the red bottle in your grip,
Touch me at the nape, at the brow,
Open the sea-door with a courteous gesture,
Use my hair for the tides.

Without a bottle, without a glass
I shall wait in this room small enough not to miss you.

MOONBEAST IN SUNSHINE

(Sudden slowworm at Totleigh)

Talonheaded with obsidian glances
He threw his tangles through the long grass
Showed me a way this side that
Stabbed his white snout into his misdirections
Switched through a yellow flower into secrecy
Dived through a flowerstem and was gone

The slowworm confused me and was gone
He looked this way and then that way
A yellow flower outstared me the grass empty

Moonlight streaking along choppy waters
The foil creases as the astronaut beckons;
This wizard pointed the wrong way and it beat me.

Cross between electricity and melting snow
Hybrid of a moonbeam and a waterfall
Son of a lizard and a white explosion
Glittering dewcloud pierced by rifle-fire
Child of a speedboat and its splitknot wake

I look this way that – I fall between your pauses,
    unravelling
Stairs I may not descend, not yet –
Who is the slow worm?

Maze-tracer ripping up your clews in one swift
    gesture
One swift backward strike so I no longer understand
No longer see the way, like a wound closing,
Like a sudden change of waveband

Quartz-sand pouring into mercury
Self-made torrent of metal milk.

DANCE THE PUTREFACT

Scenario for a Masque
for Pete Farr

'As he lay on his back, stretched out on the ground, with arms extended, he marked himself out with stones – the shape of his body, head, legs, arms, and everything. There you can see those rocks today.'

Old Man Creates – *The Hero with a Thousand Faces*,
Joseph Campbell

I

'The Avenue of the Giants,' he said calmly. Meaning the trees, introducing me to the Village. I have come here because I have a dance. All here have come for similar reasons. Here nobody pries or condemns. Your dance is not mocked, since mockery distorts the dance. Everybody here has been dance-blind, and here some have recovered their sight.

II

We were walking in the woods near the Falling Leaf Tavern, with its cellars full of liquor made in autumn. We had explored the avenue of great trees tossing their heads, with the church at the far end whose font was full of the surprising water. The dance of dust over the surface of the holy water in the font made visible the constant movement in the consecrated water. We had seen above the village the flat dancing-ground that had never been touched by a shod foot. I removed my shoes and socks and walked with my companion on to the hard flat ground dustless and warm. From this platform we surveyed the village. Tall columns of bonfire-smoke climbed into the still air, spiralling and twining from the villagers' gardens. We had descended and walked along the tidal inlet towards the beaches. The tide was low and we strolled by flat sheets of black mud, watery earth, earthy water. Secretly in my mind I hear the first steps of my dance. Warm fires glow from the windows as we return in the twilight. We pass a smouldering bonfire deep within which, as in a cage, mice of fire still race.

III

Smelling of new-baked bread and sawdust in the early sun, glossy as chocolate, soft as drifted flowers, the floor of my dance is prepared by the salt tide. I hear the great mud-drum. Its first beat ripples to the farthest shore. It is a liquid mattress, a slack trampoline, cradle and grave.

IV

I am very strict, in order that I may be very grotesque. I am very strict, because I am very grotesque. My white shirt is without spot, its collar-lappets ironed smoothly back, a red scarf tucked in the opening. My trousers of an equivalent whiteness, demarcated by a broad dark belt. Like a cricketer I am white, like a morris dancer I carry a withy, a willow wand. I am a person of sheer whiteness save for a slice at the waist, standing at the brink of capacious black. With my feet bare I advance towards the soft black mirror.

V

With the strokes of my withy and my bare footprints I dance my reflection on the mud. The mud is firm but quaking, soft as a strewing of dark flowers over a firm beachsand. This is the way I dance my figure. Leaning out over the mud, with my long withy-wand I draw stretching out as far as I can two crescents, their bulge towards me. They are the eyebrows. With a cry I leap over them and land up to my ankles. These prints are the socketed eyes. With a sliding step I slive out the nose and stand working the trench of the long mouth a pace away. With my wand I enclose these features in a head. I pass on to the throat and stroll out a left arm, a right arm − the hands come later − with a second bound I am ankle deep in two nipples, whose breasts I now scribe from my vantage points. A third hop, legs clapped together, gives me the navel, from which, swivelling, I mark out chest-lines and transverse rib-marks. Down the midriff I dance the long cunt, I furrow, I delve, I dance its extent many times, it splashes me, I am dark to my belt. I dance along the waist and make a left leg, returning to the cunt. I dance a right leg, returning to the cunt. I finish off the arms with hands that grasp and spread the cunt. I take a fourth leap, and am standing in the feet of my creature. I face the sun over the sea, she streams behind me like my shadow, the small clear wavelets advance towards me over the tidal mud. I turn, I pluck my feet out and stamp them down facing my crea-ture, my left foot in her right, her left foot accepting my right. The sun behind me from the east casts my shadow into her outlines and she configures with this part of me. It is time to give myself up to the dance.

VI

I am down, and within her! I have vaulted into her boundaries and I am as black as she is. I am buried deep in her flesh. I pull her flesh off her in handfuls and cover my skin in hers. I prance, cool and nightladen with exterior cunt. The black bed before me is rucked. The black woman-outline has risen from it and I dance within her skin. I am the black woman. I am petal-soft, and my surfaces are rounded and shining. The bosom of my shirt is heavy with mud. It hangs and flounces like large breasts full of black milk. The black lady minces sadly loverless over the mud, she smells of tar and sunlight. Where is this white lover? She dances sadly on her own. Soon her lover will return, but her disappear-ance is the condition of his return. She will enjoy the sunlight while she can. Soon her ladyhood will pour like black blood through the drains of his bathroom, she will fade like a shadow in a shower of clear water.

VII

Why do I return again and again to this same action? Because it is my dance. No one here gives reasons or asks questions. We are here in this village in order to dance. His dance is all a person has. It is his datum. But I, I cannot read my dance, and until I can do so I am condemned to enact it, and am imprisoned within it. I am dance-blind. There are so many other dances I could join! But now the season approaches in which all the dances are joined into one, the time when all the people's dances are performed together. For the first time in my life I shall perform my dance among all the others, with others watching. None will blame and none will condemn, for each person has his dance. This season approaches.

VIII

That season arrived this morning with the blowing of trumpets! Six men in Sunday black clothes wind the silver trumpets. Six women in village white bow the small dark violins. The music awoke me in my great tavern bed. I gather up my dancing-clothes, which have been cleaned and ironed for me without comment. I dress quickly and carrying my wand I clatter down the wooden stairs. Outside I join the procession of people dancing to the music up the hill to the smooth stamped platform. The Flora Dance plays from the six loudspeakers on poles that line the route. The sun shines. I hear the Flora Dance play through the innumerable beaks of all the birds.

I am afraid. How can I dance my desire on this hard earth? I have watched the others dance the dance of their own lives, the dance they wished to read. The music falls silent and they dance to the sound of their own flesh. There is a lady presenter with a forked twig who touches the heads of those who are to dance. I have watched the man who dances the tearing and devouring of human flesh; companions are selected by the lady to dance the dismemberment he wishes. They jerk and thrash on the dancing-ground like farmyard carcasses; he stuffs his mouth with the pink flesh greedily; the soaking of blood into the ground is danced with wriggling fingers. What if I were selected to dance this part by the lady? Would I do the dance justice, imprisoned in my own? I have watched three men dance the fuelling of ovens with their fellow-dancers. I have watched the old woman who dances the sewing of clothes over and over. Certain partners dance their assemblage into great costly garments as she stitches their bodies together; at last she rends them and the bodies scatter. She dances only with her rags. I watch a great company of men and women who dance a Parliament, and I watch the enacting of just and unjust laws, I see the Parliament dance its sinking into the ground, not a stone left on stone, and a new assembly arises. I watch a household dance the knocking together of a ship of great size from the bodies of other dancers, from which they exclude a certain company. However, certain dancers dance animals, who are admitted, and the remainder dance drowning, crying silently and clinging to the ark's human timbers as it sails without them. The lady presenter touches with her twig the heads of those who are to dance drowning. She does not touch my head with her invitation, even for that.

X

The lady passes among the dancers and signifies the beginning or the end of their dances; she turns them out of their courses with the touch of her twig. She is dressed in spotless white, more plainly than a bride, in a manner suitable for dancing. Her feet are bare, her skirt is pleated, she is fair-haired. She must be the chief dancer, since the others obey her, and obey the language of her wand. Now as chief dancer she begins to dance the flowers turning to the sun and the tides turning to the moon, the chief dance that lies within the others. She dances alone, the men watch her from an inner ring that surrounds the dancing-ground, she is watchful among them for a partner. She touches certain of the men with impatient strokes of her twig, and they join her in the centre. The men line up in a row, crouching, with their backs to her. The lady wanders behind them, inspecting, pausing as if to choose, rejecting, passing on, lingering on some detail of their dancing clothes, touching lightly the brim of a hat, a frayed cuff, the sailor-collar of a shirt, the bare nape of a neck, a chain around the neck, seeking, passing along the line, turning on her heel, returning.

XI

She has chosen her dancer and they dance joy! There is a sigh from all the company. She has stopped behind one man. She has thrown her wand away from her high over the heads of the spectators. She steps close in to him from behind and crouching like him rests her elbows on his shoulders, her wrists turned to the front. Her thumb-joints lie with gentle pressure on his temples and her fingers stretch out to suppose horns on his head, eight-tined horns. He is chosen as stag, and the lady will ride him, and tempt him, and he will ride the lady. There is a dance of riding and intercourse led by the lady and the man. They dance on their heels to signify the possession of hooves. There is charging and division, there is stamping and calling, there is rolling, there is slow beating with the feet until the ground and the hills rumble and the hills to me sitting in the shade, no member of the dance, the hills begin to slide. There is conjunction and division, there is breathing and sweat, there is the thumping of bare feet, there is the occasional cry as the dancers turn but no further song. There is a serpentine dance that coils figures of eight between the lady and her stag who stand making two centres slowly turning to watch each other over the heads of the winding people. I who have not been chosen cower for fear lest I intercept the glance of one or the other.

XII

Now the procession reforms and to the sound of the trumpets and violins which replace the body sounds that were the only dancing-music, the villagers descend to their houses. None of them looks at me. I fall in at the tail of the winding procession when I have seen that they wish to pass me by. The procession dances a slow step in triple time to the music. My feet drag along the grassy path. I expect the procession to disperse in the village square. I turn into my doorway but my arms are gripped. With serious faces the two hinder dancers force me to continue with them, for the column of dancing figures has not dispersed after all. As we approach the tidal mud-flats, the musicians fall silent again, and the only sound is the chafing of skin across earth.

XIII

The tides have left my dancing-floor glossy and unmarked. The people assemble on the bank, they pass me forward, and sign to me that I must begin my dance. I lean forward and trace the first features of my shadow-figure. I bound off the bank and stamp eyes. My fear has gone. With lively steps I leap and prance until I stand in the feet of my completed figure, facing out to sea, the red sun at my back. I turn and pluck my feet out and stamp them down facing the throng. They are black figures on the red sunlight sending long shadows down into the mud. Suddenly one leaps out of the sun into the mud and stands thigh-deep in the thighs of my figure. She is in white. Her forked stick stays planted deep in the soft bank, a thrumming silhouette. She crouches and draws herself knees to elbows into the trench of the black cunt. She rolls round deepening the hole and covering herself with black likeness. She flings her arms and legs wide inside the figure in a black star like a navel.

XIV

I caper with my black lady in the mud. Both lovers are present at the same time, at last. I dance earth and water. The sun dances fire. It reddens the black mud. I am a seed in her red flesh, she pulls me out of the red mud, we are trees laden with red leaves, we are glistening red serpents slithering in the mud. We dance seamless blood-marble with our sour-sweet skins joined. We interchange our red shining skins by scooping and plastering. We fashion new and surprising organs and wear them proudly for a while and then dash them away. She grows a mudbaby under her flounced and clinging skirt, and I suckle our baby with red milk out of the bosom of my shirt. We bury our baby and we stamp until it dissolves, until its very memory dissolves, then we resurrect our child. I bury her and she buries me in our world bed and we make red love in the queasy bed until the ripples of our embrace reach the farthest shore. Who are these people who signal the end of our dance with silver trumpets, with small dark violins tucked under the chins? We rise, and tear off our garments and trample them in the mud underfoot. We dance towards the crisp foam that dances towards us as the tide rises. My red lady enters the white foam, I enter, the trumpets sing from their silver throats all around us.

XV

I run gasping from the foam. The people advance to meet me and to the sound of trumpets and violins clasp a garment about me to warm my body. I turn impatiently from them to where my lady should rise from the sea to join me. The sea is empty and the foam crisps gently in hollow waves. The people draw me sobbing and shivering away from the sea and its empty foam.

XVI

This lady has ended in the sea, just like the lady I made for myself. This dance is no better than the other! The dancers dry my tears and urge me with many gestures to join in their dance. Why should I dance with people who are no more than foam and mud and tears dancing on empty bones! But as I dance loverless, I forget. Another lady steps into the circle and dances to help me remember.

XVII

Our dance ended at the tavern door, we have climbed the wooden stairs, this new lady and I, we have bathed, and slept in the great bed, and we are dressing each other. I button her blouse gently close up to the neck so that the points of her collar make a little A. I pass her pendant engraved with the A and the V inside the O, over her fine dark hair. She buttons my shirt but leaves it open so that my throat is bare in a V. The sun and the moon circle without end over and under our bed and our table. The rain beats on the hard-packed dancing-ground, and beyond it the sun sets into tango fire like a launching-pad. The moon beats out her triple-time. The clouds draw out of the waves and fall foaming, and shed their peacock rainbows as they will. The moon is an endless necklace of white ladies, red ladies, black ladies always leaving, always returning. I fasten her necklace loosely around her collar. The blood beats time in our warm throats.

XI

THE WEDDINGS AT
NETHER POWERS

(1979)

THE VISIBLE BABY

A large transparent baby like a skeleton in a red tree,
Like a little skeleton in the rootlet-pattern;
He is not of glass, this baby, his flesh is see-through,
Otherwise he is quite the same as any other baby.

I can see the white caterpillar of his milk looping through him,
I can see the pearl-bubble of his wind and stroke it out of him,
I can see his little lungs breathing like pink parks of trees,
I can see his little brain in its glass case like a budding rose;

There are his teeth in his transparent gums like a budding
    hawthorn twig,
His eyes like open poppies follow the light,
His tongue is like a crest of his thumping blood,
His heart like two squirrels one scarlet, one purple
Mating in the canopy of a blood-tree;

His spine like a necklace, all silvery-strung with cartilages,
His handbones like a working-party of white insects,
His nerves like a tree of ice with sunlight shooting through it,

What a closed book bound in wrinkled illustrations his father
    is to him!

RICH JABEZ DOG

Jabez Dog felt very rich. Smells among the gorse
And strawberries, there was a smell
Of honey everywhere, he felt at last
He was one of three persons, Father, Son and Dog,
And as he trotted into the wood he felt Apostles near,
He looked among the trees with his nose for those
    Apostles,
Then he looked at the trees, they were the Apostles.

The approach of an Apostle is like the approach of an oak;
The approach of an acorn through the earth
Is like the approach of an Apostle: but these were female,
Female oaks, like bearded Apostles with tits:
Jabez felt his piss inhibited: flowers without yellow pollen!

It was unnatural, he wanted a sunlit oak,
The yellow light attending on the sunny pollen
Through a day of expressive balsams of the trees
Emaned in changing rainbow-odours through the day.
This was unnatural: a grove of bitch-oaks!

But then a new smell like a spirit walked through
All the trees at once, it was less a smell itself
Than a doorway to one unimagined yet, like the negative
Of crushed coconut, which is gorse, or like a golden door
Of honey slowly opening, and the opening opening:

Virgin Jabez gathered himself, and leapt through.

THE WOOD

The wood ticking like a water-clock,
The drops gliding on slant twigs like funicular tears;
They hewed great tree slices, piled them up, forgot.
The wood contains a city of tables and chairs,
A countryside of doors, a continent of windowframes;
The wood is a secluded library full of shelves
And on the shelves softening books
And through the waterdrops like glistening spectacles
The vision of unborn librarians pores, of carpenters takes
    measure.
I open this book with an axe,
The grain pours within like a slice of a waterfall;

I slice open an acorn: down the corridors of power
Oak-lined parliaments approach, and votes approach
Like forests of people shedding green rain.

OR WAS THAT WHEN I WAS GRASS

I was putting a bandage of cobweb on the sudden cut
In the pain the fly told me what the web was like
The spider's face with its rows of diamond studs
And my skin crackling as the pincers drove in
That crackling pain went all over me
I knew I would never grow well again, my shell crazed,
And the acid came from the jaws and began to turn me
    liquid
And I felt a terrible pressure all over with the suction
And I was drawn up through the tusks into that face.
Then I woke up as though I were in a distillery
Humming with energy, retorts of horn and transparent
    tubes
Buzzing with juices, but I was at rest
Sealed like wine in crystal vases, and I looked down myself
With my eyeskin which was the whole egg, and I felt
The wine condense and become smoky and studded with
    rows
Of the eyes through which I saw that the mother watched
Benevolently from the roof of the factory which was
    herself
And my father whom she had eaten was with me too
And we were many flies also contributing to the
    personality
Of the eight-legged workshop, and I began to remember
    the man
I had fed on as a maggot or was that when I was grass
Or the snail slying from my shell crackled on the thrush's
    anvil?
And whenever my eyes closed or my shell crackled in pain,
It was as though I stepped out of black winged habits.

MY FATHER'S KINGDOMS

The lovely shimmering skins of water
Swooping between the lions
The gown of water of Trafalgar Square,
The hollow brides of water:
These belonged to my father;

And the policemen pacing it in their deep clothes,
Their silver switchgear on their Queen's helmets
They belonged to my father, said 'Good-day'

Saluting like the thunderous city.
All the clothes of the city-men, the umbrellas,
The sponge-bag trousers and the stiff white collars

Belonged to my father, the starched points,
The studs, the charged tie wedged in the points,
The sparkling shoes trotting down Threadneedle Street
Like city serge bright-sewing

These belonged to my father, and at the City's centre
God sat like a dome and with wide eyes
And broad wings and a smart tolerable beard
Jesus swam through St Paul's ceiling, said 'Good-day'

Saluting like the thunderous city
Which belonged to my father

The BBC's sparkling hair
Of lines of electricity that reached into our homes,
The voices that were correct from London

Belonged to my father
The trains belonged and the clocks obeyed the trains
And Selfridges and Father Xmas and Richmond Park
Belonged to my father, and his father gave it to him.

Even the bombs that fell on London
Belonged, he let a few in.

BORN

Born with a little cap of slime, his caul,
The midwife washed him, and the skin floated off,
She fished it out like a paper-bag,
Shut it in the dictionary, P-Z. Later
She peeled it off the page and folded it in a locket
She gave him on her death-bed, in the scent
Of coal-tar soap; even her death
Smelt like nurses; and when he wore it

For his own death he tried to rip the locket away:
It must be evil! for he wanted to rest
Closing his eyes but they were transparent
Like a caul and he saw the room unchanged
Except for his nurse who had arrived as his eyes shut.
She stretched out her arms as though he were drowning
But when he opened his eyes there was only his wife
Drowsing on a chair, but shutting them more people had
    arrived
With straining arms and faces about his bed,

And then the soap-smelling midwife bent and pulled at
    his face
And took a squalling red thing out of his head
With a little cap of slime, and he was awake
Among the grown-up people, his head being sponged
And the corpse floating off like tough paper in the bath.

ONE TIME

Her dress rushed and glistened as she went
She carried a green handkerchief
We walked through the first act of a great thunderstorm,
We sheltered in the silent ovens.
The clay had been built so deep and thick in the pottery
That no thunder reached us there, only the violet flicker
Through the doorways; the floor soft dry sand.
Now when I make love the memory of that time
Rises through my skin, her skin
Rushes and glistens as it goes, and the black thunderstorm
Deep in the silent ovens, lightens.

THE SHRINKING CLOCK

The pug-nosed bluebottle butts my window
Buzzing like a watch that shrinks the day
Into a hundredth of itself: now it walks
The white cross-beams and enters the sunny stage,
The light strikes rainbow sparks from its black waxes,
It is covered with oily spectra, like a black motorcyclist
It stands and preens in the hot sun-patch;
It is not clockwork: it is not filth;
It is a spark of the sun that knows the sun
And clothes itself with the sun; its eggs
Are sculptured urns of the sun, like sallow
Grains of wheat; it is a winged lion of the sun
Roaring, high-pitched and very fast roaring.

FROG-LEAP PLOPS

Frog-leap plops into the sandy water,
The water, the jouncing spring, its bubbles,
The fresh and skinny frog that dances
Upright in the spring,
The little clean legs, the clean satiny mechanisms,
The body of clean cushions and levers, lips and lenses,
Shimmering mucus and clean silky muslins;

The green cock-frog decays, still dancing
In the sandy spring while his generations
Of flickering black tadpoles surround him like black fire
He feeds them

Ah the water is a clean organ again
Dancing an upright pencil-thin skeleton.
Frogs are the cleanliness of water,
Not mere streamlined water in fishy capsules,
But water dancing in its springs of water,

It rounds in fish-shapes to flow,
In frogs to dance, and the dotted mucus
Everywhere in water like an eye of god,

Its black centre everywhere in limitless frog-pond.

AUTOBIOSTEOGRAPHY

When he was dug up his bones were found covered
With fine minute cursive writing which when rubbed
With lampblack stood out like a crabbed inventory that
    was
Notes for an autobiography composed as though he stood
In his bones with his flesh over his arm with his limp
    head
Reading what he had written over the everlasting portion
    of him;
It seemed to have been scratched with the diamond-point
Found loose in the grave at the site of the heart.
I thought that all bones had their life-story graved on
    them
Like a stony map of how I have used my flesh;
He did conscientiously what no one can escape:
Leaving stone maps of judgment. However, he
After writing that composition passed into the museum
    gallery
Where millions of soft gazes like a stream wear his bones
    away.
Dickens signed soiled collars on his American tours. Hosts
Pass through the sea, utterly changed, unscathed, without
    writing a word.

SHAVING

I regard the wet brown eyes in the stubbled mask,
Why do we all wake to the day in turfy masks?

I wet the face, I pat it, I energise its roses,
I begin the day by scraping off the dead layer of the night.

My face floats expanded in a concave dish of mirror,
Perfumed, embalmed, stung to life again,
A little streak of red mingling with the cologne.

Men with beards are wild men!
They stand around in their tangles of slumber and growth!

The shaven man learns anew who he is each sunrise
By standing in his own full view watching his own
     expression
For ten minutes while the blade sweeps away the blue-
     black embers
Of the night's fires; the tempered blade, Samurai! the face
     is born.

These faces rise into the mirror blue-black as from death's
     bruises;
Lazarus had a deep stubble of eleventh-hour shadow:

But he emerged from the cave super-fatted, shining with
     glory,
And beardless as a baby, his Jesus tomb-barbered him.

AFTER THE CRASH

My soapy meditation in my still-colliding bathtub.
I am all blurred, I am warm soapy water;
Hard edges are for dead people,
Like the breadloaf that cannot be holographed
Because it is moving, gently heaving,
Living even when sliced, cannot stay still
Till it is staled and corpsed; and the face
That hangs like a blurred mask
Behind the ruby hum, the laser,
That is an alive face: it is a trembling curtain.

The roads full of cars, pouring metal
With beating oily streams of air above
Like the syllable Graaaa endlessly pronounced,
Blurred from living death, the metal slightly blurred
With vibration, beating with hot air, then
As the solid car touches the solid car, the final
Dead stop with all the sound of the world in it,

A bird-call and a volcano, a soprano and a hammer,
All the possible tunes of metal, the trombone in the
     foundry,
And the mark of the sound wadded into a flat conch
     impact.

I lost nothing but an old tooth.
I rode the ambulance with the new moon like a keel
In hard-edge of the deadboat of souls above me.
I wash the oily skin and sound of the metal off,
I buzz still in my skin like those grinding hulls,
I see the water roughen in the buzzing bath,
Soap-clouds spread, the steel mantra dies.

The metal bees have sought their garages.
We are their honey and pollen, the sweet thing
They gather and destroy, the flesh-roses.

GOD SAYS 'DEATH'

God says 'Death' in a gentle voice
To the corpse sleepless with the wheats
That hiss on a low earth-note all night
Like a door hung over with dark leaves
Out of which the immense syllable blows:
'Death' in God's voice dressed in his spiderweb shirt
With its tassels of wheat, in his knobbly dressing-gown
Pulled from the oak; he
Says 'Death' with all his clothes,

And his mushroom buttons,
And his ponds which are mirrors
Tunnelling into the sky where he jumps up
Parting the thundercloud with electrical claws;

The reedy marshes of the railway, on some platform
Deep in East Anglia with the mire-drummer thumping
Through the lonely sky, God might pop out of the mud
Puffing a smoke rolled of flesh, dung and pelt,
And offer me one

And I could ask him then why 'Death',
And he would smile like a dago in his black cloak,
And offer me life to keep quiet about it,
'Would you call God a liar?' he hands me flowers
From the churchyard: 'Do you call these dead?'

VICARAGE MOONCAKES

The white pillar of water throws itself
Over the inlet cliff. What keeps the Moon up?
Nothing but itself, rolling over the ground,
Luminous millstone. The Vicar has made a clock
Out of balsa-wood and black soapstone,
He has a pair of pants of black bible-leather,
He has a parson's leather-jacket marked Holy
Across the shoulders, and Bible on the bum;
He has made a walking-stick
Of plaited straw: he likes featherlight things.
He lies on Fridays in a special bed
Which is a wooden plank in his large dry hall.
He writes a long letter to his Bishop, cold as a prison
    corridor.
He feeds a death's-head moth on a piece of marzipan:
He is an authority. The Moon
Grinds soft white flour over his parsonage,
The daily round bakes him like a loaf of crust,
And he feeds us with Jesus like little soft moonstones
That taste of marzipan from his lepidopterist's fingers.

THE GRAND LUNACY

The moon is the mansion of the mighty mother,
With its one blazing window it wings across the sky,
It is the abyss, sensing everything,
It is the opener, pulling up the frail spirit,
Snapping its rootlets a little more, each time.

Its glassy beverage, sticky as libido,
Oozes out of the mistletoe,
My moon-yolk leaps out into the bedroom,
Moon-beam, self-coloured.

The dead are the embryo people of the earth,
They are called Demetrians, eternal freshness
Is guaranteed for them; as the moon passes
They all stand on tiptoe, her beams
Comb them, they are like cobwebby wheat
As the wheat is, with its indefinite stalks,

Its frayed alleys of shadows, bending, tiptoe.

It is she who causes the woman's tongue in my mouth
To branch like an antler, and the wings of cupid
Deep in my body, to beat; it is she
Who twines her fingers in my skin,
Flays a layer as one pulls
A sheet off a mirror in which she stares

From the one window flying in the sky of her stone
cottage.

SEAN'S DESCRIPTION

The grave of the careless lady who swallowed pips,
From the rich subsoil of her stomach and snapped
coffin-timbers
A fine greasy crop of apples glittering

With their waxes; and Sean told me
Over a customary glass the best description he'd read
Of what a dead person looked like, actually:

'A green doughnut with eyeholes in it,' he said,
'A green doughnut with black cream,' as we sat

By the waterlilies rooted in mud of the pub garden,
And a bumble-bee in a tippet of glossy fur
Snatched a line from the air, and I brought
One of her apples from my pocket, and bit
Through the sweet flesh that fizzed with young ciders
And my toothmarks blazed white through the red skin.

'Look,' I said, holding up another firm sweet apple,
'This is what a dead person really looks like; taste her.'

THE LOOMS OF THE ANCESTORS

Cloth woven on a loom whose spindle-weights
Are made of the sliced bones
Of forefathers and foremothers.
The loom is the burial place of the ancestors:
The long bones for the treadles,
The sliced bones for the weights,
The thin bones carved into the shuttles.
As each person dies, some portions
Are fed to the birds,
The remainder buried in the cotton-fields,
The bones boiled and varnished,
Carved, and pegged with bone-nails
Into the loom, which is called
By the person's real name, which is not used
When they are alive, but is their loom-name.
Some flesh flies in the air, other meat
Is buried wrapping cotton-seeds,
This harvest also bears their name and is woven
On the loom of their bones which is placed
In the courtyard where the birds drink.
The garment is called by the relationship.
I am wearing my grandfather's aunt on my back.
My first wife is these knickers.
Sheep graze on the cemetery grass
Where the wool-people are buried, not far from the hills
Where we white cotton-people burst our pods.
When the sheep are filled, the goats graze there,
We ferment their milk to a spirit
Which speaks through the shaman's lips
Drunk on ancestors. The chief wears
A robe of woollen chiefs, many-layered as an umpire,
And the birds feed from his grandmother mittens.

I spin my father's white flesh onto my wife's fast wheel.

PLACE

The train's brakes lowing like a herd of cattle at sunset
As it draws up by Lesson's Stone, by mountains
Like deeply carved curtains, among small birds
Knapping at the stationmaster's crumbs, hopping-black
Like commas of wet ink: I could see their small eyes
    glisten.
I thought I must die in my sleep, I lay in my bunk
Like wet clothes soaking, the convulsions were the journey,
The bedroom bumped. I stepped off and the mountain
    landscape
Was like stone guests set round a still table
On which was set stone food, steaming
With the clouds caught on it; a plateau
Surrounded with peaks and set with cairns
And stone houses, and a causeway up to Giant's Table,
And the railway trailing like a bootlace. My house
Was hard by Lesson's Stone, near the sparkling Force
That tumbled off the cliff, that in summer
Left its dry spoor full of thornbush. Then the lizards
Flickered among the rocks, like shadows
Of flying things under a clear sky, or like
Bright enamelled painted rock on rock, until they swiftly
Shot sideways too fast to see. I arrived
On Lesson's Stone Stop platform a decade ago;
The place where I live is still like pieces
Of a shattered star, some parts shining
Too bright to look at, others dead
As old clinker. I am afraid to mention
The star's name. That would set it alight.

GUARDED BY BEES

The pornographic archives guarded by bees
Who have built comb in the safe; iron doors
From which the honey drips; I sip a glass
Of bee-sherry, yellow and vibrant; I came here
Past the old post-office, boarded up,
From within the cool darkness sun-razored
I heard the hum of bees; my friend tells me

That the radioactive cities of the future
Will be left standing for euthanasia,
They will be kept beautiful though all trees
And lawns will be plastic. Those who wish to die
Will drift through the almost-empty streets,
Loiter through the windows of the stores,
All open, all untended, what they fancy they can take,
Or wander through the boulders of Central Park, its glades
To hear the recorded pace and growl in the empty
    zoo-cages,
And consider the unperturbed fountains of water,
While it, and they, are rinsed through and through
As the pluming spray by sunlight, with killing rays,
Lethal broadcasts, until they can consider no more.
Germs over the whole skin die first, the skin after,
Purity first, then death, in the germless city that amazes
The killed lovers with its pulsing night-auroras.

I reply I would prefer a city constructed of OM,
A city of bees, I want this disused city
Converted to a hive, all the skyscrapers
Packed with honeycomb, and from the windows
Honey seeping into the city abysses, all the streets
Rivers of cloudy honey slipping in tides,
And the breeze of the wings as they cool our city.

This would be my euthanasia, to be stung by sweetness,
To wander through the droning canyons scatheless at first,
Wax thresholds stalagmited with honey-crystals
I snap off and munch, and count the banks
That must brim with the royal jelly . . .

And some wander through the sweet death, city of
    hexagons
And are not stung, break their hanging meals off cornices
In the summer-coloured city, drink at the public fountains
Blackened with wings drinking, and full of wonder
Emerge from the nether gates that are humming
Having seen nature building;
                                    others stagger
Through the misshapen streets, screaming of human glory,
Attended by black plumes of sting,
With a velvet skin of wings screaming they're flayed.

THRUST AND GLORY

A great longhaired hog, glistening with the dew,
It knows night by heart, sucked through blue irises,
But day it allows to rest and glitter on its skin
And its long hairs harsh as fingernails
Like coarse reeds on a hump of the bog.
It is a golden pig and its underslung rod
Is the very word for *thrust*, like the drill
Into the future, and it will run along that drill's sights;
But now, glistening with distillate, it waits
For the sun to raise moulds of steam along its back,
For the sun to warm it dry and the air to towel it
Testing its hooves meanwhile that clock on the stone,
Ready with its seed and tusks and bolts of muscle
And the grease of seed it pumps into the black sow
Like lightning-bolts into the hulking black thunder anvil
And the storm will gather until it breaks and rains pigs,
The mud glorious with rain-shine, pig-grease and wallow.

THE WHOLE MUSIC AT POD'S KITCHEN

While eating a crisp ice-cold lettuce at Pod's Kitchen
I thought of how the white flesh of cumulo-cirrus was
    ice,
How wind pulled the fronds from the seven-mile lettuce
That hovered daintily over counties, wide as a county,

I thought of how the thunderstorm whirls the white
    blanketings,
How the sheer-white terraces become a palace of
    fireworks
Like a Snowdon aviary of rainbows spreading their wings
And sparking their beaks and fucking in great thumps;

I find on my green lettuce
A tiny snail like hard snot

I think of poisons so old
That they have become precious stones
Pulling back to black earth edible men and women
And how the earth folds over them like grave
    thunderbulks
With white inscriptions startling in the dusk.

I swallow my edible green fronds and regard
My glass of water fallen from those clouds
In black thunder;

It stands still and clear, poised to enter me,
Like one long distinct note of the whole music.

A MOVE TO CORNWALL

I must raise a teashop in this place with my own two hands,
I am marrying a wife to conceive a child to adventure
Once more in these mother-lands, these hills
Like great fat mothers in green, dreaming
And as they dream sweating slightly in their sleep;

And the woods of grey oaks unravelling from their age
In green foils and glossy membranes this dawn's freshness;

The black-and-white fungus like a branch of magpie;

The radar we call trees reading the weather day by day,
Building models of the weather vertically in grids
Fining to twigs, the climbing axis of rings,
Cylinder upon cylinder of recorded weather,

Like old people crabbed with their reading,
Cramped among their books, the forking pathways between
    stacks,
Each apple a complete summary indexed in ten pips
That I shall serve baked brown and running in juice
With a core of sugar like melted resin,
With a drawer of money,
With a drawer of forks smelling of fish;

The child runs in from the swings; I gave her scalding hot
    weather-apples.

from LIVING IN FALMOUTH

I

Seagull, glittering particle, climbing
Out of the red hill's evening shadow into sunslant
At high tide and sunset; there is a moth
On the rusty table that spreads out wings
Like lichened tombstones.

A crackwillow leaf
Floats into an ashtray; we are among mirrors

And water, and the small windowed boats
Gently in the tide play with long beams
Like silent swordplay

And the gull arrives into the high air
Still full of sunshine, and his particle shines

And the boats knock gently among the shades
And the heads nod

And the good and bad dreams come swimming
Up out of the water glittering as they arrive

Sliding from under the red hills on which
The four-legged phantasms of wool graze,

Cloud-dreams let loose a moment of shower,
Dream-tides knock the fencing dream-boats
And two-legged dreams make one flesh.

II

I sit inside one of her granite tents
Praising against reason the high winds,
The stars hard like gimlets, her bronchitis,
Her onsets of winter and damp moulds,
Her spooks that do not linger,
Her magic touches.

She is only the same town from day to day
In the sense that a book is the same from page to page:
Or her water in the estuaries banked high
With mica-mud that glistens like satin garments
Ready for the spring to put on and shake out
To every colour, is the same water
That lies glowering under corpse-skies.

III

The tourists run like tides through granite houses,
Their ebb the dereliction of seaside pavilions,
Summer woods like smashed clocks, cliffs
Like crumbling cloudscape, dry-rot like wood-spooks
With white cobwebby arms: a bad smell, holding
Out a large repair-bill. Falmouth's bathing-beauties

Are sewing next summer in their dressmaking classes,
Her art-school a tenement of night-dreaming canvasses;
His clouds a tight lid God fastens on the box
Full of thousand-year-old churches and stony boarding-houses
Deciduous of visitors; her echoing mines
Terrible art-galleries for works
Of miner-death that mills tinfoil, of cars in the raw
Bleeding over the roofs of profound caverns. That
Organ-note as the Redruth wind blows over the moor
Winds on the pipes of long-dead mines,
Brings all the bad weather, all the 'flu.
This is the wind that blanches Falmouth, shrinks it
To thin-glassed tombs of drunken landladies;
Her blossoms wither, like an alcoholic flush;
The tourists ebb like tides out of the houses.

[…]

V I

A ship's figure-head bobbing in on the tide?
A floating pew, shaggy with saints?
Then I saw some of the hair was roots, it was an oak
Upended, a tree swimming ashore.
It bumped against the quay, nobody I could see
Stepped off its felloe of roots, but the town lightened
As if this traveller had tales. Two hundred years
Of voyaging oak, by its girth; say it had sailed
Round the world upsidedown since Garrick cast
An acorn into the Thames from Parliament Bridge. We got
    a tractor
And wrapped chains and lugged it from the harbour,
The gears screamed with the weight of the wet leafhead
Spread through the harbour like a green medusa
Dragged out of the sea full of acorns and foliage
Encaching tons of brine. I think the rains had clawed it
Out of Trelissick's precipitous shores upriver;
The Clerk replanted it in our Gardens. In my dreams
It is a true sea-oak, riding shockhaired over the dark water,
Voyaging through the years white-barked like moonlight,
Its branches like veins of light dredging the deep.

V I I

The whole world's water at some time or another
Flows through the Carrick Roads, bringing

197

Its memories and Chinamen, its Portuguese ships,
Its sectarians and its briny sea-fruit.
Some days the water is bloodstained with trade-battles,
Others it is birth-water running like hot fat,
Sometimes it is industrial dregs, quite often
It runs 'pure from crystal springs:

And Helford oysters
Sit in the Passages selecting these waters.
Harvested by leathery faces with good eyes
And hands like watercourses, they entrain to London,
To the potted ferns and bow ties,
Where they induce savoury dreams of moonlit water
And Ancient Cornwall, in new young tycoons,
Seductive Poldark dreams that draw the money west . . .

We watch the great cars glide by to the boardrooms,
We own only topsoil, the minerals are reserved,
The ground is sold under our feet.
The Oysters call them here, the Blooms keep them.
They will own everything. Let the land
Packed with underpalaces of gold dripping with oil
Be oyster-tales only, told to a mining penis
On a hotel-bed in London; let it be rumours only, lest all
Our first-born be made miners by the great absent landlords:
Not made deep starved miners by the enormous absent
    landlords.

[. . .]

IX

Cinder-cakes and sour beer. In the cider-cellar,
A corner stuffed with cobwebs, and a little grey drinker.
He drinks and drinks until his loins hurt, and what does
    he see?
It is what he thinks he thinks that matters to him now.
He thinks of all the stars like animals, he thinks he dreams
He snips a piece of bristling fur from each, and puts
Peltry of light into his purse to sew a suit from.
He jerks awake and laughs, in his cider-cellar corner.
When he tries to tell us about it, he gets lost
Among the processions of animals, and animal-headed men,
In among the feet and hooves plashing starlight. Amazed,
I suppose, like him, I love the moist stars of morning:

Orion with his brilliant cock shining like the wet
  spiderweb,
Like a ladder of light heavier than all the world,
Climbing in his drenched plumage like pulsing snow,
Like a silver beaten so long that it gives back light in
  pulses,
Or like a black tree over-arching, of white apples with
  pulsing juice,
Or like a rainfall so massive it gluts and cannot fall,
Or like a full-rigged black ship, sailing with all knots white,
Or like wet herringbones at the rim of a great black plate,

Or am I drunk on apples like crushed stars, potent fruit,
That turns you grey and folded one day as cellar
  spiderweb?

X

Our radio is sensitive, but there is, thank God,
Beethoven sunlight beaming from the ionosphere,

Yet I can hear rain on the radio, and I think I can hear
The sheep tangled on the hillside, and I'm pretty sure
I can hear the broad black stairs of the slate quarry
Like pages torn out of the open hillside
Rustling packets of static;

And there is thunder! far distant,
High-pitched, like cellophane;

The soft grey sacks of rain pass over
In scratchy slippers,
The water is a continual whisper
That paces all ways down out of the skies,
Plashes on boulders, puts itself together
In new ways, raising rain-smells
Over the boulders, down from the moors;
You can hear every rasp and scratch
Of water from our speaker,
Every drop in the whole sky:

And Beethoven's gone, dead
And buried in busy Cornish water.

Sea-waves that are dry
Come off the tide
Or off the rolling Redruth highlands,
Electrical Winds,
Charging us up

It is one explanation.
Waves of exhilaration,
Waves of political rich broadcasts put out by the moorsoil,
Sparkling their invisibilities, recharging us.

The real broadcasters are marching, they are a sightless surf,
There is wave after wave of imperceptible police,
Invisible black psychiatrists in coats the colour of sea-wind,
Invisible white healers in the moonlight
Charging us up

The gusty weather heaves all the leaves of the brain,
The red cells scatter, you can see views through them,
We shall be down to the skulls soon –
Recharge us!

The dead have powerful lungs,
Lungs like parks, sky lungs,
The cemetery sex-adepts at their pursuits,
Joining the worlds with their maggoty electricities,
They set my mind to work with poisoned arrows
That dance you to death like windy trees
Charging about.

From this room we see a clock of breeze
And clouds that run fast or slow depending on
How much we interest each other,
Recharging ourselves

Great dockleaves stampeding in veridian pelts,
Herds of them with muscles of breeze,
Leathery resurrectionists!
The dew crackles and sparks,
Charged up,

In this wind the Goddess kisses every child at once.

XII

The church is very real, absolutely too real,
It is realer than me, realer than where I live;
If this church is a house then I am a white shadow;
Look, there are written stones here 200 years old.
Being my senior by 200 years they do not speak to me,
Except with formal cursive manners like engraved visiting-
    cards
Quoting their names and numbers, their vast antiquity.
They are so still my footsteps must fidget them,
I expect they wish I were as still as they are,
Sitting in some pew studying stoniness until I grow slatey-
    cold.
And there is that vast cross-death that is worshipped inside,
Tainting the air with sweats and hymns so that breath,
Which is something he doesn't need on his side of the
    altar,
Is like a superfluous whispering of trees, appropriate to
    trees
Which are best cut down and employed as crosses,
Or chilled till they turn to stone; this death
Is so vast and old that the local deaths are trivial,
The people of the stones have not died, they have moved
    into the yew-shadow,
Which is a tree that has been casting shadows longer than
    I have,
And my parents who cast me are moving into the shadow:
    I follow slowly.

EXCREMENTITIOUS HUSK

In the bright light which is the sun's excrement,
That which it throws off in its processes,
I saw the big spider wrestling, intricately involved,
Wrestling with a shadow, with a filmier spider.
Was this its mate that it is sucking dry, is it
Topping up its fertilised eggs, the tight little capsules
With their juice of their father? Oh horror, I said,
That life comes out of death, and that this spider
Is feeding its children on its lover; and I saw
The spider struggle as a man might struggle

Out of his boots and his trousers soaked in the river,
And I saw the spider crooking and uncrooking its knees,
Extricating specks of claws from outworn skin,
Giving birth to itself in fits, like a belly-dancer, and having
     done
Scampering away leaving its dead self stuck to the altar-
     stone

Of St Cuby in Cornwall, mock-celtic restoration
It had chosen for its transformation
In the rosy light of the phony roundwindow,
With the little stream chugging under that altar
Where the Saint's bones would have been laved to make
     miraculous water
Passing south through his skeleton for every pilgrim to
     drink
In the fabulous middle-ages where every other bone was a
     saint,
And the spider was a nothing, and the altar too busy to
     think.

ROUGH AND LECHEROUS

The wind blows furiously through the laurel grove,
As the frost twists and shatters there are sparks of ice.
The oaks create the morning-mist that is arranged in
     shelves,
White sequence of oak-shapes as the dew steams off their
     leaves
In the sweet tinge of first sun like a staining of honey;
But he wants the harsh tastes, he is not a man
Who lives in the steering eyes, in the jelly-globes,
The geographies of coloured images without taste or
     odour.
That he left his white syrup-of-mushrooms in her
In a meadow glimmering in the moist dust
With white puffballs large as lambs, is recorded
In the memory of his palms, the soles of his feet,
His prick, his scalp. He folded the woods up,
And all the moisture with the sheep and the puffballs,
Folded them very small and passed them through her cunt
Like a painted cloth through a ring, and through his prick

Like a lance into the heart as they made love
In the hot rain that splashed and steamed off
Their bodies-in-spate full of tumbling scree.
The birds mute their white cinders, happily fluting.
Now she cooks eggs on the stove of lava-bricks;
He lifts the Mexican sugar-skull white as a seabird
Out of its red paper, and takes it to her,
With its meaning: I wish to kill you sweetly again;
The frost-crackled horse-mushrooms smoking as the sun
    touches.

THE NINETY-TWO DEMONS

The vast brown shallows planted with seaweed
Awaiting harvest: iodine harvest, the violet element,
Evening element of the violet clouds vast as the shallows,
Vast languid harvest beating in the rock-pools.
The seaweed-scyther comes, his trousers rolled,
His hands crackled with salt sea-gathering, the little rivers
Of hand-blood add to the millions-of-brown-tongues
    harvest
Licking salt, licking blood from the gathering hands.
The boulders flower slowly with stone barnacles
Built of boulders that long ago dissolved in sea-chafe,
The dissolved ancient boulders rebuild on the boulders.
There are only ninety-two elements and most of them
    come from rock,
And the violet iodine returns like hair to grow on the
    rock,
And the human feet made of seawater and stones
Splash in the shallows gathering iodine
Under the violet clouds, among the dissolving rock
Made of the ninety-two demons of existence who
Travel the length and breadth of it, whose names
Enable you to chemist them; you are they.

SILICON STARS

(Diatomaceous plankton)

In the deep of the sea, a dandruff of plankton.
In the thin sunlit layers life thrives,

As it drops into the ever-night of the depths
Buries itself in itself, in fine dust
Always-raining. Adam, look at it

With the eye that God gave you for naming the smallest.
Those are footprints of life sharp as spur-rowels,
They are silicon stars like transparent iron,

Each is a vessel growing from its own centre
And pierced with windows like Washington
And, falling empty suddenly, so raining
Like a snowfall of glass;
                          much whale-meat masters
The open ocean, whistling and plunging,
Whose turds of plankton are entirely
The massed crystal vases of the almost-invisible creatures

Hurtling down to line the ocean with mud that is fine
  porcelain.

PEACHWARE

On the stoneware platter, a peach of bloom
Faintly blushing, arse-cleft like a wet dream,
With a gathered-in feeling under the down
Of heavy sap, like a great drop of honey
Held by its fibre and a little napped pelt; at its side
A silver knife with a white bone handle and writing
Cursive on the silver, the surname, Box;
And on the one-hundred-year-old planks
Glossy with beeswax and a hundred thousand man-hours
Polishing, done in peachwood with mountings of silver
At butt and tip, with a bunch of thongs
Riveted with thin stars in stainless steel,
A whip in peachwood, a wicked little whip.

AMONG THE WHIPS AND
THE MUD BATHS

She offered the liqueur glass of Grenadine
Between her legs; the beard lapped it up;
She swooned, recovered, said
M. Grenadine's the man for me; and from that day
The establishment was known as Mme Grenadine's.
I saw her lose her temper with a punter once.
It was unprofessional, but after forty years of coaxing old
    cocks
She thought she had a flier, and it was not.
She screamed at him so furiously the sparks of anger
Danced in her teeth, picking them; she had a mouth
Of blue flame; I *think* I saw this; I was so respectful
That when she blew her top like Krakatoa I saw things
I did not believe. This went with the rumours of China,
How she was said to have learned to ease the slow blue
    lightning
Out of her skin and out of her lover's skin
So that they were sheathed in radiance, and the dark
    room
Flickered with their body-prints, like sand-dunes
    electrified
After a dry day. I did go in without knocking once
And I saw something gleaming, but it was so faint,
A kind of mouldy shine on the snoring bodies
Wrapped like beached tunny in their silken sheets.

I have flickered static out of the great bed
Its sheets clung to me and would not be smoothed,
And there is continual restless bedmaking in this place,
    but aside from that
Her power makes me see things, I mean her personality, I
    mean my love,
Among the balustrades and carved galleries of her house,
The damasks and the fur rugs, the whips and the mud
    baths:

All that sex populates my imagination and makes me
    happy.

THE WEDDINGS AT NETHER
POWERS

I

The grass-sipping Harvestmen, smelling
Like haylofts on stilts, creaking
Like wet leather; a raven hops
And picks at them through the gravel:
It has macabre dandruff.
In its spotted froth the bark-faced toad squats
Among the daffodils like Stars of David.

II

A wasp crawls over the crucifix, sting out
Searching for a vulnerable part; the savage vicar
Strikes, the usurper bursts in melted butter
And horn-slices; another takes its place
Searching with its sting out over the holy places.

III

A gold-and-black body pinned to a matchstick cross,
The extra leg-pair free, glossy with wax, their cloven
Dancing-pumps shadow-boxing with slow death;
The sting stretched out in agony and clear drops
Slipping along the horny rapier to the tip
Where a woman crops the venom in an acorn-cup.

IV

The laboratory with skylights, the glass assemblies,
Tubes, taps, globes, condensers, flasks and super-hot
    flames:
With windows wide open to the pouring waterfall
White with every colour and exclaiming with every
    word,
With roof wide open to the starfall; just down the
    stream
The Mud Shop, with fifty-seven varieties of bath.

V

Two birds singing together like learned doctors;
The dew is open on every page;

He washes the dog's feet gently with warm water;
She spreads luminous marmalade on cindered toast;
There is no tree of flies in which creamy skulls lodge,
   humming,
No dogs here have intercourse with any virgins;
There is a slug in the garden grey as a city kerbstone;
There is a cool sweet book of one page bound in
   appleskin.

VI

One hundred ship-weddings, the scoured planking, the
   pure sails,
The bride's train blazing across the scrubbed poop,
The century of marriages and a hundred brides
Pulled over the water by their blinding veils.

REV. UNCLE

The cool tankard engraved in wriggle-work.
A slight scraping or nibbling noise
In the house-timbers, like boughs chafing.
The salmon-silvery river over the red rocks.
A clockwork theatre. A munumental
Calendar musical longcase bellows-clock,
That measures the lunations and strikes
Christmas again after thirteen have passed.
A salt-saw in a glass case over the fireplace.
Rev. Uncle's 'Obby 'Oss: the rotary spark discharger,
Stinking of ozone with the blue crackling spark
Leaping among its wires like a chattering monkey.
He says: 'Teeth are the most indestructible of fossils,
And I wish to understand everything to understand
   God,
And because it is Sunday I make electrical sparks
To remind me of His Holy Ghost, nut-cracking ape
Swinging from Apostle to Apostle chattering
In tongues. I make myself
Both literate and numerate, Peter, and the alphabet
Is God's knucklebones of Pentecost
Where he fleshes himself fingers of flame, my lover,
And in algebra numbers are letters, you can hear

God's voice of creation when you vibrate the
    equations . . .'
And he did so, singing quadratics,
'Let X be middle C: now strike me an A . . .'
And I did so, on the piano.
'Not that the fossil-stone is a shut-in god,
Say rather it is a constant, something so slow
It shows its godlikeness only by residence
In many centuries. Don't tell the Bishop
But God-Mumgod made the world in their image;
Virgins like you will understand in due time . . .
Ma-God is a sea-maid, created from brine
Delicate skinned patterns of beating gonads
Like a fleet of umbrellas frailer than rain
Each like a seawater castle or mandala
A curtained pulse of bliss of the sea
And I tell you, boy, being dead is like that,
A celestial jellyfish shaped like the sky, beating, beating,
A whole eye, grazing on aether . . . but I love
Being God's vicar on two legs, lad, and the hymns,
Give me that A again . . .'

In my Uncle's library, my Mother's brother,
Every book and stone after church
Speaking his tongue, and on the brass lamp
His dog-collar swinging like a starched half-moon.

LIGHT HOTEL

The little girl riding the fallen tree like a spindly horse,
Like a queen mounted on a green spider;
The little girl's white flesh is so sacred, so queenly,
I love and fear it so much

Carefully I think only of her dress,
Her foliate dress that falls in dry green pleats,
Or think as I look away from her sunlit face
How the sunlight holds a great conference in a sandgrain
With its plate-glass terraces and vista-windows of gold-tinge,

Then how the moon will hold her conference in the same
    sealed chamber.
In between times the non-staff have no clearing to do, no ashes
    to empty,
No glasses to polish, the light simply passes, great guest,

The light simply passes from the hotel, it is left untouched,
And above the million sandgrains, the one girl swishing her
    wide green horse.

TALL HAIRDO

I

Her bronze hair beaten into a bearded face looking backwards,
She posed for her photo by the orchard, her coiffure
Stared backwards deep into the blossom where the clear stream
    raced
Full of its rippling fishes without blood, bones or skin
That wait for the apples to drop and become cider in them.
Open the wooden doors! cried that face
As her backwards-countenance stared deep into the trees.
I took my photo to purify the air,
Memory will perfect itself with its aid

Like bees sipping honey from a picture,
Painted flowers, real honey.

II

That face!
The grass grows fast in the starlight,
The sheep's entrails smell of mown grass and starlight,
The dew falls on the grass like the stars descending to feast;
That bronze gaze does it!
The rich bodies of stars
Covered with molten syrups and roasting waxes
Have dark-distilled themselves into featherings of moisture.

Remembering Jupiter's shadow
Peering out of the bronze hair-do,
In the roasting sun I smash that black
Bristling Devon fly: popping out of its back
Fat bunches of sallow eggs across the thin green window,
Like a banana-truck packed with yellow bananas in vehicular
    black,
Like smashing a flying ear of wheat which is black.

IV

The grave countenance of polished hair
Climbs into the evening;
There are clouds like Buddhas of slithering flour,
There are Butter-Buddhas of fatness, sunset-melting,
There are Buddhas of flowing pearly wax,
And now the storm, of great black-eyed Buddhas
Thrusting quick enlightenment from goffered halls.
Morning Buddhas climb rungs of frill and ruff, in the quiet air
White gulls turn, fine themselves
To a razor-line, turn back
A countenance alighting with a lemon stare,
A hooked nose, adjusting feather garments round a look
Rustling, of gold and black like apple-bees,

A waspish eye with a centre
Like the cold black earth flying a sunshine corridor.

V

She looks out of the picture,
Her bronze countenance facing backwards
Pores over the gravestones at St Materiana's:
Smooth bald slate to the east, light lichen coastwards.
We paced it out
Like walking through a great black tree
Of silver-lined leaves, changing as we passed
The colour of God's acre.

VI

The croaking frogs in the springtime:
The cries of unborn children.
The light shower sets the wood ticking

Like a great oval watch made of many oval drops.
For modesty, she looks down at her feet;
The bronze face rears up, alert:
Suddenly all the hoar oaks are chattering with auburn sunlight
As though troops of monkeys with torches ran through the
    boughs.

VII

Your inward skin studded with eyes like yonis
Looking down within you like the stars
Dilating out of blackness: there presides
Your photo-face and a bronze countenance watching
    backwards.
All the stars are gliding to fresh places,
Fretting as they glide, twirling like gimlets.
As they pass over, the dark apple-trees
Release their perfume in slow explosions.
They relimn into a new constellation
With two profiles that is the whole sky.

The moon climbs its slow hill to the centre,
Wish! it hangs there like a mirror.
Then the sun rises and does not put the stars out:
They shine still, strong black rays, and beams of perfume.

XII

THE APPLE-BROADCAST

(1981)

ON THE PATIO

A wineglass overflowing with thunderwater
Stands out on the drumming steel table

Among the outcries of the downpour
Feathering chairs and rethundering on the awnings.

How the pellets of water shooting miles
Fly into the glass of swirl, and slop

Over the table's scales of rust
Shining like chained sores,

Because the rain eats everything except the glass
Of spinning water that is clear down here

But purple with rumbling depths above, and this cloud
Is transferring its might into a glass

In which thunder and lightning come to rest,
The cloud crushed into a glass.

Suddenly I dart out into the patio,
Snatch the bright glass up and drain it,

Bang it back down on the thundery steel table for a
    refill.

SPRING

Even the bicycle-oil smelt of daffodils.
The full round drops slid into the little orifices.
I made my chain glitter.

I pumped the pedals with my hands, the bike
Inverted on its handle-bars and saddle,
And made the wheels shine like mirrors,

And they whirled like skirling puddles;
My pleasure was intense to think
Of the scented oil spun into the machine's recesses.

She came out into the sunshine from the house;
She wore a kind of bloomers and a blouse.
She mounted on her wheels like summer cobwebs.

The air was scented with my father's daffodils.
My pleasure was intense to see her cycle
And to watch the air puffing through her blouse,

Past every recess in her perfumed fields.
I opened my collar to the breastbone
Like a proper cyclist, and my erection

Was angular and pleasant on
My pointed pommel as I pedalled after
Along sweet-smelling roads, the scented oil

Spinning through my glitter.

THE BRITISH MUSEUM SMILE

None of the visitors from teeming London streets
Smiles. The deeply-lined downtrodden faces
Elbow the galleries. The sphinxes inside smile
And the colossal faces.
The face of a king with shattered legs
Smiles. And the guards smile. Their solitude
Forms into a smile and the patience
Of all the seated faces in navy uniforms
On the little chairs with the deeply-marked cushions
Smiles. They have caught it from the sphinxes
And the colossal kings and the powerful scribes
With the stone incense-bowls who smile sweetly
Over the smoky crowds. Some of the smiles
Are printed on the air from the faces of the guards,
And the stone faces have dissolved a little in the air;
Passing through and through the smiling galleries
Rubs inch by inch the face into a smile,
The smile of the king you pass (whose legs are sand),
The imagined absent smiles of the drenched nereids
Whose headless robes blow back against their flesh
In many folded smiles, whose smiling heads
Are museum air; the mummies

With their gasping toothy grins
Under the polite smile-paintings of their coffin-shells
Lumbered here by ship and block and tackle
Scattering a trail of smiles; elsewhere
The nereid heads are pebbles or sand,
And who picks up the pebble smiles at its smoothness;
(And the sleek sand is made of microscopic nereid heads
Turning and kissing in the water of the tide
The smiles rubbing from quartz lip to lip,
Dissolving in the sea and flying on spume;
The mariners inhale, and smile.)

Such smiles have flittered down
Like pipistrelles of Egypt on to the faces of the guards
And the smiling guards know something unknown to
    their crowds,
Something fallen from the sphinx that patters down
To fit you as you sit still on a stool
Polishing with your back those polished stones
For twenty years, or among those polished volumes
Not reading, but learning that smile. It took
Four thousand years to teach that smile
That flutters in these galleries among the guards
Who exchange mirrored smiles across glass cases; how
Did stone first catch it, that virus smile?

MY FATHER'S SPIDER

The spider creaking in its rain-coloured harness
Sparking like a firework. In the cold wind
Round the sharp corner of the house,

In the cold snap of that wind,
Many turned to ice:
Circular icicles.

My father lifted one off
Very carefully over the flat of his glove.
When I see these hedgerow webs

It is always with the sighing of the sea
In my heart's ear; it was at the seaside
In the smell of sand and tar that I first

Understood the universal perfection
Of these carnivorous little crystals
Coiling from their centres like the shells.

They were cruel and beautiful
At the same time; abominable
And delightful; why else did the silly

Flies dart into them to be drunk
Up like horny flasks, as if
The pints of beer had veiny wings –

If I could see those dartboard webs
Surely they could. They are doorways
To death and the mandala-sign

Of renewed and centred life. And this one,
Here, look, with its array of full lenses
(For the thread is fine enough for minutest

Beads to catch and roll the light in strings)
Is like a Washington of the astronomers,
Planned, powerful, radial city, excited by flying things,

At every intersection and along each boulevard
Crowded with lenses gazing upwards, pointing light.

DELIVERY-HYMN

(During birth the baby's head rotates against the os crucis
at the back of the mother's pelvis.)

See! the Woman is coming,
A Christ child in sun's rays
Painted across her clothing.

The Ancient of Days is in His heaven,
Dangling like a parachutist in angelic cords
Among white wings feathering and beating;

The Ancient's finger is hushing His nose,

He is white-nightied in womb-clothes,
Curled currents of birth-water are His beard;

His Mother's true presence rustles through all her veins,
He knows the whole Torah,
His skull bowed and in the mouth the small thumb,

Preaching the thumb-suck sutra from the hollow womb.
See, under her bellyskin little knuckles punch up at
    heaven!
The Mother croons over her cathedral-dome

Hymns to her Ancient who will emerge into light and
    form
Fragrance and other wonders in His good time,
But is first to be crucified headlong on bone.

Now He is full-bearded and in the nave,
His serene locks are curled pulsations of the water,
He is warm-shirted in membrane,
And knows the whole Torah.

(The Woman is coming now, and some Christ spills
Bright-red over her clothing.)

AT THE STREET PARTY

(Jubilee 1977)

Water makes her way, accustomed
Into all places, through mire as an eel,
Through the air as a hawk,

She gets past the obliterator of forms
Because she is the transformer,
Gets past clothed in food-chains,

Buckled into such sappy, stretchy satchels,
As wasps and gnats, such expanding
Revelation luggage as you. And the air

Which separates forms: to breathe with joy
Through the double nostrils, the nosethrills,
And to smell at the street-long table

Of the jubilee party in the open air
The head of my son as a mark of tenderness,
Smelling my sweet son in salutation,

Like fresh-baked bread mixed with the smell of tar
Of useful rope, sitting at his banquet
Under the street lamps with the other youngsons,

And – I could live on the smells of it –
He is warm and slightly sweating,
My sweet son, having drunk wine,

And I can smell the wine escaping from his hide,
And on the table the scones brick-brown
And the fruits arranged in castles,

And water making her way into our forms with joy
By way of wine and beer in cool pewter
As we drink to each other, and the pewter has its scent

Its faint eternal scent of tin, and the crowned
Heads above smiling wide on the flags, bending and
    rippling
Taking into wide mouths their great draughts of air.

GWENNAP CROSS

Suddenly, it is autumn,
The convolvulus chars
With a fleshy scent,

The little Saxon Christ
Stands among his ebbing flowers.
He is carved from oolite

With his arms outstretched,
He stands in his stone loop
Supported by a thick shaft.

The prehistoric seas strive
And the result is this same Christ
Speeding through the corridors of time

With arms outstretched and welcoming
As though the shaft into the ground
Were those self-same corridors of stone time,

For the sea has set as stone, and we,
We carve it into welcoming gestures.
And since the light that fell into the great tree's head

Became that plant, and the beasts
Nibbled and their bones were inundated
And sacrificed to geology, therefore

Is it any wonder that this stone
Became our patron?
Do you see a person here,

Or just a stone?
Do you see a person in the moonlight,
Or is the Moon just a round stone

With a hare carved on it
Flying without a shaft? If
It is just a stone, why

Does it fly, spreading
Magnetism like feathering wings
Whose beat you see reflected in the tides

Whose claws pluck at the water-margins?
I pause, and look up at the full disc.
Someone has carved a man there

Sitting safely in a boat
On its floodlit surface.
I kiss the head of the Gwennap Cross,

It is a hard and odorous stone
And tingling, but the smell in it
Is as though I kiss

The head of my baby with its rinsed mossy smell.

SALUTING WILLA

(The great boulder at the mouth of Boscastle harbour in N. Cornwall is sometimes known as 'Willa'.)

The warship glides in like a malicious buffet of cutlery.
Willa's petticoats are slamming under her stone dress
Like iron doors detonating deep within the rock,

Shuddering through the feet that tread her slate sills,
Her blow-hole smoking and saluting
That has buffed for centuries her inside corridors

With the sea's rifling from which they shine like glass
As for military inspection. The warship's personnel
Line their greymetal platforms at attention,

Salute with ship's guns the rock that has been firing
Its cannon at high tide longer than artillery
Was ever thought of, or steel could float,

The hollow rock volleying from its caves
Returning thunder with thunder
Back to the buoyant anvil hammering

Among the windcells and the catspaws tautly anchored.

THE SIRE OF BRANCHES AND AIR

I

The sire of branches and air.
The low waters begin
To give off their cunny smell;
It means rain is near.

We have the emergency edifice,
The umbrella, which is a cross
Between a city suit and an office.
The moist wind bends the trees

Which have acquired presence
And their extra dimension

From this alluring smell
Forced through their budding branches

From hammered reservoirs like cold pewter
    shields
To which they add their own pinch of cunning.
They are threads of pulse
To which the breeze

Puts its own beating fingers
Gently, like a bearded physician.

II

The branches toss with such question,
And swell with such abandon,
I think each tree is a child at play,

It has donned the wind
Like a playsuit that thinks up games,
And falls thoughtfully into its quiet folds,

Then the resumed wind mounts
The stiff sire of branches,
It is a ghost trying on bodies,

Streaming over the land and letting them drop
After their battles.
A great face opens laughing

In that tree-head, and in that other
Head, the hair smarms flat as a seal.

I think that elsewhere this spectre also
Is a child; that somewhere in a nursery
Just over the treetops, a child's

Sleeping body lies in its white bed,
Emptied of the small omnipotent ghost
That can overturn a countryside

Of leafy timbered rooms, like a burglar
Passing invisibly through green walls;
Now large pawmarks appear printed

Across the leafhead and satisfied
The spirit of the child condenses
From the muscles of wind,

Lays itself along the little body and
Shrugs its way back into the angelic countenance.
I open the nursery door on my way to bed,

There is a knowledgeable smell of rain;
I shut the window and notice how still
The cunning trees are on the ridge after the
     storm.

EARTH SHAKES AWAY ITS DEAD
LIKE CRUMBS FROM A CLOTH

They have smoothed their mounds down,
The dead, they have healed the soil and gone;
All is smooth lawn, a trifle long.

Where there was once an orchard of stone,
They have left, however it was done,
Only a seeding lawn, a trifle long

That works in the wind like television:
Across grass pictures, viewless sprinters run,
The prints of an invisible force flying,

Every wing-beat distinct in the grain
Of winnowing stalk and shadowing stem.
They have picked up their skeletons,

The people of clay, they have walked in their bones,
Plucked up their gravestones and not scythed the lawns;
I cannot tell how it was done;

All vanished into grass, a little long.
They have pulled up their static stones,
Their texts, and tucked them under their arms,

They have gone off like borrowers in the evening,

In the twilight returning dull thick tomes;
I wish I knew how it was done,

The graven texts gone.
All that is left is a shivering lawn;
Under it I can't tell where who was lain,

Or whether or how he is coming again,
The writing gone. Shadows hunt on the wind,
Calf-deep in cool grass I could hardly be stung

By these shadows of snakes, by these skimming scenes
Healed into a park; my feet laved in soft grasses
I wade through green streams.

Where are they hiding? I want to meet them
Now, before they are departed and quite gone.
Will they not be clean

And cool, like this wind-driven lawn,
And like the wind flying into the unknown,
Not by still text kept down, or solemn stone?

ROCK, EGG, CHURCH, TRUMPET

There is a churchy rock
Mothy with seagulls
Looking as it would fly

If only they would beat together
Their bread-mould pinions,
Fly like an angel of rock

With a stubble of wings;
Ripples pass over the rock
As though it were planted thick

With wheat that is mouldering.
The gulls mew-mew.
The rock that has indeed become a church

Is crazy with its wounds,

Having been sliced from the hill and
Blown up from it, and fitted together

On the same hill, a little higher:
The windows moan, the hinges shriek,
It is carved into weeping angels, it is

Thickly-set with their wings and open-mouthed
   guttering,
And is something between an egg and the rock;
Church is one of three kinds of feathered stone

That cannot fly. An egg is full of feathers,
A sealed stone globe, the pebble of a bird
That has roosted and will roost on a grey rock

That ripples its hide with feathers and shadows
In the creaming tide; and the church
Bellows with song attempting to take off

With the hymning engine of pewed people
Throbbing to us across the waves.
Stone is not just such an inertia –

Look at the little gymnast
Swinging to music along parallel bars
On those long bones; listen to the Tibetan

Flute of bone and the shoulder-blade violin
Strung with gut, and the creamy violin
Held high in the claws of a feathered angel;

The stone moon carved with a hare
Swoops over the feathering sea
That beats like the one tidal wing of the world –

Pull the cold bone up to your lips, Trumpeter,
Bark out with your angel-breath laden with spirits!

THE CAVE

He stands under a bright sky
With a rotten apple in his hand. It
Is a winged apple, for it is full

Of codling moths, and down the blackened
And webbed paths the seed still hangs
With its leafy corridors, its heaps

Of autumn fruit. The wings of the moth beating
Stir the leaves in the seed; the apple-egg
In his hand is struggling to hatch.

Every wing-beat is a new thought, then the thoughts
Speed from his hand and the sky is dark
With fringed wings and heavy apples, and the wings

Dip and he hears the deep breathing
Of the dead. After this, the conjurer in the head
Can develop his act. In it the clothes

Of the audience shall come to life, and strip
Themselves off the sitters, prance and dance
In the aisles, and the conjurer shall stand aside

And the clothes shall waft on to the stage
And clothes will pull chains of clothes out of hats,
Clothes will saw other clothes in half.

The naked audience, feeling their power
Stripped from them, their talking clothes, their
Eloquent masks and attitudes, shall sit

Attentive, naked as pips, while
The handless, headless, hollow clothes
Shall pull themselves through each others' textures,

And pray with hollow sleeves held up, and sacrifice
By unbuttoning and falling off the air, and fly
Like moths and lie in heaps like leaves,

The conjurer thinks of his act, holding the winged fruit
In which the seeds sit watching the moths eat.

FULL MEASURES

People sailing down the river
In wooden vessels between the magnificent trees,

Leafy cisterns of river standing in their own shadow
Like avenues of barrels in cool cellars

That grope up to feel green in the skies,
River flowing upwards from miraculous bottles

Of willow contentedly rowing the river to God;
The true source hovering, blinding white, over the mountains;

And it is moving with a note, like great brown lorries
Of goods trains rumbling full of water, though it is

Like one long umber room of sequent chambers
Sliding through each other, which are pulses

Echoed from the rainy source, the rocks
It bounds down, the turfs that hold, one long room

Broadening and full of sunlit motes
And recapitulating ripples. Quantities have paused

To fill the trees, to construct shady paths
Before they volplane back to water in the flat

Veined drops of autumn. Other water
Pauses in its stages like passengers

Passing in wooden vessels between magnificent trees.
The sky's bartender in blackening whitecoat

Prepares his biggest drops, full measures.

II

On the boat made out of trees I drink my beer
And hold it up to pledge the river; it matches,

It is mainly water, and stays a while in me
Rejoicing and transmitting visions

Of where it's been, some of which I see. The ocean
Drinks at the river's mouth, the sky

Bends down to sup the waves, and water
Runs invisibly up the wind-ladder

Disclosing as it flies great ice-ships,
Snow-rigged, spunglass frigates, until it is too heavy,

Can go no further, and returns barking,
A great hound of thunder. And on the evening river

Under the leaves the water flies
In winged drops with a sticker drinking

Freely from all a special heavy beer
Fermented in our veins for generations

Travelling in our veins like walking rivers.

FROM THE LIFE OF A DOWSER

Water is bad for him, much too exciting.
He runs away to Cornwall and drinks
From the sparkling well, *Fenten ow Clyttra*.

As he lifts the tin cup he wonders,
Trembling like the water in the cup,
What it will show this time, after so long,

They have boiled his water, made him drink tea,
That is stunned water, but he believes it thinks
As it tumbles over rock, breaking white,

Or streams into the high air, breaking white,
Or lies below its lintels in old stone wells
Pondering like some long transparent god

Waiting to be consumed and joined to more of him.
The Dowser believes, looking into his cup
Where air-bubbles in the water cluster

On sheer mirrors like silver tods of grape
And feels like that god about to drink
Some vineyard that is moonlit. He shuts his eyes,

The water is cool, and tin-tasting,
A spectre of earthy darkness brushes by
His throat, and disappears. There is nothing more.

He gets up from his knees and brushes them, regards
The avenue of long grass in which he stands

That burrows into the hillside with at its end
The stone lintel to water like an open wardrobe
With clothes of light flung about the grass

The dew-sheen and the spidery coronets
Which shiver like those bubbles of the well,
And a triple stone head on the cross-beam leering.

Still nothing more. Maybe this
Is enough to dig a well into the hill for,
To sculpt it and process, to make pilgrimage,

But then, why here, when everywhere
I break some slate in a damp cutting and water springs,
Whenever I dig my garden down into the water-table,

Prod five finger-freshets in the ferny turf.
Water is everywhere, and I think with it,
And remember with it, inside this rock

(And raps his knuckle on his brow),
And speak with it, as the clouds make scenes
And scrolling pictures, like a god

Opening his mouth and bellowing through
Lips and beards of water, water streaming
Through him like a fall or force, when

The frowning clouds in white coats came for him
Like falls walking and he forgave them. Now water
Is still in him, and well, and pondering.

GRIMMANDERSON ON TRESCO

A pocket Moonbible by the lacy shore,
A Ladybible of God the Mother,
Of ultimogeniture: the lad
Freshest from the womb inherits
Nothing but fortune's favour
And extraordinary companions
On the electrifying adventure.
These are not wrinkled scriptures
In fly-dirt size on india paper
Crisp as a fly's wing; it is
A story-teller's stout handbook
Of basic situations: the old king
Needs a wife, the great toad like a wasted moon
Waxes Queen aboveground; the battered soldier
Steals a tinderbox, and has
Dogs with piercing sight at command;
A white snake tasted from a covered dish
Imparts to the breakfasting king bird-speech.
You do not cling to the scripture,
You improvise with spirit.

On a rock above the delta where I read it,
A fruitfly shares my apple with me,
Tastes my fingers and walks about my palm
With its bicycle-pump tongue.
It has a horny frame
Dwindling delicate as a tropical shell;
It is the self-same shell-stuff
As those beautiful thin million ears
Listening inside the Atlantic fetch.
It has cobbled spectacles it cannot take off.
On this dry day my friend
The painted conch with wings,
Sips, sips at my sweat-beads,
As thirsty I puncture my apple's skin,
Drink its fountains of juice stored up for me,

Read Grimm's bible by the spumy shore
Where fruitfly swaggering like an inheritor sups
Sweat-apples of my palm's seamed thoroughfare.

RENFIELD BEFORE HIS MASTER

*(Renfield was the lunatic in Dr Seward's asylum
who assisted Count Dracula during his English expedition,
and who loved to eat flies.)*

I

He was eight when he started earning
His living in a silk factory;
The big bales, corded with twist,

The incipient peignoirs, the feminine slink.
Was he a spider at all, once?
The managing director nipped the nub

Of his silk-web, at his shiny long table
Sipping at telephones, and his workers, caught,
Buzzing and gossiping

At the endless benches of their lives along which
The silk slid in thin rivers.

II

He liked bouncing in the bales, sneezing into
Their dusty canvas hides like crabby shells –
Lying outstretched over them

Gripping the cordage with one's hands
And one's feet braced, one's loins
Buried in some special penknifed silken gash, and one was

That male spider with a bellyful of silk oneself.
He would watch the canteen flies,
All possible silk, and at home

He kept in a pearly bottle choked with gossamer
A lustrous great spider he fly-fed; he had become
Clever enough to snatch them on the wing

Wondering at how the beautiful webs
Could yet be spun out of the corrupt glues
That were the fly's food; he mused upon

Those husks caught up in orrery rounds,
Emptied of all purpose, yet white
And winged as angels. He knew

The silk of his employment was spun by worms
Of a moth, and dreamed of feeding that moth
To his spider, the silk would be redistilled, radiant

With the light and pulsing beauty of all the trembling
    moths
That spin silk clothes for the babies of themselves
Wrapped and cross-clawed like an Egyptian Karast.

III

The butterfly or the sulphur-moth sucking at her weed
Is only one of the beauties; her transformation
To thin taut threads under the same sun on which the
    spider

Dances to eat her is another of them,
The skeletal patterns of cracked shadows in the sun;
And the beauty of the crabby lichen-back

That chucks her loins from side to side
Like Lola Montez, and tiptoes out
To wrap on tautened lines her prey in bales,

Is yet another, as he thinks
Drowsily of sleep, that great spider
Bending down to suck his soul from his face,

Kissing face to face, and turning it
Into that sensitive web which fills the nightworld
And catches fluttering dreams for nourishment;

So Renfield's madness or peculiarity
That loved the creaures so
The rest of us despise, led him

Fearlessly into the night of dreams,
Young silk-factor, where he met the master, Vlad,
Who fed him endlessly from thin soft hands.

IV

Who fed him endless streams of drops on wings
Like mother's milk, choice flies, and told him:
'Be that spider whom you fear, I, Vlad Dracula,

Will so transform you, as you wish,' and showed him how
Life flows in liquid drops, through fangs,
Creature to creature, in chains of drops like webs,

And whose work he did, so long as he was strong,
Guiding the young white girls to dance
Upon the webs without being caught by Death,

Raising them to drink as It did, spiderly,
Until fly-swatting Van Helsing clapped his fat palms
Smack and said 'No more of those,' wiping hands

Stained from the stake down immaculate spun hose.

ORCHARD WITH WASPS

The rouged fruits in
The orchard by the waterfall, the bronzed fruits,

The brassy flush on the apples.
He gripped the fruit

And it buzzed like a gong stilled with his fingers
And a wasp flew out with its note

From the gong of sugar and scented rain
All the gongs shining like big rain under the trees

Within the sound of the little waterfall
Like a gash in the apple-flesh of time

Streaming with its juices and bruised.
Such a wasp, so full of sugar

Flew out within the sound
Of the apple-scented waterfall,

Such a gondola of yellow rooms
Striped with black rooms

Fuelled with syrups hovering
At the point of crystal,

Applegenius, loverwasp, scimitar
Of scented air and sugar-energy

Shining up his lamp-tree tall and devious
Given utterly to its transformations

From sharp-scented flowers to honey-gongs,
Giver and taker of pollination-favours,

A small price for such syrups and plunderings,
Its barky flesh, its beckoning fruit,

Its deep odour of cider and withering grasses,
Its brassy bottles and its Aladdin gold-black drunks.

THE LAUNDROMAT AS PRAYER-WHEEL

I

The whirling pole bound up in linen,
The Lord of the Dancing Axle-tree;
There is a resurrection with a loud synoptic cry.

We move from place to place like shadows of the
    whiteness
Of these garments which seem woven of light
As they draw out of the mechanical sepulchre.

It is the night of the Mystery of White Shapes,
The angel is here, a splendid presence, like electricity in
    linen,
I fold the double sheet up, I wrestle with its wings.

The dazzling garments like dead bodies light the tombs
Of resurrection-devices, washing-machines in lines,
There are dancers full of water in the drums

That dance their twisty music to the coins,
Elastic celebrants treading in the tombs
Unwinding reels of flickering ghost-films.

The tumbling shirts are scalded fresh,
The hankies fluttering
Like the leaves of a white oak in a blowy cave.

The ghosts that appear in sheets!
Whisk the sheets aside, and what is under? Puffed water,
Geist, *Gischt*, gust or swimming foam.

When the neutron bomb explodes, it is the garments that
    survive.
A spotless white shirt falls shuddering to the floor,
A muslin gown settles peacefully to the grass.

He is clad in a cloud of fresh clothing warm and dry.
A really white shirt feels white when your eyes are shut.
The coffin-maker of Nazareth was a snow-white
    carpenter.

II

The superiority and glamour of a candid white garment.
As though wrapped in light, like a white-washed house,
I study the radiance of my shirt with my eyes shut,

As though wrapped in lightning, among the
    thunderstorms.
Men clothe themselves in dark in imitation of the clouds,
They darken their white clothing to show obedience

To the natural courses, the tinctured farmer bends
Over his muddy fields as the rain-clouds do.
Toiling in mud will not reproduce the lustre

Of low clouds as will acacia or indigo.
The naked body is vile, and lacking in speech,
The clothed flesh belongs to a man of eloquence

Whose skin of alertness converses with the hugs,
The featherings of movement, whose skin
Instructs him that a garment is a reservoir

Soaked in strength, and fabric a tunic of kisses
Like the heavenly tube through which the earth flies,
Arraying to their seasons, echoing.

Even the rain is white, and has a white belly,
Is affable, and clasps the gowned body
With its soaking grip in lighthouses of lustre.

LECTURE OVERHEARD

A great white ear floating in the sky, listening. I say
That your hair is but the beauty of ashes of blood
Passed out through your skin. I tell you how

We all live in our manacles which are
The food-chains forged by the sea. Light
Pours on to the brine, and the little creatures

Which are green dust thrive there, to be eaten
By the larger: small creates the great.
We munch the daft-eyed herring of that union,

We lift the salty waves of its flesh off the hairy bones.
The great tree of water flourishes over the sea
And begins walking on its visible roots

And then rain storms over all the land.
Holes are blown in houses, and their roof-scales
Lifted off the hairy timbers. It lightens and

Dissolved nitrates leach into the soil, the great
Thunder-voice utters fertility. In its echoes
Rings of trees spread out and protect our land

From the leaky repeated visits of the white water-engines
Of dazzling rain cranked out of the depths.
Grass spreads its tablecloths, and the cattle feast,

Our feast feasts. We pocket ourselves
Under open stone books and gravestones
But our substances distil in needlework

Of water back to the sea and there become
Dust-creatures and the shock-eyed salmon.
I have carved a large spider in wood

I have incised its globular body with the food-chains
Which wreathe about its jaws. See, the spider is hinged
At the edge of its carapace – open it – there is

A little carving of a baby, smoothly-grained,
Nestling deep in its spider-box, the future
Nested in the spider. The great white ear

Passes on, having overheard. We listen to the sea
Which renews, you can hear the reversal
Coming and going, with its sighs. The great ships

Pass by in chains, loaded with provisions.

GUNS AND WELLS

I

The artillery-men wait upon the big gun,
They have its banquet piled
And ready in greased pyramids,
They serve the long fat shells like cannelloni,
The gun munches with an explosion.

Molten tears silver our countenances,
Vomit of metal plates the cornfields,
Men blow away like smoke in the ringing brisants.

No doing of mine, says chef-commandant,
I feed the guns only when they are hungry.

I I

She tells me the polished skull of a traitor
Lurks in this well still,
His comrades gave rough justice,
Over the parapet laid his bare neck,
Cutlass-sliced that smuggling head,
Which dropped like a boulder
And is down there to this day, she said,

Polished nearly to nothing,
Bobbing in the well-spring,
Folding and unfolding in the polishing water,
Almost glass, and papery-thin,
Ascending, descending on variable cool water,
Nodding upon a current which is a spine,
Spinning like a film of faintest shadow
Or flexile churchwindow,
Reflating when rain fattens the spring;

Then a sunbeam
Strikes down the brick shaft
And there gazes upwards, revolving in the depths,
A golden face; then the sun

Goes in and the water goes on polishing.

THE WHITE, NIGHT-FLYING MOTHS CALLED 'SOULS'

I

Their bodies all uncanny slime and light,
I brush silvery maggots off my white bible.

239

We are copies of each other. Bound in leather
The book crawls among us with a loud voice,

Dead men's matter wormed into chapters
Between the first communion doeskins.

Worms are the messengers rustling in the print with
        quills,
Masters of God's word, the bible bookworms;

We are dead men's matter, gene-edited,
Say God's bibles, covered with worms.

II

The moths flutter at the candles like clothed ladies,
Like long ladies in Assyrian gauzes;

The moonbeams twine through the flowers creating
        nectars,
The moths sip, and reclothe the moonbeams in light
        leathers

And dusty gauzes like Assyrians for their dances,
And these moonbeam moths sup at the candles

Like soft explosions.
The sunshine falls on meat, creating liquors

The blackflies sip
Dressing bright sun in greasy leathers,

Tight shining leathers, and like Assyrian dragons
Trample on my bible-hide and kneel roaring

At top pitch, dabbing with their suctions.
The little bony flies come to the Bible

Because it reeks of sacrifice. O God,
Burnt offerings like blue candles of the ghats

Twirl in smokes of fat to Your motionless courts,
And we brushed the stout Baal-zebub flies away

That wished to wing Your meat, and clothe it, God,
In white maggot-skin, like bibles. The Lord's talon

Out of thunder slashes meat, scorches off the skin
Like opening His book, and He snuffs the odour,

Clothing the meat-nectar in the Lord God; and Who
Brings His own untouched flesh to His pregnant Bride?

III

The wireless at midnight gives out its hum
Like a black fly of electricity, folded in wings.

A moth like a tiny lady dances to the set,
This hum is light to her, a boxed warm candle,

This set has inner gardens full of light.
Our baby, like a moth, flutters at its mother,

Who mutters to her baby, uttering milk
That dresses itself in white baby, who smiles

With milky creases up at the breast creating
Milky creases, and milk-hued water

Hangs in the sky, waiting for its clothes,
Like a great white ear floats over us, listening

To the mothy mother-mutter, or like a sky-beard smiles
And slips into its thunderous vestry and descends

In streaming sleeves of electrical arms
To run in gutters where it sucks and sings.

SONG

I chuck my Bible in the parlour fire.
The snake that lives behind the bars there
Sucks at the black book and sweats light;

As they burn together, the codex
Flips its pages over as if reading itself aloud
Memorising its own contents as it ascends curtseying

Like crowds of grey skirts in the chimney-lift,
In particles of soot like liberated print.
The vacant text glows white on pages that are black.

The stars, those illustrious watchers
Arranged in their picture-codes
With their clear heartbeats and their eager reading stares

Watch the guest ascend. Around us in the parlour
The inn-sign creaks like rowlocks.
The drinkers glower as my book burns,

Their brows look black
Like open books that turning thoughts consume.
Then all at once

With a gesture identical and simultaneous
Of reaching through the coat right into the heart
They all bring out their breast-pocket bibles

Like leather coals and pile them in the fire
And as they burn the men begin to sing
With voices sharp and warm as hearth-flames.

The black pads turn their gilded edges and
The winged stories of the angels rise
And all that remains is our gathering's will

Which assembles into song. Each man sings
Something that he has overheard, or learnt,
Some sing in tongues I do not understand,

But one man does not sing. I notice him
As my song takes me with the others. He is
Setting down the words in rapid shorthand

In a small fat pocketbook with gilded edges.

PHEROMONES

(Pheromones are 'external chemical messengers' given off by the body. They are said to communicate profound emotional and physiological effects from person to person.)

Dreaming of a dog, whose nostrils
Are his lightless eyes, means
Murder and riches; under the sunshine

Blazers bright as bluebells
With brass buttons yellow as butter;
The strong light

Shooting down the polished walking-sticks,
Running in sticks and streams,
Calls like trumpets

To the game;
The sea hedgehogged in gold,
Frogged in it, like a great blue blazer:

The great doorman with the labouring heart.
In this heat your scent is a snapshot,
Your spoor streams from you like a fragrant picture.

Your fingers
Sniff down your glass and walk into my lap.
It is so hot

My sex is a shelled snail,
And I excuse myself from You
For my nostrils wish to savour

The self-scent of my own sex
This gathering promotes,
And so my smelling fingers tremble first

At the eternal curry-smell of the brass handle
Of the metal of trumpets of the Gents
That it never loses or ever could lose;

Doubtless a dog would know its master
For over the brass in thinnest films are laid

The identities of all who have here touched
themselves.

I bend my nose to the knob, for I swear
The champion of tennis employs this place;
I would know his sweat anywhere

After that magical game:
He filled the court with the odours of his perfect
game,
Excellent musk, wiping his handle;

Let the trumpets call his prize!
I enter and am girded with personalities,
Long ghost snailing from the bowls

And gutters; my own genius mingles with that
Of the champion and the forty-seven assorted
Boozers I can distinguish here in silent music,

In odorous tapestries. In this Gents
We are creating a mingled
Essence of Gent whose powers

To the attuned nose
Are magnificent indeed
And shall affect the umpires

Who shall agree with what their noses
Tell them strides viewless from the urinal
Where the gentlemen sacrifice into stone bowls

In silent trance. Oh how
The tennis champion strikes pheromones
Under my guard with his far-sighted nose;

He has brought us to heat which calls him
In blond hair and buttons to his trumpeting prize.

DREAM-KIT

Shut away here in Cornwall
With these provocative black
Materialising cabinets: TV or radio set,

That raise horrors and slight
Glories in the mind with
Invisible rhythms caught in

Their lightless black interiors
On skeletal fingers. The whole
Earth's atmosphere is a pond

Of trembling waves made
Of invisible colours, a river
Of transmissions full of

Coloured images of where it's been,
Its receptive water peering into cities
Full of troubling troubled ripples

The news makes and the dramatists
And the rainbowing commercials, and packed
With invisible creatures that swim

Plainly into view on the
Aquarium of your screen.
The set itself is like the window

On to a great tank of sharks,
Or one set into a swimming-pool,
Or into a river's banks,

You switch from place to place,
You have so many windows; it is like
A diving-bell searching over ooze

Or a tumbler pushed into a stream for you to see
The sportive minows footballing
Back and forth over the green watery colours:

But they are all phantasms: you are watching
Vibrations only, rhythms, which are

Nothing shaking the radio-ether, which is

Nothing also. Racks and racks
Of goodly-looking nothing in a broadcasting
    hypermarket
Transmitting centuries of miles away,

And not at that moment either
Since these are only phantasms of reflections
Stored on tape, strips of plastic

Lined with finely-powdered forms of rust.
And these rays penetrate our brains,
Like God's rays of outer space

That warm us, but unlike those
Asking only that we remain
Distracted. The TV set

Is an artificial dreaming-kit.
The true instrument
Is the dreaming mind

That pushes its tumbler
Into the river that flows
Under the skin: the groping

Caressing fingers enter
The neck's skin and grasp words there
That cry out.

THE JOURNEY

Carriages sealed, and marked 'reserved'.
In the dining-car everyone turns
Frowning at something that slips out of sight

Past the window among the thundery horizons.
The clouds are like black cliffs streaked
With torrents of lightning, with the rain

Flying against the panes like an explosion in a glassworks.
Clouds like great white moths, wet moths
With the voice of an old lady out of control,

Mist riding over the gravel-pits like white Christians,
Mist on the steely waters like the cliffs of heaven.
I see stream past the window

A magpie like a black bible partly open, fluttering
Its white pages between black covers; it arranges them
So that some text is always showing; the wind

Flicks its pages and the bible spins past, and everyone
Turns to look again. One bible? What bad luck . . .
But here comes another, slowly rowing after the first,

Catching it up at last. Bible and counter-bible,
Man bible and wife bible: good luck for eternity.
The thunder has a human voice, now it is coming close

To having a human face: the clouds fold
Into a benign countenance, turning away. Behind its
    skull,
A bright shaft of sunlight breaks through.

On the rubbish-dumps I see the breeze still blowing
And the many feathery plant-seeds like travelling candle-
    flames.
They are burning rubbish-heaps like vast

Lantern-faces set in the hill, like a
Village of windows. I think that a city should not
Be hemmed by its disjecta, however beautiful

At night, but that it should be surrounded
By a wall carved to sound a fanfare on the dawn wind.
I observe this to the young lady opposite; she does not
    reply;

Her toes wriggle guiltily in their open-work shoes
Like a little stream over its rubbishy pebbles.

THE SECRET BREAKFAST

The secret that was her marvellous beauty;
Sometimes he saw it everywhere, when he least expected it,
Though at any moment the bad habits would wear thin

And it was there in items of his person, or in what
He had not thought to look at before. He might suddenly
Catch a glimpse of it among the birds,

Not the song merely, but the flicker
Of white excrement muted
Between the legs could give it;

Just that phrase, 'muting a white
Excrement', with its flicker, could
Do it. 'Why,' he said, 'my world

'Is broken up in patches, little
Windows. The domes of the acorns
With their polish as of some Islamic masterpiece

'Infinitely jointed: they will have it. But
The oak is not my lover, only my friend.
Snatches of a friend's speech open to the beyond,

'The touches of a lover's hand are guaranteed!
But I will keep my scepticism,' he shouted,
As he walked into the breakfast room

And the table set was a sudden playground
Of toys, arbitrary and laughable shapes
That demanded to be played with; the spoons

Like paunching fairground mirrors on handles;
The boiled eggs like sealed skulls, full of a runny thought;
The salt like a caged swarm of pure white flies

In a fluted aviary; the pepper
Like beige gnats each with its pungent sting;
The fried eggs shining like the sun and so defenceless,

Blood of greasy gold; the napkins folded
Each in its ring like the silver thorax of a snow-moth;
Marmalade like an aquarium of orange eels;

The butter shining like a sweating steed
In its small loosebox; all the forks
Tingling with their tunes; 'Hum,' he said,

Watching the zoo parading and his actual breakfast
Coming and going, like poetry
In between the factual lines; 'Good,'

She said, not bothering about his hesitation,
But knowing he was happy, and that, in his case,
Meant seeing things, while

The eggshell fluttered in her white hands.

THE HOUSEKEEPER

The long esparto of the nether world,
The grass avenues that rip you to pieces
Whispering *Isis, Isis,*

Go there a second time
And they restore you whole;
It is worth risking all.

The left hand of God is clothed
In a whispering glove of rushes,
Or it is clothed in a bed that creaks

Like leather; I found a great spider
That held fast like straps of leather tacked
Behind my picture of the Vicar smiling.

In the high wind, in the churchyard, he and I
See that the spiders are having difficult landings,
They have become caught up in their parachutes

Now their flight is hampered by a light drizzle –
They cannot raise their soaked webs, their windrows,
Their skyhooks, their gossamer strands

That lift them into the unknown by their
Bottoms where the spinnerets are; these matters
Blaze at me because my buxom pillow

Waits for the kephalia of my teacher, while the yews
Distil their flashing poisons over the indifferent graves.
I will seduce him from the church

With the empty foxskin
That wraps my full white bosom; after
Through the mists and jet black graves we'll wander

With the light gone out of holy marriage,
Religion changing hands, and all the old
Arguments gone. The sea goes on

With its distant signing on all the beaches,
White writing on gold. I draw off his limbs
Jesus' black shroud of cleric's cloth.

My master of communion
Lies flat on the pillow like a snake flattened
On the superspeedhighway, crushed

And recrushed by the speeding traffic,
Its venom evaporating
Harmlessly. I have tried

The taste of the cloth mask of his chest,
I have loosened his linen collar with my teeth,
Rustling *Isis, Isis*, and he comes

Like an express-train, calling on
The thousand-windowed name of God; and now
It is the yews distilling slowly on the mirror-graves,

And the marriage gone up the chimney where the cats
    shriek
On slanting roofs in midnight moonlight. My cup runneth
    over

And my house is as if full of holy bread new-baked,

A tough flaky roof and inside
One entirely beautiful white bed that must be eaten
Smelling of love's light alcohols and yeasts

Before staleness hardens it like holy marriage.

SILENCE FICTION

The late houses are built over the early caves,
The foundations and cellarage are where the first people lived.

We have fitted stout doors and hang their keys
High in the chimney-vaults where, out of sight,

They gather from the flames great swatches of soot,
Bunches of soot-flowers out of the food-fires,

Like the brushes of black foxes through the generations.
Then in the especial bad times a besmutched woman

Enters in defiled white to fetch down our keys
And open the earth to us. As she stands in the threshold

We know we must cast over our hearth pitchers of water,
And she treads through the warm ashes and with black sleeves

Reaches into the hanging soot,
Unhooks and rubs across her skirt revealing

The bright metal under the black grease. She
Throws the key down ringing on to the stone flags,

Leaves into the dusk for the next house.
We unlock and descend into the cellar-roots,

Light in the chimney-roots our lower fires,
And begin our lives on the unadorned earth floor

Some of which is sheer sand, elsewhere silky clay.
There we find shells of earliest cookery, and our fingertips

In the dirt encounter marvels of red-ochre bones,
Our torches tossing shadow like black potter's clay.

The wind blows through the upper houses, and the rain blows,
Cleansing hearth and porch, rinsing chimney. We know

By no messenger when to return; under the tangled
And matted hair, and the grime, and through the rags

That have rotted, a look shines,
An acceptance. Then we return

To the sunlit chimneys and the whitened hearths,
Out of the earth cradle; quenching the flares,

Troop chattering out of the cellar stairs,
Draw baths and strop to mirror-glass the rusty razors,

Secure the lower doors with their immense keys we hang
Shining bright in the chimneys; light our upper fires.

The black soot feathers through generations on the long keys.
We recall wondering, occasionally, that in those cellars

We never spoke, not at any time; once through the door
We were to keep and breathe the silence

That had gathered there like foundation water
In the roots of the chattering houses, deep and pure.

THE APPLE-BROADCAST

(Meditation-experience at Boscastle, N. Cornwall)

An Apple a day . . .

I

A valley full of doctor apples,
A valley-stream like flaming straw,
The valley blushing from its roots, and rustling,
The hill-roads cobbled with red fruit.

Some hidden bird blows his dry trumpet
Under the oaks, hoarse as an insect
Crying, under the crisp fretted oakleaves,

Hoarse as a fly walking in its hair,
Its swishing skeleton, its crackled footsteps,
Over the tusked leaves, hoarse as broken bone.

The air goes taut on water-strings
To dirigibles of thunder riding, it splits,
We see the lightning packed with apple-valleys,

All the insects shaking, and their shutters shine
In repeated flashes, under the lightning.
There is the dry trumpet from the rustling leaves

Of some bird chopping at the oak-line
Full of green caverns with the dew
Running over every twig forming

An eye wherever it can,
Walking up from the sleep of water,
Shaken into the sudden light,

Tall water-being shaped by fretted trees,
And the hoarse bird trampling over the leaf
Under the green caverns with its dry trumpet,

While I lie intensified among the grass-sheaves
By cobwebs in their flashing wheels,
An instrument among bird and insect instruments:

The oak-walker scrubbing with its throat,
Or the spider's wiry grasp
In its silk aerial hung, catching parched transmissions

That cry with dry coughs
Out of their saline drops
That moisten their batteries of wings,

The moisture that looks out of their dry eyes
Which the spider blots up with its tusks.
A bird speaks like crackling porcelain,

Like the crunching of its sky-blue shell,
The lightning flashes over the apples,
The black birds skid across the red roads,

And I lie as if transfixed by the lightnings
Amid the stiff dry arrow grass
Near the Spider with her crisp handclasp

In her glass ladder rocking the empty fly.
A dog barks a command from a cottage yard,
The apple-college shakes

Over the entire valley.
On the upper road a quarry-lorry
Hits a bump, its boulders bark and spark.

II

The valley full of doctoral apples,
Round doctoral books among the spider-webs,
Scarlet with white sugared pages;

The oak-colleges ponder in their timber halls
To the bird's music of the dry oak-trumpet,
The wasp demented in the apple-crags

Turning over and over the red book
Of tattered skin and fragrant learned oozing,
The bird barking under the trees from far off:

That standing wave called 'Bird with Dry Voice'
Held in branches, broadcast in echoes;
The broadcast 'Valley Water' flashing and rustling;

The birds sailing on their silky circuits
Among the laddered robes of water,
And transmissions whistling in these vivid outlines,

Their skirts that brush us constantly
Hanging from stars, their sparking silks,
The enormous white voices over the wet apples.

I listen to the voices in the rock cottage
I dwell in which is a radio-set,
I go outside and watch the planets brush us,

Their wakes of birds and insects, their broadcast
Called Spider in her silk antenna.
The stars shine down in their long dresses,

Every cell of the grey house becomes glass,
The skin clears of each red apple, every seed
Like slow lightning spreads in orchard-boughs,

The enormous white voice over the apple-valley
Beats in echoes orbed like spider-webs that shine
In broadcasts hung with appled water-drops,

Its electricity races down all streams and stems
Like flaming straw and mirror appleskins,
The stiff grass stands on end.

I am electrical for ever with these sights,
This broadcast uttered from the apple-storm,
Beneath my skin its lightning runs for always;

Like cobbled groves of rosy apples
I will transmit my programmes,
Like insect-eyes glittering under lightning.

IV

In the valley full of doctors,
In the weather full of round young doctors,
The lightning is a white priest hurrying
Past fat black convocations far above him,

And the red doctors knock heads conferring
Like the rolling green heads of the sea close by
With white beards and rumbling snowy rafters;

In my granite cottage which is a crystal-set,
The walls flashing with their ancient broadcasts
Recorded as the rock flowed, then set in wavelengths,

The baby sits with fingers weaving programmes,
Sitting in a broadcast which is a jersey,
Picking up a programme which is a rusk,

Mouth full of dew, fingers which are aerials,
Sitting on a wavelength which is a blanket
Woven out of meat and starlight on some far hill;

I will give my baby an apple which is a doctor daily,
We shall tune in together to what it says,
Breathing apple-scented air-transmissions,

For with my tender knobbed antenna
I tuned into a certain star babe-broadcast
Deep in a girl's receiver

As every bird and beetle and doctor apple
Does, on its own particular waveband.
There is so much unseen, and so many tuning

To lightning broken over the apple-orchards,
   responding
To lightning spun through white-skinned orchards.
Now the thunder has closed his humming station,

The moon-band rises, moths dressed like moonbeams
Take wing into the excited grasses.
The Spider plucks some for their floury blood,

Good bread, but many couple
Lamb-faced in their woolly wings,
Tumbling like moonlit monarchs in their ermines,
And printed across with black star-signallings

Flutter the constellations on their wide white wings.

XIII

THE WORKING OF WATER
(1984)

SECONDS, DROPS, PENCE

The river green as its trees that stand
Up to the breeze in flounce and ferment.
Every drop accounted

Not as by a miser,
But by awareness, somewhere,
Or green awareness everywhere.

The water creased by colliding ringlets,
Every feathering accounted for,
The fishmouths plucking the smooth stream

Tucked with buttonhole mouths
Which leave shadows and ghosts
On the mirror, colliding ghosts,

Scudding shadows. And the mud,
The plush green mud
The close-set velveteen

Combed everlastingly, electrical
With the river combing by, its slow
Green sparks dancing

And flashing between sky-pole
And water-pole, water
Brushed through grilles,

Deeply sliced currents
Through railings and through chains,
And the rows of sluicewheels

Like gardens of steel flowers;
The green walls built
Of the courses of leaves,

Some panels hiss,
Others are shuttered still.
A river of leaf-colour liquor,

And in the Works, repressed water,
Misery counted in ledgerly sinks,
Concrete tanks like catalogues,

All their leaves unturned
Mouldering in the unread libraries of water.
Suddenly the people in the town feel dirty

And turn on their taps because
A dirt-coloured cloud glides overhead,
And the countermanded water stirs,

Great librarians of pulse reach into pages
Tear relevant passages off concrete shelves,
Slices are taken down and drawn into baths.

The clear texts are dirtied again.
Water lies in its hearths
Like an ashless fire,

Like a great glassy puppy ready to play
If the taps whistle at him;
The river-current plays with its bone of sunlight.

This is how you adjust the water-set. Six
Sluice-wheels on a gantry over a brick-lined pit;
The swirling images of all life

Flowing into the square chamber;
And at the bridge of the brick ship
To watch over the eternal wheels and spirals

Forming in the water
And wheeling there like the stars;
Turn the wheels upon the wheels

To pull yourself into the world behind the world,
Which in its sudden cold snap
Sets in innumerable six-sided wheels,

The cogs of the universe of the planned water-city,
Time set and visible like an Einstein precinct.

XIV

THE MAN NAMED EAST
(1985)

CALL

for F.

The shipwright's beauty, who butchers the forest,
Dresses it again in shining sails,

Garments like blossom,

And nailed with new iron like budding grain,
With big ship-bosoms full of wonderful fruit
And men of unbelievable expertise
Of knowledge of the stars and sands;

You serve branching ocean routes
As though the whole sea were a sailing-tree
And the ships were blossom on it
Gliding slowly
On its world-embracing boughs
Transferring goodness and prosperity,

You give them yare names:
Ocean Moon, Tidesource,
And their travellers a berth of womb
In the big-belly blown along
By blinding blossom;

And others dig
And uncover the scarlet iron
And with fire forge sounding hulls and bells
And the great mines of iron feather on the waters,
The heaviest stone sails the wide seas,

Or in the dusty dry dock
Resounds to its remaking
As a cathedral calls out to its glad city to serve.

IN THE PHARMACY

for Wendy Taylor

A moth settled on the side of a bottle,
Covering its label, a marvel. The embroidered wings
Of the moth called Wood Leopard. It flutters off

And settles on another bottle. The label of this violet
Fluted container with the glass stopper reads
Lapis invisibilitatis: it would make you disappear.

The moth like a travelling label walks
From bottle to marble bottle with floury wings
Embracing each and tapping with fernleaf tongue

Sugared drops at neck and stopper,
Built like a fat rabbit with gaudy wings extracting
The essence of pharmacies, the compendium,

Staggering from jar to sculptured jar and sealing
Into capsules its own cogitatio,
Implicating in its eggs our explicit medicine.

And the draughts of invisibility, the poisons?
The caterpillar remembers to die, and disappears,
As the labelled stone declares,

All melts to caterpillar soup inside the wrappings
Where the pupa cogitates,
Just the nerve-cord floating like a herring-skeleton,

And round those nerves lovingly unfolds
The nervous wings on which is marked
In beautiful old pharmacy script, the formula.

THE HEART

An autumn bluebottle,
Frail winged husk with the last squeezings
Of the year sealed up inside,

The last juices and saps of the fruits
Crystallising inside the stone gaze
Of the insect-mask, countenance of sugars.

It sings softly, in search of sugars.
The maiden sings softly,
She whose red blouse

Is blowing on the line,
Its buttons glittering like sugar,
Full of the wind's tits,

That I saw her filling yesterday;
As though she had given one of her bodies
To the elements,

For the weather to fill,
The red blouse pulsing on the line,
Emptying and filling like a heart

In the strong gusts,
The wind's heart beating on the line;
And the sails of blood,

The stout red-rigged yachts competing on the estuary,
Red for celerity and heart,
And the transparent word breathing everywhere.

The maiden and the fly sing softly,
It butts its drumstick head against her window,
She stares out at a heart of hers beating in the weather,

The fly so full of low sweetness it hums like rubbed crystal.

THE GREEN TOWER

(Carn Brae)

Leaves on their wooden shelves
Like shelf after shelf of shiny footgear
All marching on the wind,

Boots without soldiers,
The battleground of wind
Under one blue helmet,

Spirit soldiers marching in their winged boots,
The sycamore of the churchyard full of ghost
By this broad calm church

Light and airy and white with plain windows,
Built in the seventeen hundreds
Like a rational cabinet of light and praise

And at the nave-back a step down into an old tower,
The old bell-tower with the map of scores of churches
All the bell-able churches in Cornwall.

As I stepped down into this area
I thought that a high bell must still be ringing,
Have lately been rung,

Or its late echoes were caught still in the crystals
Of the dark stone blocks of this elder tower,
And like an electricity a slight

And relaxing current passed through my whole skin
And I stepped out into the broad church and there was
    nothing
And I stepped back into the stone tower that was tingling

And I stepped out and took her back down with me
And she felt it also, like the near presence of water.
And outside the tall tower was green from weather,

And with its gargoyles that looked like piskies of the rain,
Like a towering haunt of piskies, the green tower;
And every Sunday the tiger of blood

Lashed its tail on their altar,
The bible turned its pages
Over and over not wearing them out,

The souls all marched in the big
Thumping boots of their hymns,
The congregation roaring aloud with their cunning

Who have that sweet relenting pagan
Bell-hung current at their Cornish back.

THE QUIET WOMAN OF
CHANCERY LANE

The blind girl points at a star.
At night, she says, when all the stars are out,
She feels their rays feathering on her face,
Like a fringe of threads.

She stands by the beehive's low thunder.
There will be snow, the bees of ice
Will swarm from their darkening hives. I see

Clouds are gliding, and becoming, in the moonlight,
Mountaineering from nowhere, as the mass of air,
The town's hanging breath, soars into the cold
And is ice in dirigible bergs
And apparitions of a terrain they have created:
Cloudscape. How, under these glories, I wonder

Can men stroll past in deadblack suits, signifying
Ignorance and blindness of the skin,
Swinging griefcases packed with inky briefs,
And a spring in their step from this uniform?
They have a blind confidence, she says, in their power
And in the courts cry 'Proof, proof!',
They can make all others' skins go sightless,

Blind with worry, yet mine, she says,
The Quiet Woman without eyes,
Not living in my head,
The Headless Woman, my skin
Is open as the night sky, with the remote stars
And nearer glories easing across; my eyes
Are blind, but I know these people
By the no-shapes of their numbness as they go,
But since, blind, I am not in their power,
Being afflicted by God, they will not touch me,

With their penal pleading, for I belong
To Another, Who has my eyes. These lawful men
To her are like stars that have gone black, turned
Inside out with the suction of nothingness,
Empty sockets walking the Inns of Court.

The blind girl points to the stars
As if she could see; she informs me
How a special breath from space
Tells her they are out in their moist fullness.
Yet the sky is so packed, how can she not,
Pointing, light on some constellation or other?

But I believe her when she tells me how
Her life without eyes is so full. I take
The blind girl by her night hand.
With her fingers raised, she traces in the air
The slow rising of that mountain that hangs, the full
    moon,

It is like the presence of a fountain, she says,
Like the fresh aura of falling water, or like
That full head of the thistle I stroked in the park,
And its sound is like a fountain too, or like snow thistling.

UNDER THE DUVET

Sleep-feather, the sleep-feather
Comes drifting down,
Rocking the child to sleep,

The child sleeps covered
In a bag of drifting sleep-feathers;
Eider-plume, the ducks are flying

Loftily through feathered clouds.
She sleeps flying through their death,
Their flow of plumage, bag of the whole flock.

Just as we realise with care
That we are dreaming, just there,
Entering the Self, and leaving, just there,

That we are asleep, and watching a dream,
And just there, waking, but entering
The small door of a second, the opening of a tick,

The nip of a cog, and watching,
Our Mother above shakes out her bag and the snow flies,
Or the dew manifests, like stars

They are suddenly there, a multitudinising of the grasses,
A heavying and a lighting-up,
We glance down, and the dew is there,

Like all the still seconds
There ever were, stopped,
Each one seeing into the morning, deep

In the interior of its glance, the morning;
And it is a dream of feathery embrace
Like a cloud pluming a mountain,

And the fleeces of sheep too heavy to walk,
So they must settle, and sleep
As the cloud settles

Grazing the mountain, among the silvered grass
Where all, air, mountain, sheep
Is a feathered being, silent with fog,

And within a fleeced pinion
I see the dark mouth of a cave
And enter the cavern

And am immediately among
A feathering of echoes
And I remember that Goddess

Who hid her child to conceal his cries,
Hid him in a cave known for winding passages
And galleries among which the echoes

Never ceased to cry, and surely
This is the passage along which the cloud retires
To its mountain's interior in the daytime,

To its inner pasture, and I find
That my hair and my dress
Are plumed with that cloud's dew

As the spiderwebs and the grasses are feathered
On every fibre with the water
Of the mountain's grey brain ever-distilling

Among its cool granite convolutions,
And I squeeze droplets out of my sleeve
On to my lips, the cloth is rough and the taste

Is of cloth, sheep, grass, wings and ancient water
Stilled over and redistilled until it shines
Again like the plumage

Birthwet from its egg of the newborn angel.

SHELLS

See shells only as seawater twining back
To the first touch, of seawater on itself;

The water touching itself in a certain way,
With a certain recoil and return, and the mollusc

Starts up in the water, as though the conched wave
Had been struck to stone, yet with the touch

Still enrolled in it, the spot was struck
And life flooded through it

Recording a thin stone pulse of itself,
Its spiral photo-album, its family likeness

Caught in nacreous layers, as if
Your skull grew spiring from a skull-button,

Your roles coiling out of your smallest beginning,
Full of shelves of selves

Turning around each other
Like a white library that has been twisted,

Like a spired library turned in the tornado
Unharmed, keeping the well of itself

Open to past and future,
Full, like the mollusc, of the meat of sense,

The briny meat, twirled by the tornado;
And this, whose fleshy books have swum away,

Emptying the magnificent pearl-building,
All its walls luminous in the sunlight,

Empty stairwell full of sound,
For since the books created the shelves

To fit their message and their likeness,
Echoes of books remain, resounding,

Printed endlessly around the shelving,
Like the seasound of seapages turning over

And over, touching themselves
In a certain way, echoing, reminding,

Evoking new themes of old sea-shapes. A new shell,
A new skull begins again from its speck

Echoing the older books made of water.
See how the clouds coil also above the eggshells of cities,

Touching each other in certain ways, so that
Rain falls; clouds invisible

Over the sea, but when the watery air
Lifts over the land, the white shells float

Crystallised over the hot cities, muttering with thunder.

TO THE WATER-PSYCHIATRIST

I

The water-psychiatrist: the plumber
Who will come at my emergency,
So that I can give my head another good wash.

Mice, porcupines, sloths and shrews:
All the same core-mammal, the obsession
Of all species, the family face,

So different from antelopes who are
Skittish as butterflies, leaping wise-faced
Like an astronaut at the end of his silken string.

In the gurgle of the urinal
I took a charge of water-electricity
Straight through the end of my penis;

The cistern was discharging with a white noise,
The cleanly electrix went right up my tube
(Now I have something to tell my plumber)

Leaping like that antelope through my mouse,
A charge right down from the waterworks
And through the fresh green hill of springs

Where the deer leap, bounding over streams,
Down from the clouds fluttering with lightning.
I shimmered with electrocution harmlessly,

With urinal lightning in the beer-smells
Enriched like a boudoir by gathering, in their passage,
All the perfumes of the magic galleries

They had passed through, drinking up
The pictures of thought painting themselves
And repainting over the red walls, enriched

Like the balsamic inside canopy of a great tree.

(Then there is the pacing puddle of her shiny shirt;
Her way of slapping together a cheese sandwich:
As she does it a figure of lancing light
Flashes across her shirt-back;

This shock went up my generation also;
I became skittish; the antelope
Of light was in the shirt; my mouse ran;
I was a hedgehog with prickles in my skin.)

III

I went out resolving to trace the source.
The little stream rippling down the hillside
Entered the urinal, so I travelled up

The glittering electrical water I had felt in my generations
(Some lightning flashed into a tarn held in the hilltop?)
Towards the source. It was a spring

Overarched by a tree, the source had reduced
The relenting mud to black because so full
Of all the colours of lime, leaf and bough;

The electrix of the tree had clambered up my spine.

IV

Dare I wash my head again, with lightning
In the water, starlight
In the source? I went out to the stars,

Hedgehogs of light; there was no surcease,
Nor did I need one, like the thunder-source
The lightning in the black

Followed by creative shadow, the black
In which light forms and daylight breaks,
The lovely shadow kingdom, ablaze with shocking light.

THE PROPER HALO

In those glad days when I had hair,
I used to love to smarm it down with Brylcreem.
In those old days this was the definition of a boy:
A scowl, Brylcreem, and back pockets, admonished
To refrain from pomades at one's confirmation,
So that the Bishop would not get his hands oiled,
Greasy palms, laying them on. My uncle laughed at me,
And called me 'Horace!' with my flat-combed parting,
My head shining like a boot; though, as a Navy man,
He liked all that sort of thing himself,
Shaking a kind of Bay Rum out of a nozzled bottle
Labelled in Arabic that came from Egypt,
A brick-red Sphinx on yellow sand for scene,
Spidered with Arabic like uncombed hair. Retired,
He would send to London to the importers for it,
And I asked him what the spider-writing meant. He told
      me:
'If you want to be like Horace, employ our oil.'

When he died, he left me his personal things,
A wristwatch with a back pitted
From tropical sweat, studs and cufflinks
Glorified with tiny diamond-chips, a dressing-case
With hairbrushes useful to me then, his shaving-mirror;
I mourned him, but enjoyed using his things,
Conversing with his shade, taking both parts in the mirror,
Remembering how we talked, fascinated by this grown-up;
And I remembered catching the habit of hairgrease,
He dropping a little in my palm and showing me
How to rub it in with fingertips, 'You'll
Never lose it now, keep up the massage,'
Which wasn't true. Still, when he died
I did have hair, and liked the barber's shop.

A university friend staying with me
Translated the Arabic on the bottle,
Laughing. I said '*What* spirit? and he said
'Definitely religious advertising; could your uncle
Read the Arabic?' I thought not, though he had
Many spoken phrases. 'Then he picked up "Horace"
From the vendor's gabble; it reads:
"Horus comes to greet you through this oil."'

I liked the barber's shop; the man
Stabs the pointed bottle at his palm;
My dark hair is cut and shaped and forests felled
Over my white-sheathed shoulders lie like toppled pines.
The oil shivers in the barber's palm,
He puts the plump bottle down, and that hand
Descends swooping on the other; they rub together
Like mating birds and as they fly to my head
I see they shine. His rough fingertips
Massage my scalp like the beating of a flock
Of doves; now it is my hair that shines
And stands up as though an ecclesiastical charge
Were passing through me; I laugh! 'You like
The scent of the oil, do you, Sir?' I nod,
Though I don't. It's the shine I love;
I shine with glory! and this is worth
The barber's shillings, many times. I shall feel
Of age as down the street I pass
In my shining pelt and glittering shako, my hair
Cut and shaped like my natural urges, properly, proudly,
In a halo of light and scent, godly contained.

THE FUNERAL

For N.

I

Clouds and mountains were invited, both the conscious
And the unconscious creatures. The trees
Like visible outpourings of the stream's music,
The urine of the animals in the dawn frost
Puffing like rifle-fire. The dark meat of the sun,
The bloody meat, the cremating sun.

II

Ninety-two percent of what we eat is from direct
Pollination by the bees, he tells me this
To cheer me and if true ninety-two percent
Of what he says with his mouth is said by bees. The first
    light
On leaves shines like apples hanging in the trees,

The whole forest a vast orchard, and all things
Are more than they seem, for they may fly away,
And disappear like Mother pausing on the threshold
Of the fields of light, which are like dew
Thick in the grassy meadows, for the light hangs
Dripping in the leaves, stands on the wind.

III

There is a Witness, I think, who has magnetic wings.
First it seemed to me at the funeral service with the
    terrible
Useless brass handles that would be saved screwed to
The veneer cardboard coffin which was much too small
That my emotions such as these swirled round my flesh
And some of them spurted from my eyes but ninety-two
    percent
Were beating in my back in a sensation like spread wings.
Since mine were sprouting I was able to see
The wings of others, such as my father's, standing next to me,
And his were ragged and tattered like those of an old moth
Close to drying up and drifting away, it seemed my duty
To merge my birth-wet wings with his, and this I did,
Entwining them in an embrace with him that he would
    never know,
And sure enough he, the widower, perked up,
And I felt tattered, but not dry, for back at the house
I sobbed my heart out in the little white-tiled loo,
And there was still a little angelic witness lodged in my
    spine
At the small of my back, in Jesus-robes, little calm watcher
In white, which I cannot explain, merely report.

IV

The other thing the funeral showed me, unpromising
    seance,
My Mother, subject of it, at the door ajar
On the field of light, looking back over her shoulder,
Smiling happiness and blessing me, the coherent veil
Of the radiant field humming with bees that lapped the
    water, and she bent
And washed her tired face away with dew and became a
    spirit.

276

WARM STONE FOR N

I

Death as pure loss, or immutability.
A watch falling into the well,
Ticking a while in the cool spring, distributing

Its faint shock; or death
As a diamond-second in the year, set
Glittering cold in the anniversary,

The tiny diamond in her ear
Surviving the cremation?

II

Death suddenly appearing, like a spiderweb in the fog,
A piece of paper opening into a house, the snapshot
Through an open door, and at the table sitting still

Somebody; the house
With one room and no kitchen,
The house with the card door;

The disposable house.

III

I turn my back on the ascensions,
The unscreened smokestacks, I do not wish
To watch her ascending, the knots

Solving themselves, fading,
Climbing into the antechambers of rain.
Besides, her smoke should be white,

Blinding!

IV

And the colour of lost rain escaping!
And the photographs white
As the clothes are empty.

I open the prayer-book;
It is empty.

So, with her death,
I will baptise this small
Quartz; it shall stand for death

Like a glass room
Of which only a spirit knows the door,

Which only a spirit can enter
Turning and showing itself in the walls
Lined with warm mirror

Knowing its form in floor and ceiling,
Able to say 'I am here!'

V

It shall become a custom,
Warm room ringed to my finger,
Warm so long as I am warm,
Then left to my daughter

To keep warm, and bequeathed
To hers; warm stone
It will house multitudes.

TRANSACTIONS

I

The waves break on the shore with a scent
Of briny cellars of sea-fungus shrouding
Drowned shiny forests. I have a white door
To my cellar which when I crack open
Is as though the house were a wave, stopped,
Overhanging, and in the still
Round cellar in that moment's time
The mushrooms manifested. I put them there.
A pulse of phosphorescence keeps the house up.

278

The little mushrooms are salt
And they smell of zest and venom.
I swim into the yesty air of the cellar
And see them stand like white circular messengers,
Helicopter-winged angels.
Stiff one-vertebra spine.

The pylons choiring in the wind
Marching like the X-rays of cathedrals
Along their zesty ozone spoor like the odour of
    mushrooms,
The earth spinning within its mother, the waters,
Around its father, the sun,
Within clear sight of its godmother,
The mob-capped, nectar-rayed moon.

Whose white patched cap resembles a mushroom
Flying in its helicopter wings of magnetism
That raise the metal-sheeted tides
And crack them open scenting the sea-air with zest,
The pylons choiring,
Her silvery blouse flashing with electricity
Through its opening leaking her ozones
As the moonbeams scent the night-opening flowers,
My white shirt like an electric ghost
Specially laundered to enter this darkness
Under the cellar stairs where the white door stands open.

LIGHTS IN THE MIST

Lights in the mist branching across the water
Like fruit shining out of an orchard.
Then the mist clears, and the waves are disclosed
Stacked to the horizon, each with its poised sound,
Visible sound.

Her sleeping glances, her sleeping gloves,
Her body like some soft delectable debris
Awaiting collection. He breathed her odour in,
The carelessness of her relaxation overcame him
As no planned seduction could. He tastes the apple
She was eating when he began touching her.
The explosions of sea on the walls,
Random shell-bursts, traversing. Now she dreams

Of putting the final touches to the firstborn,
Knitting the baby's only garment with bone needles,
Engraving on the flesh the fingerprints like a colophon.

Dewy cobweb frozen like bone-of-lace; the orchard
Doing its one thing: creating leaves and fertilising flowers
And rounding fruit;

The water of the well twisting back into its brick socket.

Tasting alternately the cold earthy water, and the cool
Earthy fruits out of the apple-tree rooted in the wall.

The fenestral mists branching. The new veins branching.

CLOUDMOTHER

to D.P.

I

Several hot days,
The one after the other.

The standing cells of sunshine, lofty sunshine,
And in them blossom black thunderstorms.

Lathering clouds.
The wind tumbling in chunks.

The yachts tacking through the cells of gust,
Rigged like crescent moons, scudding.

The clouds the accumulated sails
Of the invisible wind-boats.

They throw their lightshadows,
Their visible loomings,

And they throw their windshadows,
The dark splashmarks of gust hurrying on.

The mountains in the distance
Steer the evening wind towards us.

The notes of bells
Blow towards us from the ravines of mountains

That halt the morning wind, and so
The long hot days, and the thunder

And the necessity for thunder, piling up
Like invisible pillars of the law: over the sea

Invisible and mere vapour, but over land
Which lifts the wind, it crystallises

Like silent moored navies awaiting orders.

II

A gap in the hedge which is a dry stream
Awaiting thunder. A footpath of dust to a wet valley.

My skin needed the wet meadow, I wanted to be
In that state of rest after thunder.

I considered the tree that gripped waters deeper than
    the dry stream
And the hedgerow in its roots, it

Considered me. The Cloudmother was glad
I noticed her, the invisible streamers

Pouring up from her boughs like
A reversed waterfall, patterning over the city.

I overheard a thought: 'The unmoved mover
That wishes to be moved,' then from her own

Accumulation of clouds her upper foliage fell
And shone, the Cloudmother hissing with the pleasure.

MOTHERS

The Mothers elect to keep their hair
Cropped quite short in close caps.
It is as they pitch their voices close,
Near voices without coiling timbres or
Disturbing undertones, just so their faces

Shall not be swung across with hair
Nor with unpredicted modulations the expression alter,
Nor a curtain sweep to give the child a glimpse
Of the other half of her feelings
Instead of the whole libration, the balanced face.
Another mother may well peer out of the left-hand side.

That would make Mother unreliable, or
Seductive, and stunt the growth. She
Must carry everywhere that certain voice,
And with her a certain structured cloud of fragrance,

A pleasant regulated scheme of odours
That are bedmaking, and kitchen,
Clean paint, and freshly-cut bread,

Like a balsamic mother-tree growing
Behind everything; that oak-avenue
Of Father's book-lined study, that
Alphabet-tree in the playroom tuck-box,
Joined at the Mother-trunk

Behind the appearance of everything,
A balsamic tree of odour everywhere,
A tree of flowering home. The Mother's hair
Is short and frank; and, recollect,
That maiden that she was had never learnt to swear
Or curse either before she made herself a Mother.

THE WILL OF NOVEMBER

The millionth leaf blowing along the path.
The sea white-headed, white-tailed.
Sky of wind-pounded ice.

Frozen bees shaken from their hives,
Rattling from the box like gravel.
The travelling shadows of the gravestones,

Oblong slots of mortal sundials
Among the puffs of young fog
Out of the brown wet grasses.

Oak like a telephone exchange
Full of birdcircuits talking,
Full of birds and no leaves,

Birds, not leaves,
Look higher: there the aeroplanes fly south, scoring
Skaters' tracks across the raftered ice.

SHE BELIEVES SHE HAS DIED

She believes she has died
Has become a spirit, naked as air,
So she steps out of her front door, nude as a peeled wand,
With peeled eyes, observing like a spirit.

There is an old tractor, a stiff fountain of rust;
She salutes as one invisible the squirrel, representative
Of the creatrix of the British Navy,
Who created the wooden ships by planting oaks,
Her presence passing does not hinder it, the rusty
Squirrel gnawing on a nut confirms her spirithood.

The elaborate bodies of death that people bequeath!
The house behind her, with its rustling wardrobes,
Those fleets of oak tall-masters, the oceans of clean water
Enough to float them which hasted through that body!

If you could see the perfume of the wood
Come rolling from its aisles! Older spirits might.
She passes through the meadows underneath the pylons
That flash and hum with their electricals, skeleton castles
Trapezing with ghosts, past the docks, the black
Spanish query of the great hook, the steel hulls
Booming with their riveting, like spirits
Battering to be released from flesh, or hymning,
On to the magnetism and glitter of the marshes, the little
    trees
With their backs bent laving their faces in the mud,

For she wishes to live again, and lave her body
In the mud, to make it heavy
Enough to live again; she straightens up
Her face glittering with it. The green lantern cabbages, the

Spotless mushrooms, are spirits compared to her now.

THE MAN NAMED EAST

The dew, the healing dew, that appears
Like the dream, without warning, hovering on the blades;
The motions of his wings bring dew and light,

The man named East. The ghosts have lost
All sense of perspective
In the drinking-water, twisting and turning,

Shaped by too many vessels, and furrowed
By too many fearful vessels, for we
Drink the water of a drowned village

Of a drowned College from College Reservoir,
And across our drinking-water goes
A small yacht like a lighted kitchen,

A fishing-boat like a ruined cottage,
Dinghies like little violins
With squeaky rowlocks, with violin-voices,

With the devil's music written on the waters.
I stand by the small stream which contributes.
I kneel and dip my hand in, it insists

Into my palm with a slight pressure
Like a baby's hand, which is still
The elasticity of yards of water

Reaching down the hill
From the clouds on high; I crouch
With my hand in that baby's hand

Feeling the slight movement of its fingers,
The light clasp which is love,
The little bony stones rattle

And the cool flesh of glass sinews;
It babbles like a baby, I bend
My ear to the water and now I find

Underspeech I did not hear before;
With the forest like a vast moth
Settling its wings on the hill,

I dip my finger in my mouth and taste
Forests and air and the ice
Of the white rain-wing and its power-pinions.

IN AUTUMN EQUINOX

Black cat sitting in the scotch mist
A white sheen over her, every single hair
Piercing a water-bead

In a high magnetic autumn of electric sunsets,
My heart leaps in my chest like a cat
With a silver sheen on it jumping over a wall.

The sun, the enlightener, the whitener.
The snail has made his silk track over the berries.
Summits of water rise above

Cold summits of water.
The crowd, the myriad, the millions,
The region beyond the tomb,

This day on which the ghosts of those
Who have died during the year assemble
And prepare to follow the sun

Through the underworld as their leader
Into light, does not feel like death,
The white sheen over everything, that was mist.

On my walk over the hill I meet
A buddleia of the skyline
The blooms the same hue as the early evening sky,

So there are rooms in the bush
Where the sky seems to hang
And there are white butterflies at the flowers

Tugging and fluttering
As if the sky with its clouds
Had assembled like bloom, the bush hung

Thick with bunched sky and fluttering cloud;
While from time to time the silver underneaths
Of many leaves bend giving their sheen back

Like an electric shiver on this sky-tree;
And the long grass is full
Of big gunpowder-coloured birds who take off

With a detonation of wings, and to its thunderclap
A thunderhag rises out of the hills
Sliding sideways and gunpowder-hued,

Making our feet tingle
With its electrical presence, and in this field
Crouches an idle tractor visited by bees,

Great flower throbbing
With its metal scent, and a wasp
Nibbles at the grease ruched from two great pistons.

Now the mist returns:
All the spiderwebs – waterbeds! in the hedges
Every bush a contraption of sheen and waterbed.

At home in autumn
The dog's magnetic body
And its dynamite health abounding

Marking with its delighted pawprints the sensitive sheen,
Drives winter sickness from our blazing hearth.

WHITSUNWIND

The aerodynamics of the hold of the house,
Our wooden, cello-voiced ship,
The hull of the house, its grip on the wind,

The sheets and rigging of the beds
As they dream their noisy voyages,
Its heeling in the seaweather,

Marvel of nailed timber,
My carriage which thunders:
The dead trees of it resurrect and

Howl through their corridors
Like huge fires passing by on either hand.
I draw a tumbler of foaming weir, let there be

Weir foaming out of all the taps, I run
From tap to tap to augment the sound,
And all the lights on too, trees of lightning

With fruits of thunder,
Wagner on the recorder;
There are ghosts enough to rattle all the bolts

Like nuts in their wooden cases, and the nails
Bow silkily their grains; such bottles
Of stouted fire, and the charged air,

And the sea wind rushing with its manes
To leap the mansards packed with light
And groaning like string orchestras.

Now, the calm of Whitsunday. The waxy seed
Of grasses that shines over the field
Of light laid down like mother o'pearl,

And the sea still rocks, and in the ears
Water-radios in stereo sealed in a cave,
Two coiled shells like cockles locked in chalk,

Small twin blowholes taking the air's full fetch;
The sea quietly puffs tons
Of white sound at them in Whitsun.

THE BROTHEL IN FAIRYLAND

(Madame Twoswords – Goddess-patroness of brothels)

The courtesan with a taper guides
A young man to her mosquito-net.

There is a river-party in full swing
With hired geisha, and three courtesans
Dance their winding dance on the
Landing-stage of a teahouse. It is called

A teahouse where we drink the girls
And meditate on the tea, the women
Dressed like peony-gardens fill the fairyland
Of painted screens and doors, their shadows
Lie solid on the layers of mosquito-net

Where a woman holds up a stone saké-dish
With cherry-blossoms in it and beckons to a client
Unseen behind the mosquito-net, the stone steps
Shine with the little hovering lamps,

And a lighted-up pleasure-boat like a wedding-cake
Iced with light, a 'fairy-boat',
Does its winding dance

Like a torchlit procession down the guts of the river;
It passes on the current swiftly; we glimpse
On the deck a woman holding up a bamboo cage
Of fireflies and pointing at them.

In Japanese, 'fairyland', in English, 'brothel'.

The fairyland is full of candlelight, perfumes, and
    electrical skins,
You can feel them as they pass by on their currents swiftly
Entering your skin and leaving it, gliding by
In their visible skirts, touching you
With their invisible clothes, their electrical dress
Such as a forest also makes, or a wooden scow
Blazing with candles, or a swift-flowing river makes;

With a screen by the enclosure announcing business
And a shaped electrical neon picture of Madame
    Twoswords,
Lightning in a peony gown. Many holy ghosts

Crowd round her to see the outcome of that fight.

MOTHERS AND CHILD

I

The soft modelling for hours,
The soft handling.
Undressing, she forgets to say her prayers.

The town of wives, promenading,
Staring among the lighted beauty-shops
Which are shadows of the beauty that is above,

That is too bright to look at
Except in the shadowing of lipstick and powder,
Painting with colour, camera obscura,

This in the town of the two electricities,
The powerhouse, lighting the shops,
The wives, stiff in their orgasms

With fingers stretched like starfish
And eyes going like electric bulbs,
Witch-hair cracking the taut white pillow;

And the stiff filamentous reach of the powerstation
Incandescent also in its circuits
Like some miraculous gestating glow-worm

Or silk-spinner of tungsten
That shines with that power,
The elastic of magnetism,

For whirl wheel within wheel
It comes spitting
Into the lamps, over the sheets

Of the great metropolis of rooms
And the lighted villages of wives
With the lover wanting the skin off

Wanting the electricity in essence,
The stripped wires,
Electricity with its rubber off,

Electricity more naked than last time;
He strokes for hours
Mowing the magnetism,

The sheets crackling,
The soft handling over and over,
And gradually the first skins loosen;

And the wives observe this recreation
As the mother her rounding belly
And wishes her child to be naked of it

Herself now willing her own birth
As the fish skips out of the wave
To be nude of the water

Water that peels off water as it marches
Nakedness off salt nakedness,
So that, undressing, she forgets to say her prayers,

As water forgets, and reflects
The beauty above her.

II

Or does she beam beauty up
To be bounced off the ceiling
Or off the man above her,

Transforming her beauty
Into his (and he needs it);
Her fighting-gear

A silk shirt,
Excellent accumulator of electricities,
Admirable rubbing battery of orgasms,

Or, as they say, Static,
For time stands still.
Such heroes as there might be

Awake when they touch her skin,
With a silent shout of recognition,
Skin which flutters unbearably

When they touch it sufficiently,
Like a moth beating in the light of the sheets,
The moth whose wings are flaming

Without being consumed;
And the wellspring where the more it is drawn
The more it flows;

While the wife as mother of herself opens
And draws herself off
That which steps out

Over the sill, the berth, the landing-place.

LIKE A ROCK

Rain marks cold coins in the water.
When she wears a shirt, a blouse,
It is as if she were dressed in water;

The whole river turns with her
And crinkles with her breathbeat.
I have seen a rock in the

Fast stream dressed
In a beautiful shawl of water
Hunched round the shoulders and

Open in front; I have seen
A smooth rock standing
In a waterfall, dressed

In a never-ending weave
Of water-trails down the stream,
A twisted glass shirt like flame,

Like a personage
On whose head light beats
And refines him utterly down to the tail

During many centuries. When
She wears a shirt, or blouse,
This is saying: thus

I glisten, and ripple so,
Under my skin and in my secrets,
And I am dressed like this for you to

Prepare your entry and stand
As a rock does in flowing water.

WOODEN WHEAT

As the ear of the wheat, the cone
Of the pine. A bunch
Of wooden ears, the wooden

Honeycomb dripping with balsam
Tasting of cough-drops,
Ligneous cog; and aphids

In swarms like a tremendous crop
Of green apricots with legs, big
Glass bums of clear emerald syrups.

Over there a modern hotel
Among the terraced needles,
Like a luxury liner washed up in wooden tides,

The green-shadowed fish of air
Vaulting through their rollers, feathered fishes
With ample wings, and everywhere
A pine cone, like wooden roses
Perfumed with cough-balsam;

Or a cabinet of ears that prick up in the sunshine,
Or a comb of wooden eyelids curiously jointed
Opening upon honey; a cabinet

Of wooden eyelids most marvellously jointed
And overlapping like an Islamic masterpiece
That falls open with a click, spreading;
A cabinet of a hundred lids that all at once
Unlock. It is full
Of yellow dusts and sherberts, each grain
Elaborately carved, carving within carving.

Unripe it is green and like a spindle
Of green fingernails tipped with red,

Of green fingernails that begin to tap and click
As falling off the bough this gift rolls
Into the patch of hot sun and starts to stretch.

Many remain fastened to the tree
Like dark lanterns engraved
All over with sealed eyes.

THE YOUNG AND PREGNANT
SPIRITUALIST

By mere breathing, she sees her own shape,
The solemn tranquillity of her naked life
Under her clothes, the day-long caress.

The tie of each sitter like a crucifix
Nailed to the throat, their heads
Being washed in blackness; she is

Washing their heads with night
In her chant, her moaning chant,
They bow their heads and take it,

All of them, in their circle, the sitters.
She has a baby in her womb that sways in its bonds.
In trance, that baby is, communicating with her;

And she tells herself this child is of such a virtue
I am made a prophetess. Accordingly I speak
From the womb to these nice young chaps

Who serve in country offices and shops;
I help them jump the counter into this world.
The room is psychic, the whole space answering,

The draperies flutter at the windows in grimaces,
Straining to speak, the great sewn faces,
The very air is living with currents like her birthwater,

And tapping out her heartbeat there climbs a disc,
The luminous tambourine, to which there floats
An ectoplasm that grasps the shivering drum

Like a foetus in its robes,
Or like a lily unfolding, and from the draperies
Steps out a spirit naked as pips, with

A few wisps caught up for modesty; and to herself
This is the grown-up image of her baby
Adult and unspoilt; I pray I will meet her

In our afterlife together; but now
She is the centre of this circle, they may ask
Their questions, and to one it is

The dead wife returning, to another
His sainted grandmother, seeing her drapery as age,
Those wisps clinging to the face as wrinkles, but I,

I know she is the future
Growing in me and talking round this table

XV

THE MUDLARK POEMS & GRAND BUVEUR

(1986)

EYE-BESTOWING

(Mudlark III)

Down the small path to the winding marsh
Where the alders bend and lave their heads in mud
He visits for a predawn ritual prayer.
He hoods himself in that same alder-yeast of spring,
Makes of himself a sculptor's rough of mud
With a clod face in which the live eyes beat, rehearsing
The entrance of the sun into the wood, the eye-bestowing;
In the marsh's bubbling spring that feeds
The ferment from a rock, washes off the worst.

For breakfast, bacon
Like sea-sliced strata eaten in the bath.
The child, blood relative
Acting on his behalf in the future, God Willing,
Is learning to read by putting out
Long trains of coloured pictures: witch, jelly, giraffe;
She is also learning vocabulary, it seems,
By touching her Mother.
The ships are drawn up close to the shore;
Great felled trees, are they sleeping, or dead?
The ships are sleeping. The vine
Has smuggled a dew-scroll through the half-open window,
Is shooting arrows made of bees
On a bow made of flowers and bines. In the harbour

Men have busied themselves inside the whales
With their paring-tools; they are drawn up close to the
    shore
With open mouths and lighted bellies like the naves of
    churches.
With her, there is the time for playing horse
And the time for stringing pearls. Her blouse
Opens past the pearls into its vaults.
I wash the mud from my head; she says
'You are all eyes.'

DRINK TO THE DUKE

The Duke of Burgundy, who represents
The drunkenness of battle,
With the deep purple of its soldiers,
Those bottles of hot blood
Caved in immense tuns
Under the battle-field, bottlefield,
Where it travels with its iron into the grapes;
Burgundy, you are drinking soldiers,
And have always done so –

And the Duke in his iron rage,
His moustache erect, his eyes bolting,
Reining his horse so she stands
Huge on her hind legs,
And the great insect carapace leaning sideways
With its white eyes in the coal-scuttle helmet
Glaring like the soul of a mantis,
And the noble sword scything down,
Uncorking you, drinking you by the neck.

GRAND BUVEUR I

Two barmaids play by squirting beer,
Soak each other from the taps; a miniature
Of champagne shaken by a bar-squire,
With his finger as a nozzle, leaps in spray so
The room floats with zest and spiritous dew
Like the holy Celonese festival of white-shirted girls
Squired by squirted coloured waters
So that soon everybody is rainbows after a ritual storm.

Drunkenness arrives
As in the darkroom
Fluttering in alchemical trays
The vision on red paper in black silver is suddenly
    complete;

Or as the dew
Forming with perfect bell-roundness
Like bells of glass in harmony

Rings echoes of itself on every grass-blade,
Harmony of lenses, each reflecting all,
Dew suddenly there like knowledge,
Over the surfaces of the brain the perfect nerve-drew
Arriving in the grey meadows of brain,
Like drunkenness, complete.

And the depth of his drinking suddenly fits
End to end like all the pints fastened
Into a glass-lined well that reaches through the years
He calls down it and echoes call him back
To a Sunday walk on a Somerset hill by an orchard
Where the boy lay down having bought cider
From Farmer Gregory, virgin cider
Harvested by virgins, purchased by them, and dreamed
A fabled animal pacing through the trees,
A deer with silver antlers between which spun the
    moon,
Pacing through the big dew of apples formed to
    perfection,
Every bristle of its pelt sharp, but within
The black dews steady in the violin velvet skull
His image trapped.

GRAND BUVEUR II

An impure
Draughty tourbillion opens in my throat
With the desire for a smoke. I resist
For a space, and only for a space, otherwise
The evening would be spoilt. The spirit of tobacco,
    sure,
Is a greater power than the individual cigarette,
And there is an abyss between immaculate and filthy,
Cause for rejoicing; I pollute myself carefully.

Drunk, and smoking, he sees
The qualities of things and not their consequences;
Friends, I was afraid, the swift-drawing flue
Of her white neck in the soot-hued dress
Is of such quality, and I cannot know
The consequences. The little pat

Of butter melted between her thighs,
The butter. I had the feeling of my seed
Rooting, a feeling of rotation
As of parachutes winding into groves
Of bamboo, thick-set, the summation.
She shakes the rain off the tree-pattern on her blouse,
She shines like a peacock in the wet,
In the rain, she flowers, her cigarette goes out,
As I tread in her stream
There is no space or time, my hand passes
Into her collar, a clean wet tourbillion.

MASTER PISS-ON-HIMSELF

(Universal Pissoir)

It is the garden
Of Master Piss-on-Himself
Who made the dew.

He causes the trumpets to roar
As he indicates the falls
Abounding in their multitudes.

His votives are the grassy shrines of tiles
In continuous baptism and imageless union
With the dew. He caused the lashing tempest.
He rounded the fat drops of the unctuous shower.

The wet turns all our rags to silk.
The rain rings lightly on the rims
As the squall drives through the belfries.
It is the park of Master Piss-on-Himself,
His groves are big grass whose mossy trunks
Glitter with peppery springs all night, all day.

LEGIBLE HOURS

The legibility of the evening,
The union of grapes,
We drink it and its spiritous consummation
In this brandy that shines in the dark within,
With the lamps blowing,
The flames like enraged tigers
Roaring in their thin glittering cages,
Ravenous oil-eaters.

The stinking shadows fly out of the wooden windows.
In the dawn, the brittle machine of salt,
The salt bread of the sea, fish for breakfast,
Feathery skeleton, pinion of the sea;
On the smooth-spun sand
Imprint of constellations,
Starcast of the brine, starfish.

Then the evening made legible
By the recording of a ghost
Or an opera of ghosts, the impress,
The mediumistic conches attending, the ear-shells,
The ghost's whorls spinning in their skirts,
Her contractions and ululations,
Her abyssing to her still axle,
Her repeats, her expansion
To the night sky, circling,
The display and occultation
On the night air of her grave that turns.

The legibility of the house.
The courtyard tree,
Green harbour of ten thousand ships
Tending anchor, optical toy of deep shade;
Can you hear the light hum circling in echoes
Around the stream, and the reflections
Caught in the woods and the inextricable shadows
All combing one way, can you? and there!
As the tide turns the weir-sound changes
Its pictures and the tree-head lightens
In the legibility of the grape and the new morning.

GRAND BUVEUR X

To endeavour by drinking to condense
As far as possible the all-pervading
Mother-body of water, to become

One of her whole and rounded bald glisters.
As the web drinks the dew
And displays its coruscations

So the body brims
With burning internalised
Self-interest, like light in drops.

The mind becoming water skims
With transient patterns like the waterflies.
I stroke her web, says the fly,

Which is pearled with icons,
I stroke her glittering moisture,
I stroke her silk,

I am captivated
Says the falling-down
Glass-reversing brittle acrobat

Of the lipped trapezes that tilt
On slow ropes that have elbows.

LOCAL

for G.M.

The Quiet Woman; the pub where men sat suckling
In the silence; a joke against wives. She was headless
Yet her benefits flowed; she was tongueless
Because we would not listen to her. A joke
Against drinkers. The Son it was
Who listened, whom the womb magnified from His dot,
Who entered shining with it, and returned, the Word
Arising always from the liquid mind, again,
There, as you see it, again there,

The Ever-Coming One, the same
Again, please.

The Ash outside the local is the tree of life
Because it hisses in the wind like serpents;
The midwife takes a stick of green ash
And thrusting one end into the fire
As it burns, receives the sap from the raw end into a
    spoon,
And gives it to the child for its first tipple;
That was a fortunate child who then could see
And remember with more than the five senses
Of Aristotle; and the lochial ash dropping
Its little veined keys into the warp of water.

His bedlinen upon rising smells of cucumber
And nothing more. Orion stands at ease,
Unbuckled, just above the horizon,
All the moored yachts swaying slightly,
Rattling their bolts and tackle on a tide
That tastes pleasantly, with a savour of cucumber;
Was this how a Saviour might taste?
In this light breeze that smells of cucumber,
The thousand trees that moan because they could be
    made
Into a hundred thousand yachts or violins.

This is his milestone, by the ash. The Moon
Sinks into it every midsummer. I lust
To sleep, and dream; out of the windows
I watch the misty dunes that are moored
And suddenly on a cold wind their low cloud clears
And their sands pour with its distillates,
The cool dunes, the immense quartz distilleries
Like a multifarious waterworks condense the dew,
Foaming suddenly with dew-brooks and freshets,
A gigantic fractionation. How can
Such beauties be tongueless! Listen,
The great dew condenses in the Quiet Woman's belly,
The unborn child, the secret sharer of the bed,
The inward drinker of The Quiet Mother,
The child who when he is crowned will light the whole
    city.

XVI

IN THE HALL OF THE SAURIANS
(1987)

PNEUMONIA BLOUSES

The iron ships come in with hellish music
They are dedicated to golden oils and engines
And explosive riveting, their hulls heal
To tattoos of guns or iron drums, riveting.
And they worship the horse-mackerel and the sardine,
And why not, it is a living,
And a multitudinous beauty, that brings the souls in.
You see the machine-shop glitter in the tin,
They are water-moths flocking in their thousands;
The packers fit the silver engines in
Laid down in olive oil that is golden;
The key unwinds. Girls
In pneumonia blouses greet the fishermen
Whose balls are brimmed with nitroglycerine of souls,
In each lacy belly the embryo buoyant
As a nenuphar. In the sunlight
The old stone watches sweet and yellow as honeycomb.
Holding the milky child
Is like holding sleep in a bundle,
Which seeps everywhere. There is still frost
In the early morning shadows like spirit-photographs
And like the lace of girls in pneumonia blouses
Ruffled as are the wakes of working boats, fishermen's eyes
Open in all directions, but the shadows of night
Trawl them back again, the nets
Invisible in the black water.

HORSE LOOKING OVER
DRYSTONE WALL

for S.C.

A horse dips his nose into dry shadow
Gathered in the chinks like water.
He drinks the coastal dark
That dwells behind the wallstones
In the dry boulder caverns.

Light lies along his muzzle like a stone sheath.
From skull-darkness kin to the dry stone wall
The eyes watch like mirrors of stone;
This horse is half light, half dark,
Half flesh and half stone
Resting his silver muzzle on the shadowed wall
Like a horse made partly of the silver of clouds,

And partly it is a boulder with mane and nostrils
Watching over his wall the plentiful wild boulders
Maned with shaggy weed in galloping water which are
    kin,

Coralled boulders nostrilling under their manes and
    lathered with brine.

IN THE HALL OF THE SAURIANS

In the Hall of Saurians, the light worked the bones,
The shadows stamped. I was haunted
With the heads colossal in death.
My father brought me here
In his bright shadowless car,
His jewel which he drives everywhere
As a coffin is lined in white satin
Brilliant in the darkness, like mother of pearl.

The wall of the Insect Gallery is splashed
In a butterfly shape with all the British Lepidoptera
And there are five times as many moths shown
For the Shadow in these times
Is correspondingly more significant than the Light.
What goes on in the darkness sees by perfume.
They say that to go out in the noon
Is to lose one's shadow,
To lose the moth of oneself.

My seed, my moth, was torn from me
Like gossamer in the wind
By the lady curator of all these bones,
Mistress of the Halls of Patterns of Death,
Keeper of the probable forms,

The underworld that is delivering constantly
The forms of life, at night like mud
That is a turreted museum, with endless galleries,
But at dawn, nevertheless,
The rainbow glides close to us across the water
Until we stand within its coloured shells,
Its sequent halls. This is our form
Of transport, the ecstasy of these halls,
The forms displayed. My father in his jewel
Scurries away among the beetles.
The corpse of London transforms in his mouth,
His tales make of it a winged thing
Full of custom and surprise.
But these are winged buildings
As we make love after hours
In the Hall of the Saurians, and the flickering light
Works the bones and the shadows stomp
As up to a campfire smoky with jungle moths
To warm themselves or crush it out.

HER SHIRT OPEN

The great batholith under the soil.
The line of farms followed the springs
That leapt from the edge of this batholith.
They had built the town
On the remains of the plain
That was the ancient harbour silted up,
The plain of fine grey soil
That is a mixture of tiny shells
And granite dust. Behind the town
Were the great grey granite quays
From which the buildings had been quarried.

You could join the sea-people still, it was said,
By following the salty path.

I felt so active
With these changes in the living places,
With the rain springing up all around me.

She slipped with me into the alley
Which smelt of the good rain,
All the narrow streets of the town
Wound to that alley.
The rocking tides of perfume
That sprang from every slate and stone,
And the mass of static
The sun had piled up by beating
On that old stone, played everywhere
In its patterns like a sunshine from the earth,

Invisible sunshine and upward rain,
From the torrential earth
Its electrics leapt up the rain,
The pylon of rain.

She opens her shirt, which is wet
And heavy with its drink like a superb silk,
And an eerie feeling superimposes
From the stone electricity and that vertical smile,
Like another music, or echoes
Exploring buildings not yet visible,
The metallic echoes of the slate-lined alley
Erotic and holy, as when we watched
The slow-growing sea-drowned grass
And she turned to me again, her shirt open,
And the current changed around us, and in the canal
The underwater forests switched direction
Showing that sluices far away had opened up
New reaches of the waterway, with varying tides.

AT THE COSH-SHOP

Hard rubber in its silk sheath like a nightie:
The assistant offered me a small equaliser,

A Soho Lawyer that could be holstered
In a specially-tailored back pocket,

And he would introduce me to his friend
The trouser-maker. I did not think this

Necessary, but I asked, Why the silk?
It seemed luxurious for such a hard argument.

Oh, Sir, so that it will draw no blood!
He seemed surprised I asked; I thought this not right;

I believe it was the blackness
The makers did not like to show,

Like an executioner it should draw on
Lily gloves, or like a catering waiter

For an instrument that performs a religious service,
Letting the ghost out temporarily with a shriek:

While all is peace within
They steal your worldly goods

Settling the argument by appeal
To deep non-consciousness

With a swift side-swipe, the Bejasus out of him –
Or an act of sexuality, equivalent?

Do the same people make the instrument
That will put the Bejasus back into a person?

The silk then would be the finest, for silk chafing
Hard rubber rouses electricity, it would be

Moulded to the individual sculpt of her lover,
Providing wisely for a longish trip, could seem

Dressed in his silk pyjamas, hard and tingling,
Or as the white silky cloud conceals the thunder

And the black current
That is going to shoot its white darts up and through.

THUNDER-AND-LIGHTNING POLKA

to J. H. Barclay

The fishmonger staring at the brass band
Offers us golden eyes from a cold slab
And silver instances of sea-flow. The birds

Which were dinosaurs once blanco the stone hats
Of pale admirals. The bandsmen puff their looping brass,
The music skating round and round its rinks

Of shiny tin, the hot trombones and the cool
And silvery horns, light
Sliding like the music along these pipes

And valves, curlicues and flaring tunnels,
Shells, instances of sonorous
Air-flow; we take a piece and present it

On the cold air to the staring ears
Of the sea fishmonger with his wet pets, our part
Of the hypersensitive cabaret. The river

Slides past all the feet; opal mud
Full of sunshine, some dead eye
Caresses the watery catacomb. A hot

Mailed fish has greased windows in the paper,
We eat to music. Above,
A cool high mountain of piled snow,

Its halls stuffed with thunderwork like wardrobes
Of black schoolmasters' gowns and lightning-canes,
White-painted; it turns to one immense

Black gown full of a booming voice from empty sleeves,
And shakes, and shakes its rain down,
And I kiss the thunder-water still booming in every drop

That strikes my face, I hear its flashing brass.
The bandsmen play on in their pavilion,
The instruments flash with lightning,

Their music is full of rain, and fate. I will not go indoors,
My sleeves are wet and heavy
Like velveteen; the trees are shaggy

With birds and lichen, singing in the leaves
In light tones and falling drops that break again
Like little thunder, and cold rain streams across

The wide golden eyes staring from the white slab.

INTO THE ROTHKO INSTALLATION

(Tate Gallery, London)

Dipping into the Tate
As with the bucket of oneself into a well
Of colour and odour, to smell the pictures
And the people steaming in front of the pictures,
To sniff up the odours of the colours, which are
The fragrances of people excited by the pictures;
As the pair walk down the gallery
On each side of them the Turners glow
As though they both were carrying radiance
In a lantern whose rays filled the hall like wings
That brushed the images, which glowed;

Into the Installation, which smells
Of lacquered canvas soaking up all fragrance,
Of cold stone, and her scent falters
Like cloth torn in front of the Rothkos
Which are the after-images of a door slammed
So blinding-white the artist must shut his eyes
And paint the colours floating in his darkness.

He chose the darkest of the images for that white,
That green; red on red beating to the point
Where the eye gasps, and gives up its perfume
Like a night-flowering plant; and with many
Thin washes he achieves the effect
Of a hidden light source which smells
Like water far off in the night, the eye
So parched; paintings you almost can't see;

As if in painting
The Israelites crossing the Red Sea
He painted the whole wall red, and,
Black on black therein,
God somewhat like a lintel. We brought
The lanterns of ourselves in here
And your imagination blotted our light up, Rothko;
The black reached out, quenching our perfume
As in a dark chapel, dark with torn pall,
And our eyes were lead, sinking
Into that darkness all humans have for company;

Standing there, eyes wide, her lids faltered
And closed, and 'I see it, now' she said
And in her breath a wonderful blaze
Of colour of her self-smell
Where she saw that spirit-brightness
Of a door slammed open, and a certain green insertion
Shifting as her gaze searched
What seemed like a meadow through the white door
Made of lightning, cloud or flowers, like Venusberg
Opening white portals in the green mountain
Stuffed with light, he having used
The darkest of all that spectrum almost to blindness

And in his studio in the thin chalk of dawn
Having passed inwardly through that blackness,
Slitting his wrists, by process of red on red
He entered the chapel under the haunted mound
Where the white lightning of another world
Flashed, and built pillars. We left
The gallery of pictures rocked
By the perfume of a slammed eye, its corridors
Were wreathed with the detonation of all its pictures
In the quick of the eye, delighting into
Perfumes like fresh halls of crowded festival.

PLAYING DEAD

His dead-white face,
The eyelids of chalk
With the bold black cross marked

Cancelling the eyes, declaring
Hollow-socketed death, and the
Marble-white countenance

Declaring death
And the red nose to admit
He had died drinking

And the vertical eyelid-stripe
Telling us not only can he open
His eyes up and down but also

From side to side in the stare
Of a real ghost
Who does as he likes

Because Death breaks all the rules, and is
At very best an outrageous joke, and almost
Whatever Death does is quite soon forgotten;

So the Clown pratfalls on the skeleton
Of a banana, and two well-dressed Clowns
Accelerate with custard pies their mutual putrefaction,

As if it were funny to worry overmuch
About these bodies we wear like increasingly
Baggy pants with enormous knucklebuttons, especially
If like that sepulchral makeup they wipe off
In cold cream to white sheer speechless laughter.

A DEWY GARMENT

The shower withheld matures to thunder,
Such activity, then such rest;
I walk out in my worm-coloured shoes
Through the puddles where the worms luxuriate,
The bone-coloured worms
In the fallen skies of the puddles;
My love of thundershowers was given to me
By Odeon University:
Such downpours in the tropical forests,
The great leaves catching the rain by its lips

Hanging poised in banquets,
And the repose was as wide as the blank screen
Still crossed by the images.
And there was never a storm without a wet girl
Shiny in drenched tropicals
Flickering to those lightnings, submitting to Tarzan,
And the film a black-and-white thunderstorm
Flashing eighteen times a second,
Which welded its lights to a seamless narrative,
For the demonic or the divine is the sudden,
And the cinema soothes the sudden.
Katharos, the putting on of a fresh garment
Even of jungle-grass
After soil and toil, the repose
In a fresh garment clean as an imagery screen,
This skin across which the thunder has played,
This skin
Of discharged rain and stretches of water;
A dewy garment covers me,
Restless manhood is gone.

THE GIRL READING MY POETRY

This is an impossible event!
This melody is my extensive lechery –
The girl reading my poetry
Launders it;
An impossible accomplishment!
Cleansed white, in London –
The beauty distilled of this dreck
Washed in a maidenly mouth . . .

And moreover the audience
From the facing 200 gilt chairs
Witnessing the ablution
Stay entirely quiet,

And as they warm to the mouth of this new muse
Give off first a perfume in the breath,
Then from their entire tapestry of skin
So that
I cannot believe this blossoming,

Like a baby fresh from its bath,
Like flowers nodding
In the quickened breath
Along the polite rows –

And then they spatter it by applause,
The fast detonations of applause,
The rattle of musketry in a flowering garden!
They charge it with kinesis
And propel it like bullets
With bravo and encomium –

And she stands there spattered with it
And glowing with the fine smell,
And takes her smiling breath
Of the cloud of quelques fleurs and cordite
And drinks up these chemicals and the electricity
Generated by applause inside the invisible
Air-hued cloud of alchemy
And imagery poetry-gas.

Overwhelmed and saturated by this opera
I glance at my printed words,
They are a taciturn libretto,
Yet I must have said something right,
My own smell small like a damp railway station,
The iron-flavoured air of it waiting for the local train:

While she, and they,
Were like the express roaring into Truro,
The doors shooting open, the holiday plumage alighting,
Boarding, the terrace of doors slamming,
And the whole symphony rowing up the line out of my
    ken,
Articulating with its rolling stock and its headlights
    blazing.

FAR STAR

It is like living in a transistor with all this radio
Which is the inner weather of the house
Presided over by housegoddesses who turn

Everything that happens into perfume and electricity;
Oh! she cries, what a blessing – and I smell the
    blessing
Like a candle lighted, a scented flame that spreads
Through closed doors, opening them;
And when she curses, sulphur blackens all the knives.
We have tuned our circuits by living together so long
And the child, never having known another house,
    deepest tuned:
She was broadcast into this world via the lady
    transmitter
And mostly plays musical comedy, though now is of
    an age
For an occasional tragic aria about the sister she has
    not got,
Who will not now be broadcast from that far star;

And I wish heartily we had more loos – our tuning
    is such
On the same channel that we all three must shit
    simultaneously.

A SCARECROW

A scarecrow in the field,
Dressed like a King
In streamers of tinfoil
Which flash in the sun
And glitter;

And in the deep night
As the moon rises
That glittering again
Appears in the field
As if a fountain
Were standing guard
Over the furrows;

A tattering robe
Of strips of tinfoil
Ragged and gorgeous because
Of its liquid facility with the light,

And so multiplex

That it is a squadron riding
With swords out saluting the light.

The birds rejoice with their song
At this wonder of the sun
Willowing on its cross-pole,
And in this presence of the moon
Raggedy in the fertile field,
And nip therefore their share only
Of seeds sown out of the loam,
And do not multiply their kind
Desperately being content seemingly
That an alchemical balance has been
    achieved:

The tinfoil rebus in the open field.
Even the vicar, passing the scarecrow field
Is reminded of life
That is not only dust to dust
But light to light and air to air,
Shooting his cuffs,
Flashing his watch.

DRY PARROT

The Parrot of Warlock's Wood,
Of Peter's Wood,
It leaves wide twiggy footprints,
It walks in its cinder wings
Like a tight-buttoned fellow
In oyster-grey tailcoat;

A Parrot has no blood
Only calcium filings,
It dries a room;
Peter keeps the Parrot
To dry the house out;
It was a clinker egg
Before it was a thirsty Parrot.

Now it taps on the clear dry mirror
And with its beak begins
To loosen the mummy plumage
And shake the egg-sand out
And utters an Egyptian cry and flies
Taking to the air up the chimney
Like a roaring hearth-fire
In its anhydrous glory.

THE BIG SLEEP

Sea, great sleepy
Syrup easing round the point, toiling
In two dials, like cogs

Of an immense sea-clock,
One roping in, the other out.
Salt honey, restless in its comb,

Every-living, moving, salt sleep,
Sandy like the grains at eyes' corners
Of waking, or sleepiness, or ever-sleeping;

And when the sun shines, visited as by bees
Of the sun that glitter, and hum in every wave,
As though the honey collected the bees;

The honey that was before all flowers, sleepiness,
Deep gulfs of it, more of it than anything,
Except sleepy warm rock in the earth centre

Turning over slowly, creating magnetism,
Which is a kind of sleepiness, drowsy glue
Binding the fingers, weakly waking fingers,

Or fingers twitching lightly with the tides;
And the giant clock glides like portals, tics
Like eyelids of giants sleeping, and we lie

In Falmouth like many in a bed,
And when the big one turns
We all turn; some of us

Fall out of bed into the deep soil,
Our bones twitch to the tides,
Laid in their magnetic pattern, our waters

Rise like white spirits distilled by the moon,
Can get no further, and turn over
Heavy as honey into the sea

To sleep and dream, and when the big one dreams
We all dream. And when she storms
We all weep and ache, and some fall

Into her gulfs as she tosses, and we weep
For the lifeboats toiling on the nightmares . . .
But in those beds waters touch each other

Coiling, in a certain way, and where they touch,
At the very point, a mineral spark,
A bone begins to grow, someone is

Putting bones together in the gulf,
In her accustomed patterns – and in their season
The women walk about the town, a big drop

Of the Dreamer in their bellies, and in the drop
A smaller dreamer, image of themselves,
Who are the image dreamed by the ocean's drop,

By the two clocks, one roping in, one out.

XVII

THE FIRST EARTHQUAKE
(1989)

THE FIRST EARTHQUAKE

The birds squabbled and fell silent
In their million trees like colleges of monks
With their mean little ways and their beautiful songs;

The yachts like moored forests,
The yachts rocked in their haven
Like women in long dresses

And invisible feet
Bowing to the earthquake.
The mist had rolled in

And developed all the spiderwebs,
The trees in the groves draped
Like pearl-sewn yachts,

The million spiders in them asleep,
The spiders in their white roofs,
The dew-lapping spiders,

They nodded their toolchest faces,
Beards wet with dew,
Dew brimming their webs and their claws;

Complex water shivered everywhere like a single ghost.
Lovers, smelling of almonds and new bread,
Roused from their beds, pointed

Rubbing their eyes at the copses of yachts
That tugged at the tremor and dipped,
Shivering rain from their tackles,

Lovers who shivered like silk
As the rafters groaned
Within their white ceilings,

This earthquake shoved up fifty new fountains!
After the first shock we are ravenous,
The little silvery fishes grizzling in the shiny pans.

SUMMER

The summer mice are fat as butter.
There is the waste of a silent bronze-smithy,
Tightly-curled lathings, and the everlasting

Scent of brass.
There is a fly listening to an egg in the kitchen.
There is a child sipping warm blood in the womb,

In the hot bell-fat womb.
Auntie holds up the smoothing-iron
Polished like a mirror with its work,

She looks into it and spits,
It satisfies, she peels
The knife-edged denim off the ironing board;

It satisfies, his tomorrow's shirt,
Blue as the sky faded with its clouds;
And as the river goes to bed in leaves,

In ten billion leaves flowing through the summer,
So must the nephew sink into the feather-bed upstairs,
Wallow in its lavender laundered marsh.

The nephew sunk in the feather-bed upstairs,
Nesting for summer in this feather-bed,
Dreams of the women of the house that all night

They braid their hair and chat
And sweep the kitchen for tomorrow's chores
And they never go to bed at all,

Since they are still there in the morning frying breakfast.
Munching his fried bread with shining lips,
His smile pocked and sintered like cuttlebone,

The uncle rubs his big hands in the boy's hair.

III

Past the river jammed like corduroy with logs
Which have been there so long their shoots
Are bushing into hedgerows, locking them,

There is a bluebell-wood by mudflats
And within it a comb of soft long meadow that delves
Into a flank of Shivering Mountain;

The shuddering cloud-shapes shake over it,
The small springs shiver down its slopes,
The scree slips day and night a little,

Expanding in the hot sun and holding,
Slipping a little further in oily dew of evening.

IV

The shades that pour down Shivering Mountain
Are irresistible to me,
Its grey locks, cloud canopy,

Its cap of invisibility;
I climb into insubstantiality
Like an old Chinese effacing among his chasms

Sliding through empty ghost rock-cities
Repopulated suddenly with shades.
I am not an old Chinese for long;

My uncle comes with dogs and shotguns looking for me,
And slaps me back into his world,
And cuffs me down slippery scree with his grinning acne,

With a pock-mask like the bottom of the sea.

HARVEST

The greatest possible touch, to bathe.
The wind bathing in the wheat,

The great invisible woman plunges
Into the heavy tassels, into the wheat-smell
That is like straw baskets full of new bread;
The wheat splashes round her, it must cry out,
All the stems chafing, like an immense piano plunged
    into
Which continues playing as she swims,
A piano full of wheat, a concert grand
Whose blackness opened on a field of wheat
And the music swims in it, and in wide waves descants;
She does the overarm crawl from one stone hedge
To the far end, and climbs out, invisible, dripping with
    rain.

II

As though all the wheat in the world
Were her hair, in which she bathes.

III

The Miners' Brass Band concurs,
They are a procession of buttery lotuses,
The sunlit air pours into them
And coils around their instruments
Like lotuses evolving from their lungs
In the sound of mined metal vibrating
With human breath, earth and air
Married: its child, music.
I wonder if the great churches
And concert halls mark standing waves
Where the weather stills as over mines
And you can blow your golden lotus and be heard.

III

The metal walks and sings. Pausing
Halfway up the house stairs
I can hear the two radio sets at once
Tuned to the same music; we call that 'The Well',
A well of music sounding between two floors.
At present we have a well-known soloist
Playing with an anonymous orchestra
Unknown to him.

I think of a buck-naked
Skinny young fellow at the piano
The sunwarmed air of the music
Like a golden wheatfield brothing around him.

TO THE BLACK POET

I

The lightning flashes
Over her silk suit, the silk
In repose in which she dreams;
Now I am afraid she is out in
The garden, out in the rain,
In her pyjamas, again; and her skin
Jealous for that silk especially;

It is a bad sign the evening before
When she dons the stiff broadcloth trousers;
I am bound to find her wet
Out in the garden in white silk
That next morning. It was in silk

Open at the legs
She gripped her birth-pangs
As the Goddess gripped mountains; I stood by
Awaiting her pleasure and passed the time
Considering the tank where the fish glide
Kissing the water as they swim, their lips
Rosed by the tropics.

II

She has invited her lover
The famous black poet
Whose beauty she told me
Was in his nostrils
Which expand marvellously
As he inhales to speak poetry;
There is no filthy rubble
In there, no kind of
Misshapen surprise, no hard
Facial shit in such a nose.

One can stare deep into it
Without fear, inhaling
The sweet smell of his discourse;
She swears it was how she conceived.
It is rose-coloured up there
A rose twilight in black depths
Blowing with articulate winds
The raw material of his poetry speech,
A breath like a marvellous
Air of the tropics reversing in a black conch
Scented with hibiscus and mango-sweat.

IV

She says, It is for longing
Of him that I go out in white silk
To stare up into the southern rain
In the rose-coloured dusk
To feel it clasp my body's form
As it slowly falls, in my pyjamas
Like a warm bed-embrace.
It is scented with the perspiration of mangoes;
I inhale that rain
Into my caves of poetry,
Our child will strip me off
Like silk clothes drenched with labour;
It will sneeze me out of its black conched caverns.

V

It is my privilege to know him
To stare into his nose
And listen to his mouth,
To be surrounded by his tropic air,
And, instead of having to meet
Him in the eye, as with the pink men,

To greet him by staring deep
Into his insufflating nose, his place
Of inspiration, myself a whole skin
Silk bandana to his spermatic sneeze.

STARLIGHT

Her menstruation has a most beautiful
Smell of warm ripe apples that are red,
And an odour of chocolate, a touch of poppy,
And bed-opiums roll from her limbs
Like the smokes of innumerable addicts between the sheets,

A morpheus tampon like a tomb of spices,
Full of spirits, red firework.

It makes me feel like Hercules!
Who spun the wheel in the house of women.
Indeed, the wheel spins, a crimson thread.
Suddenly, the stars are out,
Ripe, like the apples;
Menstruating, with the stars out.

CARCASS

In the bellies of the soft bronze flies
The carcass of the magpie flies again,
Humming like a fast song,
A gong hushed but purring to the touch.
The aviary of insects chirps with juice
They are working with their faces
At the white branches of the carcass,
Pungent little resurrectors, pepper-fruit
In bronze of false orchards slipping away
Full of their pips in lariat flight,
The magpie flies again
Through the churches of the air,
It breaks its dome
Laid by a fly in a black-white flurry,
The reverse stork that devours eggs and nestlings
Wings backwards down the gullets of resurrectors.

The navvy bows his head to the freezing asphalt,
His pneumatic thumper pounds the road
Belling with the decelerated fury
Of the wellington-boot tongue
Of a blowfly on its pitons hacking like a hero
Hard at a slab of refrigerated giant.

333

ROUND PYLONS

The clouds of luminous mist from the sea
Laying the round dew everywhere in the hedges
And the coils of innumerable dew encircling the spider,

The circuitry of the brash spider
In round pylons
As in a castle of awareness,

Many curtain walls and cistern keeps
Guarding the centre
And, down its lines of gossamer

The round helmets of light
In their slow march,
The land hung with these sheets,

The sheeted sea coming ashore
And hanging its pictures up in the hedges,
Its unsalted portraits,

The surface of the sea doubling
As it opens into sleep,
A source among white sources, cresting.

WOODEN PIPES

The hands in the womb,
The invisible hands serving at the feast,
The round banquet in the high domed hall,
Shaping the child and serving her,
Combing her body to the right shape;
This is going on now.

I believed I heard Zoe
Playing on wooden pipes as plain as plain
But as I woke fully
It was a seagull crying.

There is an inner, and an outer daughter.

My sleep makes me as my waking does,
The sleep of invisible hands
Of servitors, the music of wooden pipes,
The tree-song shortened for human ears,
The blessed ghosts of that feast
And the drunken guest at it, the reveller
Who wakes in the cold air
To the music of seagulls.

There is an inward, and an outer daughter,
And the outer girl sits, combing her hair,
The mother watching, takes the comb
Soothes her head, gliding out of it
Aches of the day with her visible hands,

For with invisible hands the same woman
Below and within is combing
Another daughter into shape
Among the birth-currents
A womb of full tresses

And the outer daughter speaks to the inner
Through the mother,
The inner daughter speaks through the mother's actions,
The two sisters are combing each other's hair,
The mother is the interface,
The two daughters kiss her.

ZOE'S THOMAS

A young leggy cat, so glossy black
He might in that instant have leapt
From the pitch-egg of night; his eyes

Golden as yolks. He scrutinizes
The room-dew of our breath running down
The cold windowpane as if it were mice.

A cluster of drops scuds down the glass
And shatters on the sill, his paw darts out
And inquisitorially turns the meagre

Water over and over – and then his tongue
Darts out and swiftly laps it up,
The innocent water which squeals with light.

QUIET TIME

The spider of the wainscot
Fell to the pliers newly arrived
Of a centipede out of the WC pedestal;
This aggressor was like the last bones of a God
Waiting for resurrection of the whole body,
Like an Osiris pillar, a small one,
A small god's spinal column
Running independently, as a God's might do –

But also like a long twist of toffee
Of that colour as I sat remembering
When toffee was the gold of my boy's mouth,
And would not pluck the fillings from my teeth;
And this long twisted toffee has its own jaws
With which it strikes down the defenceless weaver
I have watched patching his sail
For several days in this same cloistered toilet –

My quiet time; a cloister's clyster, that centipede
Is like a dark cloister running on its own
That has loosened itself from the Abbey stones
Incorporating into its twilight many brethren
Sprinting all together on brotherly legs
Like Chinese masquers chattering in their dragon –

Hunting for all the tremulous spinsters
And all the lockchesters in the world,
Hunting for the alchemistic spiders
For they have within them a Benedictine
Stilled from the swarms of prayerful night-moths
One of which now splashes the cream walls
Easing the fretted constellations of its cream wings;
I thought it was a speckling of ink, like –

DOMESTIC SUITE

The central heating buzzes
Like an apple with a wasp inside;
Water-tree-house with a bark of copper,
The taps flower white water,
Dribble glass moss.
Outside the sea spreads tablecloths over and over,
Is full of milt,
The strong pure eggs of fish;
In the shops the pure pleated eyes of fish,
Salty goldfoil, open to all their troubles.
I slice the orange; it is a round table
Its place-segments designed for knights,
Fitted with sealed goblets of juice as for astronauts.
Our hen squeaks like a wooden sash.
The shore breathes like a horse
Running under the shade of trees into the sunlight,
In this wind, white horses or blossoming trees rush
    inland.
The meadow-breathing of a pony, the strong
Leathery lips as they nip up the sugar-lump,
The strong warm grassy flank;
There is the central heating with its low pulse,
There is golden foliage and a glittering wife, there is
An unweaned child that smells of honeysuckle in the
    nights, and
Subdued water-music of horses and wasps all winter.

THE DYNAMITE DOCTORS

The dynamite doctors
At the explosives factory
They nurse the melted stew

Like greasy gravy or mutton tallow,
A grey potency in its bowls
That must never be stirred too fast

Or else the door opens on a star
Opens on a sun, on creation
And the fire-blast hurries in

337

Like an angel of death with hair burning.
The ticklish doctors
Skimming the bowls

Tilting them over the kieselguhr
To contrive that virile mud
Called dynamite,

The precious stream that must not break
In its droplets like a stick of bombs,
Otherwise the medicine will suffer an attack

Which will take everyone with it.
One doctor takes the pulse
Of the machine and turns it down

A little, the vibration is excessive;
He dips his finger slowly
Into the gluten and sucks it most gently

So his head shall not explode:
He nods, he must not shake his head.

MENOPAUSA

The change of life in her
Was like the escape of an animal,
Escape of a lizard maybe, like a fast
Comma escaping the sentence and jumbling it;
Like buildings where the main beam snaps,
The broken floors and the rubble descending
In their clouds of pepper. I will build

A new hall of statement, she said; I am tired
Of all this blood. It was the lizard
Which had wounded her, and lodged,
That now departed. She pointed
To the Moon rising, and the man in it
And said: there he is, my lizard,
Sailing away.

Or was it the woman had escaped
And offered her shadow to the dark gods?

Shadow or lizard, both slipped quickly
Like silk over the ground,
Would swerve and misdirect and disappear;

And often it seemed
As if she herself had gone
And the lizard remained,
The dry sand of the lizard
Pouring. For she
Could sit long minutes not stirring,
The eyes blinking

Seldom; then she would reach out
For an apple with an arm so graceful
It seemed a tongue; and a film

Wiped across her eyes as if to cleanse them,
A second eyelid, and then the film departed
And the eyes sparkled like gems in dry sand;

If it were a lizard, it was a seer,
Like a sphinx; after these reveries,
Munching apples, she would write long poems
To her friends, each one enclosing a letter.

ENTRY FEE

When I stroke her arms
There is a smell of bread;
Her legs, of lilies.

There are fragrant marshes in her skin
And there is a pulse in the ground of it.
The Mine called 'Isyours' is open today
On payment of a small compliment.

This is really
Very extraordinary value;
The lights are blazing underground,

Gemstones stud the walls and floors;
I walk there amazed for hours, it seems.

At the very bottom of the shaft
There is a dark pool with a white swan floating

It rouses its wings

It beats over the water
Pleating it to its depths
Raising a new odour charged
With the deep and with the extreme
Cry of the bird as it ladders across the pool.

AT HOME

I

The spider combs her beard.
One gave me cobweb-pills for the shakes.
There is a black Rasputin-fly that can't be killed,

There is a dustbin boiling with its worms;
My mother scrapes more porridge into the faces.
The flies buzz with swollen lips,

In a Russian, in the translating sunshine.
Dew scuttles down the panes
Like the shaky ghosts of crippled spiders.

I try to rub the glass free and clear
But they are running their races
On the further surfaces. The dry spider

Will raise the wet flies and drink out of them,
Like Bellarmine jugs, like horny flasks
That have wings and faces. Convolvulus

That smells of nice blancmange
Twirls about the dustbin lattice.
My father rushes through the kitchen

Flapping a tea-towel, ushering a ghost of flies
Out of the kitchen into the cool green lane.
There are still flies that circle stolidly

Keeping the pattern just below the ceiling.
They pass through my father's cloth, evidently,
Like spirits of the pattern. He returns.

II

He returns wiping his brow spiderous with dew
And breathing heavily. He shakes his fist
At the immovable fly-pattern round and round the
    lamp;

My father hefts a shuddering pail of water
And turns it into milk with disinfectant.
He pours it in the choiring bin of maggots.

Their smell of coconut and pus
Fades behind the blanket of hospital pine.
The maggots skip in their stringy boiling.

My mother folds her arms and nods her head.
We settle once more round the breakfast-table,
There is a baby brother hoisted in a high-chair.

The silent changeling grasps the shaggy rusk.
He was born in a smell of pine-needles and maggots.
I was not allowed inside the curtained room.

Its shadows were odorous, and deeper than a cave.
The doctor brisked the taps to scrub his paws.
He smelled of her, and the nurse smelled;

Pine and maggots. In the cave of bedroom shade
Where she has gone, her voice deepens like a man's
Then shatters, and another voice

Lifts in something which is not a song,
And she returns,
Gripping a maggoty bundle, not the same.

341

This terrible head suited her as well,
Distilling tears and wax and drool,
Lying across the pillow stained like brown paper,

Stamped and water-marked with sweat,
Just unwrapped, this parcel, on a fresh head,
The ginger hair in feeble ringlets,

The mauve lipstick, the broken veins in the cheeks,
Severed at the seamy sheet. It
Begins tossing, lets out an accustomed cry;

I start back, and clamber under the bed.
Here there are long lattices of dust
Rolled up against the wainscot from the blankets,

Fibres minutely ground through the springs
That coil above me, the mill
Of nightmare sickness and copulation,

The flour of germs and fibres rubbed
From bar and dance-hall all loafed together
In long limbless clooties which drift at me,

Shift very slightly in the mattress-wind
That puffs as she turns over in her sleep
Of the medicine alcohols that net her dreams

Blackening in the broken veins
Exhaling tinctures into the fresh window air
That begins again to smell of pine and coconut

And taint her appeaseless, helpless ghost.
It is in the boards and bricks.
The room and house will always smell of it.

JOY GORDON

The death of my mother, it
Doesn't mean she's gone for ever,
It means she has crossed over;
I cry because I have tears, and there seems to be
A joy in the air (she liked
To call herself Joy, it was her
Dancing name, Joy Gordon, thus,
When she danced she was my Father's Joy;
His name was Gordon.)

What are ghosts? The medium said
Whenever you think of her,
Greet that image kindly, say
'I'm glad to see you' it will give
The spirit Joy; to be fluxile
Like air, but
Constant as metal,
Not keeping to the one world,
Seeking unity with the living:
I see her now, she dances,
I am very glad to see you dancing,
Joy.

I see spirits, and try
To greet them kindly; and there is never
A company of the living
Without its spirits mingling:
There they were
Doing their Tai Chi
Under the dawn trees, the living
In their loose linen jackets and white ghost-trousers
A ballet of clowns moving as the trees move
To the dawn wind and the dawn chorus,
And among them, spirits,
Like air coiling, as though
Certain enhancing lenses had swept
In front of trees
Or between the dancers;

Under the dawn trees collecting
All the natural forces that do us good,
Gathering the metals of the trees

In manual alchemy, in sequent poses
Adopting the shapes of the vessels
Of human distillation, the hushed
Receptacles, and without, within,
The condensation of a magical dew;
To gather Joy.

The fair-haired one in the long skirt
A portion of the gnosis
Dancing slowly under the dawn trees,
She was the first one there, she was dancing
When I arrived, slowly under the dawn trees
To catch their bright metal, the distillation vessel
Itself dancing.

Just so might my daughter
Call herself Zoe Peters
For dancing or other joys
And signify 'Peter's Life':

I went to fetch her
From a friend's birthday party
In the long upper room of the Church Hall;
Some eleven-year-old lingerers were murdering
'Happy Birthday' on the old piano by the little
    platform;
There was a memento of iced cake in a twist of
    polythene
To take home, and there had been dancing;

There was still dancing,
The room was full of dancing, no girls were
    dancing,
There was dancing up to the ceiling, the air still
    paced
With Joy and I looked up and greeted them kindly.

XVIII

DRESSED AS FOR A TAROT PACK

(1990)

GEODIC POET

Since the flamen dialis was not supposed
To spend a single night away from his bed, and since
The poet likes to keep tradition, he arrives at the site

Wrapped in his surrogate bedsheet like a toga'ed Roman
Or a brisk ghost in its crackling aura. One book
Opens another, one grotto leads to another, he has made

Fast friends with the speleologists who are
Retired miners, and astronomers in reverse; they will open
New grottoes for him, the baby; on this miraculous day

They have opened five, one after the other,
With picks gently through the walls of each, the poet
Quivering in his sheet, his hair electrical, holding up

His lantern, the miners taciturn, hacking
At the quartz-back of the just-discovered cavern, then standing
    back,
The poet creeping through the ragged crystal hole and calling

'It is another grotto!' as a shining smell
Diffuses out, all smile, surrounded by scintillae. It was like
Excavating a gigantic bunch of frozen grapes

Whose juice had crystallised, chamber upon chamber
Packed with millennial crystals, and with an odour
Of chalk and alcohol which had distilled

And lain there undisturbed a billion years;
The poet should take first breath, in case of poison.

SIXTY STAGS

The serpent was more naked than any beast,
The biblical serpent rustling through the tree,
Who walked upright like a sheen or glory,
A light and turbulence spinning round the temples;

It slipped its skin off enamelled wax

347

With a snake-smell of naked blessedness,
Sleeping by its cast skin, its decanted sin,
Its magical companion, its killed self.

There was no curse.
The curse was fear, fear cursed them,
This is the self-renewing poison –
Which when reversed
Is like the boy

Who said to his father there were
Sixty stags in the forest, and when the man
Told him he lied, asked
'What, then, was all the rustling in the woods?'

MARMALADE

I shift my shape into a shirt, and that
Adjusts my skin, which before was shapeless
Having sprawled all through the shapeless night;
Once I had an orgasm at my elbows because of that
Focussing device called sleeves. I read that
Brazilian Giant Otters trample riverside
Vegetation to a quag where they urinate,
Defecate, deposit anal sac jelly and generally
Squirm about in the marmalade. That's what I call
Family life. Marmalade
Is the distillation of mud through
The tree's alembic, the great pure drop
With its glass-lizard skin swelling in the boughs,
That ripening alchemy. They come down again
To breakfast and find me staring still
Into the marmalade jar as into an aquarium
Of orange peel, the nights passed
In a flash of black, and now again
The sun shines through this jar. Right, I say,
Some toast; I spread the luminous plasm
And my anal sac quivers, I start to think
Of a woman running naked who needs
Body-painting, I put coins
Over her eyes to protect them, and leave
A small unpainted patch on her back
Through which she can breathe, and in orange

I paint marmalade everywhere but there,
Over her soft peel. My elder brother
Sits down, discharging hot cross smells
From his armpits, he is thinking: 'This innocent
Is gleeful because he doesn't know he can
Be destroyed, and therefore escapes destruction;
Because he believes marmalade is
For ever and ever and creates itself besides.'

WAVE-BIRTH

The young spiritualist giving birth
In the spirit of a seance full of sheets,
Drapes and milky plasms,

Such plasms as will appear, the birth-water
Moving of itself, the uncanny
And erotic slime, and attended

By serious Sunday-school men
Whose mannerly rituals she is accustomed to,
The mysteries of the seance being

So womby, the atmosphere that seems
To transduce questions into forms
And suggestions into shapes

Who know more than they might; but the shape
Of this emission cannot be questioned,
It is a tiny child putting off its veils,

A child manifesting covered in wax
With an almond birth-place of her own
Clean as a mushroom. The mother-made

Smell of flesh is supreme,
Out of the collision of forces that meet
In the tidal chamber of this woman;

(For the manlike waves
Pound below the seance-chamber
Which is the accouchement-room

In the house on its sea-poles
Of the old docks; where better
To guide the spirit-ships in

With their fresh intelligence?) And I walked
Up her drive in a heavy sea
Where the blowhole spume like a plume

Of steam from a horse's nostril,
Immense spirit-steed,
Rose about me on the path,

In which huge light hung split
Like banners of rainbow,
Or an enormous rainbow bending down to drink,

The he-waves hollowing into their she-waves,
The carriages of foam that shake
The resonant foundation-chamber,

And the seance-room tuning all those waves
Piled to the horizon of our intelligence,
Our mortal state;

The tongue of brine sounding the bell of rock;
And we replying to them in their own tongue
So far as we can, in labour-cries and hymns.

She speaks of 'My seance-room
Now occupied by my baby's high fragrance;
I adjust the resonance of her chamber in me

With my holy yells to guide her,
When the tuning is just right I hear her cry out,
And here she comes all gurgling

Smiling and playing with the spiritual slime
And she looks straight into me
Her iris pleated like the coloured

Wave-pictures stacked in every direction
Straight to the celestial heights, in vox humana.'

XIX

UNDER THE RESERVOIR
(1992)

THE SMALL EARTHQUAKE

The birds can't soar because all the breath
That carries them has been withdrawn
Into this great hush, the sea and sky

Calm as two mirrors endlessly reflecting.
Then the stars flicker like candles where a door
Is opened, and closed, and the ground

Bumps slowly, like a ferry as it is steered
Into the quay, bumps on its rope fenders;
And afterwards you cannot believe

The ground shifted; except, high up in the corner
Near the ceiling the white has cracked like a web
Until you try to smear it away: the spider

Under the earth spun it and threw it
Into the house; and I recollect a certain
Tang passed through the air, like

A champagne elixir passing from the abyss, creating
A freshet that soaked the grass, a web-crack,
And a jammed window in Zoe's room upstairs.

THE SECRET EXAMINATION

The wooden desks, the wooden stools
Inscribed with their flow. The examinees

Inscribe their flow. The invigilator
Has a special smell, kindly snapper;

The examinees smell of a good wash
And clean ironing with no black marks;

There is a lean smell of cream and treacle,
Or, as the Bible says, of milk and honey,

For the examination is going well
And distilling by its queries passionless thought

In small puffs from the alembics
Of sleeves and collars

With the tiny writing motions
And slight nods of head; everybody

In this well-lighted room
Of sharp pencils and dazzling pages

And cleanest clothes is exhaling subtexts,
Is inhaling information secretly colluding;

The invigilator knows there is no copying –
But how can all the answers be identical?

He is suspicious of the brightest boy
And the dullest, equally.

BLACKTHORN WINTER

A blackthorn winter. The trees lighter
Than at other times, showing
The inwards of their leaves; the stars
Because of the bitter wind
Twinkle fiercely; the masses of air
Create a hollow echoing in the woodland;
Sunset's slant light rebuilds ghost villages, echoing
In their shadow-plane out of moist deep foundations,
And celtic boundaries pulse in ceaseless wind-markings;

To smell the touch of the wind, to hear the contours.

UNDER THE RESERVOIR

The reservoir great as the weight
Of a black sun radiates through the cracks
In the concrete, expresses water supercharged

By pressure and darkness, the whole body
Of water leaning on the hairline cracks,
Water pumping itself through masonry

Like light through glass. Water charged
By the mystery of lying there in storeys
In transparent tons staring both upwards and
    downwards

(His coffee hand spills on his shirt the regalia
Of his worried mind in linked splashes like medals
Of a muddy war)

The reservoirs in their unending battle to flow
Turned into steely strain like hammered pewter
Endure their thousand tons of mud, as though

They held their surfaces open like Samson
To the dust that sifts on to their cold pewter,
And rejoice in their dark linings, as they might

Rejoice in plentiful seed,
Black seed of illimitable forest cracking
Open the stone rooms when the water has gone.

FALMOUTH CLOUDS

I

The weather, opening and closing
Doors in the head,

Opening them gently like
A gradual suffusion of sun, or
Slamming thunder-splattered doors shut,

II

With a jangle of chairs disclosing
A writhing chain-locker of cloud
Slithering away into itself.

A chalky bust of Beethoven breaks open
 On rows of ruffled theatre-chocolates which gleam
In the lightning; then, the stars
Walking in long chiffons of rain

Where later chiffons are unrolled
Along a blue counter, a bolt of silk thumped down
So it unrolls with an astonishing perfume
And a blaze of white.

In the high wind implosions of dark-cloaked cloud
As through the stage trapdoors called 'vampires', plunge.

An exploding herb-garden or laboratory
Shoots across the sky,
Arrests one's head and simultaneously
Across the inside of that dome
Plants horticultures of changeable perfumes.

That ice-cathedral which built itself from nothing
But faith, is being shot from a cannon
For charity, with silver candlesticks and sonorous
    arches
And clergy scattering in their whitest surplices;

The cathedral was full of dazzling tablecloths
Which come rolling everywhere above on which are
    thrown
Dark shadows from much higher, of personages who
    appear
To be eating supper at a long table in an upper room.

These clouds are packed with white gulls, while those

Are an aviary of dark rainbirds; when they collide
There is suddenly nothing but sun, hey presto.

X

Skywalkers with immense tension of presence
And extreme visibility and invisibility as well,
The cascades roll past, turn dragonish and then
They are all simple lace very high
On a blue robe which darkens with emergency
   generating stations
 Black as floating mines of coal.

XI

I wake from a dream of crowned and grimacing white
   faces
To my bedroom window which crowds with vast white
   faces grimacing.

SNIFFING TOM

One who goes to and fro in summer
Sniffing the saddles of girls' cycles:
A Sniffing Tom.

The same chap (I know him well)
Farts in the bath and bites the bubbles:
He doubles as a *Snorkist.*

To secure his rank, the prince
Catches in his mouth the rank breath
Of the dying king: this is the *Air Apparent.*

He is crowned soon enough
And married with Holy Rites, which should
More properly be called *Holy Ruts,*

For after copulation the rank dream comes,
And he that dreams also sweats, farts, snores
And erects and should *revere*

357

Le rêve, its reverie, for he has dreamed
A classy one, that he unlocked
The school shed among the daffodils

And it contained 100 girls' cycles,
So he sleeps to dream again, and sweats,
And he is juicy; that is, *sapient*;

By Jiminy, this is sooth! by the twins
Of the two worlds, soothe, sleep
And wake; *by Gemini!*

IN THE LAB WITH THE
LADY DOCTOR

The Old Woman resembles a fairy-tale princess
Who has stayed too long in her tower unrescued,
She precedes me among the benches, she puts
Her protective goggles on, and in this mood
Resembles that gnome who captured me; I look closer:
It is that gnome. She comes in again
With a flock of young men in white flapping coats
To whom she is goosegirl. I insist that the chemicals
On this side of the bench are strictly mine, and this includes
The bottle of gold salts, and the retort distilling
An infusion of bull-semen. There will be a fight, it's plain,
One of the young Privatdocents has his white coat off already
Underneath which he is naked, and in mock compliment I
    reach out
And shake him firmly by the wedding-muscle, upon which
He hits me all over maybe sixty times
In five seconds with karate blows, one of which
Catches me near my Person but safely thuds
On pubic bone, and I declare 'This assault should not
Have helped your case, but nevertheless this does not mean
That certain experiments cannot be performed in joint
    names . . .'
At my resolve, a spattering of applause, and the Old Girl
Crosses over from her young squires in dazzling plumage
And asks to see the bruises, so I strip off my shirt.
The marks of striking hands patter across my chest
And already the dark bruises are rainbowing like pieces

Of peacock tail. The young chap who inflicted them
Stands by, sniffing my retort's nozzle; with a shyly winning
    smile
'Will you give me a drink of this?' he asks. I feel like a fruit
Which has been bruised in order to ferment
Some delicious rare liquor; I say so; they applaud again.

from FOUR POEMS OF LOVE
AND TRANSITION

I

Her great thoroughfare,
Her sunlit valley; from the testes

Pass multitudes of liquid pearl. Her clitoris
Is a pearl stud on the jade step whereby

The jade pavilion is set on fire.
Thus the train was laid,

The rising stair, tides, docks, sluices,
Saltworks; now they drink

At the fountain of jade and raise
Their heads, dripping, and look around

At the chambers of paradise richly furnished
With the perfume which are prayers

Said on the prayer-mats of flesh and bone.

[. . .]

IV

The cat returning after his night's foray,
All the smells of it about him,
All the dews soaked deep into his midnight fur

By passage through the midnight grass
Which is the multitude observatory of the sky,
Each blade a green telescope poring upwards

A tube of green ichor-lenses
To which the whole earth puts her eye;
This observatory absorbs within itself

The rays of moon and stars, they sweat
Green recording-dew, these vessels,
A liquor which contains their transits,

And these cassettes of crystal are transferred
Like unction to the cat's black coat.
He is a walking astronomy.

He is liquor-of-moon in its animal form,
He is one whole-body deep-perfumed black
    moustache
Wandering thunderstruck full of kisses

Of astrological perfume through the grass verges.

from BUVEUR'S FAREWELL

Afore Ye Go!

II

The brown light of God all around,
The mature autumnal light, soaked
Into the eyepods of pure ambrosia,
He says, leaning back, his elbow
On the bar, and sucks his cigarette,
An impalpable meal that will not stick
On a fork, a satisfactory intangible meal
Of talk in syllables of tobacco ash,
A communion in a temple of fellowdrinkers
Sharing the one round belly, one acrid breath.

III

Like Gods, we relish
The burnt sacrifice,
A meal of grey ghost
Inhaled, and we scatter

The yellow ashes
Of earth-brown beer used up
Pissed out clean,

For we are plumbers and purifiers
In the place where women
May not enter and which is dirtier
Than they would believe; we gaze
At the ceiling like astronomers
As we grab our pub-tackle
In dreamy relaxation,
Tributary stream, contributing,
Sings Piss-on-Boots.

V

The benefits receding
Cigarettes and beer
Make small turds;

And the poet caught on a shingle
Seething with fag-ends

And dead men, which is what
With prophetic insight
They call empty bottles;

The dead men outnumber all the stars.

VII

And in the abrasive return
To the house of children and regular meals
Do these spirits satisfy actually?
It may be not, but it is still the way
To achieve the serenity of the woman
In her temple with her child
Where the raw is cooked and spooned
Into the hungry mouths sweet as flowers;
Accordingly we like hunters quaff the raw
Blood of the world out of barrels, the darting
Lightning of brandies. I say it is a womb-state,
A gentleman's lodge on the way home, and
    communion,
This meal taken in a male Sabbath

Or sewer, as you prefer.

VIII

Not just a meal
But a frenzy,
A three-and-a-half-hour's feast
With messages from Booze Country;
The poet will get an idea, with trembling hand
Unhasp the small pocket pad or tablet . . .
The morning after – what disgrace!
The script too shaking to be read:
It is in Doctor Death's handwriting
Illegibly prescribing from his own pharmacy.

IX

Buveur
A gallon-an-hour man,
He is a river below the waist
Sliding towards the sea
He has drunk up his legs
Staggering from this church
Its stained glass
The quaffable brown light of God
Of the Real (meaning Royal) Ale Hall;

The depth and sheer well
Of opening time not deep enough
Not if it were all the beer in the world –
Why, he could leak it!

Or the globe of the world turned to beer
Whirling about the sun
In one great tun,
The cloud-capped towers of alcohol . . .

X

The skin tight at extreme
He has the notably bad idea of taking drink back
For the wife and the daughter –
In the brown earth-light
Of the spirit of earth
Passing through him,

At last he has the Sight!
The town is a harmony, the people orient wheat,
Each man is a spirit, the ships
In the harbour are one ship
Containing the same spirit
Who is three hundred men
All piss-pals.

XII

The liturgy is out of hand,
The brown eyes of God shining
From all the tables
We sit round tables
Furnished with pint-eyes,
Brown eyes in glass sockets –
We blind them all, one after another,
To obtain the Sight.

XIII

The dust interests,
And the ashes,
The goblet of dog-ends,
The sheer well of all beer

Interests

The brown light
Which is all places on earth at once
And the Mass of ships on the estuary
Interest, every detail seen
Through a precise microscope of pints and at once
Forgotten, because of the greater interest
Of the next grain of dust,
Or sufflation of the breeze, forgotten.
I am a wax face through which beer pours
Into a self greater than I can understand
Or remember, I feel eternal and young,
For I drink up the brown child of beer,
All beers are young beers,
I drink up the adolescent,
I drink up my childhood,
My health, my wealth, my safety.

XV

To stroll home from his church
After purification by pickling,
The brown light of God about him,
The khaki earth-light, the cackie air,
The women in their skirts of fine foam
And light ale in bottles of pubic hair,
All clothes drinking-clothes
The company of saints swaggering and staggering
From home to pub to home to pub
Pace down the bottomless well
To the brown basis of things.

The women shine, it is something
They distil from the booze
And redistil as they talk
Filling up the retort sip by sip;
The brown leather benches shine
With the polishing transit of
Boozers past, present and finished,
Things shine of themselves
At the bottom of this well, it is
Neo-platonic and like the brown back of books,
Study-pub, the volumes bound in glass
And with a handle and all precisely
The same length, or a prescribed length
Like easy books, and you can tell
In this library who is well-read by their gait.

XVII

Taking new surroundings
With each pint,
The feet carrying me without my volition
Back to the drowning-place
Where I sit under flavoured brown water
Drinking from never-empty glasses;
The whole air is my tears and urine;
We converse as the fishes do
By gobbling and presentiment,
The entire room is our bubbling voice

We are a school of people who drink
Like fish and are pissed as newts
And piss the brown of exhausted blood,
The mud of nicotine and decay,
Brown years, brown bread, mud bed,
Brown moss; the curtains
Sweep open, they have let
Too much light into this place, the drowned
Corpses puff up to the ceiling.

XVIII

Bed to pub to bed to pub
Despite wife and daughter –
They will take you on again,
Like ships, under their white sails
Blinding as blossom, masts of cherry-tree,
Who, blown along by their blossom,
Sail in willing to take you
Aboard again
Brown sailor
Bronzed by his voyages
Through his sabbaths and sewers
As ballast
Brown as the hills
Resolute to stay at home
Give it up, or maybe sup
On a few cans, or maybe
Out for a quick one
With that press-gang.

XIX

The moon smiles;
She knew it would not last;
There is drinking money where that came from;
She shines with her white meed
As though she were covered
With cherry-blossom, and, he swears,
A fragrance from the full arena
As it glides from behind the hills
And this clear sensation will surely last,
This cannot fade, he must catch it
In his glass, like the coin of a pint
Lying at the bottom of the pint

And he drinks the moon up, where
Is the next moon coming from;
The woman reaches into her lap,
Into her handbag; she will forgive
And she will buy him a last drink,
Even now, after all that, so he can
Catch his feeling and tell her about it,
And she will tell him back again so he can believe it,
And drink no more, in the small garden
At opening time among the blossom, watch
The moon blossom with her and in to bed;
Even now
With further silver coins
With further wells of tears
Reaches into her bag
For further wells of tears.

XX

All our sailing songs, our stamping
On deck-planking under sail
Of glass with reverse lettering,
Our voyages in the mirrors
Sounding to the well's note
Which fills the glasses not shatters them
With brown sweat of tuns, we live riotously
In this well until we are liverish bones
Wheeled in at opening-time, covered
With brown-spotted liver-moss and
There are always men off the rigs delighted to pay,
The beers flow through our fingers
Covered with Scandinavian calls
And German labels sounding like moss
And green halls and flowing dwarves' gold,
Pungent with their foreign colognes
Which in an international spirit
We absorb right into our bones
And deepest tubes, while
In her belly, a quart
Of pure water lies, containing a drinker;
Persuade her in pure fellowship
To have another mother's ruin and make her baby
So drunk he will sing all the way home.

XXIII

Time please, she chants
Breaking open the bubble room
Like a piggish litter,
Tumbling them out
Into the too-bright street
Snatching them from their rows of teats
For the sun to devour.

XXIV

For he has attended the sinister BROWN MASS,
The secret Mass of St Stagger;
He counts his steps home like time allowed,
Like mortal days remaining;
He must wait them out in his kindly bed
Where his ears fill with beer-sweat;
He tosses his head
Like a drinker throwing away pints;
I turn and turn again
Emptying those shells
That stain my pillows
With their murmuring waters;

I have drunk my inheritance;
That which disclosed grace to me
Closed it almost immediately.

XXV

Later, and maybe for ever,
I lift my glass,
And salute my fate;
My Grail
Which shows me everything at once;

I write of this as I drink
And find in the morning only spidertracks:
A few winged ideas caught,
And drunk up.

Pallid animal, resembling lemmings,
Or the long-drowned from the sea inside,
Myself enclosing the womb-liquor I swim in,
Hauling myself on feeblest limbs
Out of a headache of my whole body,

I have stolen my head from myself,
I have stolen my hands, my legs, my liver,
Being stolen they are no good to me,
My hands cut off, my feet cut off,
My mouth sealed, my bride eloped.

Secret brown roots
Tap my night water, I sleep
Like the tuns in the cellar, fermenting.
Is this bed or bar-cellar?
Time is called again. I walk back
From the pub like blind Oedipus
Sockets weeping brown ale,
I will return again to these bars
In the town called Colonus, again and again
Until I can no longer be found;

Do you call these sanctuaries gracious
When they show me as I am to my lover and child
    first
And to myself only at the very last.

XX

THE LABORATORS
(1993)

PIGMY THUNDER

With a supple action
Of the wrist he extracts or pulls
My front tooth making no more
Of it than the snipping
Of a button off a shirt, though
That would not make me lisp.

I take the little cavernous
Fragment of stained ivory
Home and upstairs. In it one could
Carve without much alteration a Taoist
Temple with a staircase of its own,
Bamboo plants and cranes,
Set it under a minute
Glassy dome for a spirit house.

Unknown invisible
Personages would stroll conversing
Up and down the staircase
With feet bare and sensitive
As my tongue which already knows
Every cranny of that
Lilliput precinct, though this stone
When it was fastened into the stones of my head
Always seem to me the condensed
Form of a powerful mountain
Lodged in its rainswept range
Booming with my pigmy thunder.

STENCH AND STORY

What a child fears most
In a parent is fear. When the maroons woke us
I lay in bed talking to my children

The whole night long, in the steep house
By the dock of ships under repair and the
Fish-packing station that fills the whole air

With invisible dead fish swimming in

Odorous shoals; these smells, I swear,
If you smell them sleeping, cause nightmares.

My children feared their dreams, was this the cause?
My stomach noticed the stench, then my heart fluttered,
My nostrils told me why; it was a presence

Rather than a stench; the moon was full, it smelt
Decidedly of fish, the moon-goddess a fishwife
Bending over her tides and shoals of ghosts.

My children wanted talk of ships, not goddesses,
Which were and are spontaneous painting in steel,
Still-life great as a village of rusting fruit

Tall as three-storey houses in their dry-dock. Ships
Had read the ocean, and printed it on their vertiginous
    sides.
I lay talking with my children, all night

In bed, in the house with the tidal atmosphere
And the warm south-easterly blowing off the plant,
Overlooking the Roads where in summer the small boats
    race

Their sails smelling only of their storms, where
The water runs in long clean sheets like decent dreams.

THE MOUNTAIN

The beefarm on her sloping meadows, the sweet
Exacting spaces spinning honey;
Under the elms and the sycamores

The light leaves cherish many flowers,
The light air under the boughs threaded
With the vivid bees who return

Speaking excitedly by dance
Like soldiers in armour yellow with pollen
Instead of bloodstain from the battlefield,

Buttercup field. On higher slopes
The banks of pines with their silent smell
In serried battalions, their needles

In thick hushing carpets; here only
The solitary wasp lives, or the rotund
Humble bee, under that dark green light

In that cherished silence as under
A thick fabric gathered up and pleated
Into trees on the skirts of the mountain.

ORPHELIA

Orpheus' swimming torn-off head
Babbles its prophecies as it speeds
Upstream to the source, an entire river

His muscle-rippling body that flies
Mission to the clouds which are a river
Winding above, and the muslin petticoats

Of drowned Ophelia reaching into
Every rainy chamber of the rapid sky
Pouring into the river; her sole dress

Water, from mouth to source; there is
A certain fugitive countenance in water
Which shakes its locks and utters a penetrating

Small voice or voices, called Orpheus,
Ophelia, Orphelia, Ophelius (but how can one
Be mad or bad any longer in water's presence,

Be of anything but magnetic water?)

POPULAR STAR

He was hounded from one bride-chamber
To the next, because somebody dreamed of him

Every night, and used him; or was it
The weather used him? When it was not girls
Or married women, it was the clouds – he pulled out
On racks of clouds, and stretched carefully,
Lovingly, limb from limb, the white intestines
Parting, the rain falling like glass blood, putting
Him together in the calm reflecting puddles; this dream
Better by far than those where the girls
Dressed him in leather and whipped him, or he them,
Or revealed that the next stage was
An acid bath, or maybe that cruel sawhorse
Set with the butcher's cleaver upright so that once
He was astride, with weights pulling at his ankles, he was
Very slowly sliced in half, upwardly, the severance
Of his right and left halves complete
Long after he was dead by the blade passing
Of itself through his navel and after that
All the way; or the wire jackets waffling
The flesh, or the body-cages which let in rats
To partake of living him to the grating bone.

The frequency of these bad ones made the good ones
Quivery: being married to the Princess in St Paul's
And bedding down in Buckhouse for the dream would
    never
Let him settle in case she changed her mind
And had him decapitated in the Tower or defenestrated
In Whitehall. It seemed that the whole human weather
Used him in its seasons for its dreams, passing him
From mind to mind or more likely
Featuring him in many minds at once,
So, if he woke to all the dreams
He would be the anthill of himself being
Branded, butchered, fucked, knighted, blinded, deballed,
Wedded, delivered out of royal bellies so She could say
'You're mine at last, truly mine,' putting him
To the nipple and stopping his cries; so popular,
Passed from city-mind to city-mind across the globe,
His head torn off and winged like Morpheus,
Or like Orpheus the torn and raw wound of the neck
Connecting him to his dreambody which is every-
    Body.

ANNALEE AND HER SISTER

I rainwalked to Annalee in Lower Lodestone,
I met her sister and felt the wells
Of friendship rising in a great daylight
Which pictured the recesses of her clothes
Like private rooms where she strolled naked,
I pictured such intimacies because of their scent,
The fresh smell as she turned of the wind turning
Over a bed of flowers with the infrasmell
Of dark soil that is the buried garden
Containing all possible flowers.

II

When I rainwalked to Lower Lodestone intending Annalee
It was her sibling's clothes that hung
Around her sisterly blue stare, and upon
The triangle of her throat
By means of flowing ties;
It was because of this that in her presence was bent
The scent of things, as light is bent
By the mere presence of the magnetic rain.

I felt the wells of friendship rising in a great daylight
Dwelling on Annalee's sister, for when she dressed
To meet me, it was in her sister's clothes,
Creating thereby a new world. In that scent
Of flowering soil I pictured intimacies
Alternative to the clean bright sibling
Who would not walk in her caryatid clothes
Which her sister borrowed; their apartments grew damp
And clung in galleries emitting
Earthy wetness, creating in that scent a personal world in
    which
Only the one sister walked as the tall rain walked.

TOAD AND OTHERS

The butterflies pause to sip at nectar-
Stations, their spiral tongues
Like watches' hairsprings

Poked stiff into the nectar-wells
Of amaryllis, rose and myrtle-flower;
Time stops as you watch

The floral wings pumping full of insect wings
Drinking up the flower-nature,
Becoming it. In the garden,

A well silk-lined by water-spiders,
A white sleeve to the well, supporting spiders,
But I choose toads; and, above,

The aeroplane sounding with its purr the abyss.
Among the dusty ivy-creepers
A toad makes its apartments

Feminine and studious;
I will bring her, so she seems to purr,
Into her twilight, dusky grapes,

She will eat the nimble
Grain-sized flies that breed in grapes,
That will be her banquet in her rafters,

That will be her beauty,
Reaching in to scoop
The grapeskin see-through with a dainty claw.

XXI

MY FATHER'S TRAPDOORS

(1994)

EIGHT PARENTS

I

At the climax of the illuminated
Book of Hours the Trinity is seen in truth to be
Three self-same white-clad bearded figures
Of Jesus on three identical thrones.
It makes the eyes go funny, like trifocals.

II

This devotional picture resembles
My mother's triptych dressing-table mirror;
When she sat there, three other mothers appeared.

III

The fourth turned round to me and smiled;
The three simultaneously looked back over their shoulders
At somebody out of sight down the glass corridors.
Then she got up, and the thrones were empty.

IV

Nearly a decade after she had emptied her throne, my
    father
Sat himself down in front of the same mirror and died.
He paid his Access- and paper-bill, laid out
Like hands of cards folders on the dining-room table
For his executors, climbed the stairs to his widower
    bedroom,
Sat down at my mother's mirror and saw there were three
    more of him,
Then his heart burst and shot him into mirror-land.

V

Where is that mirror now? you may be reasonably sure
If you buy a second-hand house or bed, then
Somebody has died in it.

VI

But a dressing-table triple mirror? Can you
Enquire of the vendor, expecting nothing but the truth,
'Who died in this mirror?' Death
Leaves no mark on the glass.

ARGUS

Argus, in a pulse of waves,
Closing some eyes here, opening
Others there; the long
Light lashes shake out an air
As if his skin were breathing.

Were all the eyes closed
At one time, then he would be
Pelted like a beast with those
Thick womanly lashes, but, no,
The soft-lidded darkness travels
Over his skin in bands;

Were all his eyes wide open
At any one time, then it would be
Like surprising a peacock
Whose whole skin was vivid with eyes;

But they are not, in the iridescent man; those
Which are shut are opening and the open eyes
Are flickering drowsily, and beginning to close
In brindles over the skin, of sleeping, waking:
The opening eyes admire the world outside,
The closing eyes surprise the inner world, and
The opening and closing of the eyes
Winds inner and outer close
And ever more closely together,

Like ropemakers on their long productive walks in sunlight
To and fro between the shadowy boles of avenues.

GUARNERIUS

For a moment take into your two hands
The spacious violin, the precious Guarnerius;
Feel a tone in the wood as I speak
Which runs through into your fingertips,
Turning sound into touch, touch into sound;
Put your ear to it, as you would to a seashell;

The tone you feel is an echo of yourself in the
    instrument.

Like a shell on the shore it is always singing,
The chapelled and multi-mansioned instrument
Plays of its own accord.
Put it on the table; this woman-shape
Needs no maestro,
Sings to bats' cries on the low-voiced wind.

The maestro dilates
Out of its auricles and atria
A cathedral of sound with a thousand altars;
And a million candleflames shattered by applause;
As he bows his head to the audience
The cathedral-ghost vanishes
Into the instrument like a genie into a bottle.

After the applause, laid
Into the shaped velvet of its case,
Open on the bedroom table, it still plays
Notes and tones, like a melodious house
Contracting in the cool night, as his triumph-heat
Fades; he brings his lady back to his bed, it plays
A thermo-acoustic tune which is hers as she enters,
And a sonata as she undresses, and an obbligato
As they music each other,

And it plays to them in their dreams
For the dreamstate can hear it;

It will play over and again his death-sigh;

It is a box carved in the shape
Of a windflow angel;

All the maestros who have ever used it
Play somewhere still in this hip-shaped box.

AT RICHMOND PARK

A coppice of strobing pillars and young deer running.

A major deer with twenty tines
And the face of an Original American.

The long grass by the road
Is full of reclining antlers.

The young does as they run
Seem made of glass because their markings
Are like the marks the wind presses
On the flowing grass;

A transparent deer-tapestry with eyes
Blown by the wind over the grass.

FISH

Ate mackerel last night;
Dreamed of fish.

Two great fish, taller than men,
Hitched to a fishmonger's ceiling,

The tails still full and stout
Like mermaids' tails,

The scaled carcasses entirely hitched
On two Spanish queries through the upper lips,

The technicolour entrails excavated
Out of the snowy caves of flesh,

But the eyes calm and dark
As though brooding on seas far away and depths
    unplumbed.

As the fishmonger spoke in overalls as white
As fishflesh of fish far bigger than these,

A rich man entered and bought them both,
Had his chauffeur heave them to the car;

One was silver as ocean, the other
Golden as the rich man's abundant hair.

A PASSING CLOUD

I

They tell of thunder picked up on the teeth,
Or radio decoded on a filling, one's mouth
Buffeted with Sousa; but this was a dull ache
Pouring from a black cloud, I could get
No message from this broadcast, I must have
This radio pulled. 'No,' said my father,
'Keep your tooth, this is but a passing cloud.' I knew
It was him, because that was the brand
Of cigarettes he smoked, 'Passing Cloud' by Wills, and
'Yes,' he said abruptly, 'It's me,' and turned white;
By this token I knew he was dead,
Knew it again.

II

When I had flu I always sweated his smell; his two wardrobes
Were exhaling it from hanging woollen shoulders like a last
    breath,
This ancient eighty-four-year-old sandalwood was his
    presence now,
It soaked into me and travelled home and stayed some days,
Grief like flu; but I could close my eyes and use it as an Inn
To meet up with this wayfarer and imagine him.

III

The cat's way is to spray
And then rub her head in the odour
Like a beautiful woman admiring her mirror-image,
Her portrait thick-painted in impasto pheromones;
This is a cat of magic and she lives
In smell-spirit land as the makers of De Retzke
Printing a black cat on their packets, understand.

That was the other brand he used to smoke
Spraying the tinted air like ostrich feathers,
A chieftain's nose of nostril-plumes,
A rainmaker's cloud he passed, admiring
The sensation in the mirror of the smoke,
The sooth-ing oracle and breaker of time,
The redolent satisfaction that snaps the chain
Into peace and the smell of him
Smoking somewhere quietly in the house.

IV

His presence fills the house when he is smoking,
His nature reaches into every cranny,
Into the carpets and eiderdowns and squads of suits;
The chain is broken now, finis,
And though I can smoke in his house now without consent
The smell of cigarettes does not bring him back,
As he is ashes and has been smoked and stubbed out
'A passing cloud . . .' so that time
For him never forges chains again.

V

Except I notice that being under the weather
I sniff my hand-back and his scent appears; my whole skin
And atmosphere remembers him, the rain falls
And my toothache turns to tears, while the world fills
With reflecting mirror-water fathered out of rain-smells.

CLIMAX FOREST

A neat sunlit room
Filled with country arts –
Needlework and quilts.

A backwoods school of architecture:
Frame, a wide porch,
Deep eaves, a heavy

Gently-pitched roof –
Perhaps the house
Of a sawmill operator

Predatory of the huge
Climax forest that once
Blanketed nearly all

Of North America, but
He living within its construct,
Flesh of its flesh.

It had been a beautiful
Day, and the beauty deepened.
In the orange light

The long grasses at the edge
Of the garden seemed spun
From gold. The two

Had promised not to speak. She
Got into bed and like a vast
Nesting bird settled on him. It became

Like watching the river
For hours, watching
All the places it had wetted.

BLACK BONES

That is a human skeleton under the cataract,
The jet bones shining in the white noise,
The black bones of a man of light;

It is a cascade that accepts
Human form from the bones
That have walked into it, and stand;

It must have been his method of death
To walk into a waterfall and be washed away,
Licked clean down to the jetting bones;

And the bones articulate the roar
Of the cataract that seems to speak
Out of the ribs and skull:

His white-haired sermon from the pelting brow,
The unfathomable water-lidded sockets;
Clad in robes that are foam-opulent,

And never the same clothes twice.

STAINES WATERWORKS

I

So it leaps from your taps like a fish
In its sixth and last purification
It is given a coiling motion
By the final rainbow-painted engines, which thunder;
The water is pumped free through these steel shells
Which are conched like the sea –
This is its release from the long train of events
Called *The Waterworks at Staines*.

II

Riverwater gross as gravy is filtered from
Its coarse detritus at the intake and piped
To the sedimentation plant like an Egyptian nightmare,
For it is a hall of twenty pyramids upside-down
Balanced on their points each holding two hundred and
    fifty
Thousand gallons making thus the alchemical sign
For water and the female triangle.

III

This reverberates like all the halls
With its engines like some moon rolling
And thundering underneath its floors, for in
This windowless hall of tides we do not see the moon.
Here the last solids fall into that sharp tip
For these twenty pyramids are decanters
And there are strong lights at their points
And when sufficient shadow has gathered the automata
Buttle their muddy jets like a river-milk
Out of the many teats of the water-sign.

IV

In the fourth stage this more spiritual water
Is forced through anthracite beds and treated with poison
    gas,
The verdant chlorine which does not kill it.

V

The habitation of water is a castle, it has turrets
And doors high enough for a mounted knight in armour
To rein in, flourishing his banner, sweating his water,
To gallop along this production line of process where
There are dials to be read as though the castle library-
Books were open on reading-stands at many pages –
But these are automata and the almost-empty halls echo
Emptiness as though you walked the water-conch;
There are very few people in attendance,
All are men and seem very austere
And resemble walking crests of water in their white coats,
Hair white and long in honourable service.

VI

Their cool halls are painted blue and green
Which is the colour of the river in former times,
Purer times, in its flowing rooms.

VII

The final test is a tank of rainbow trout,
The whole station depends on it;
If the fish live, the water is good water.

VIII

In its sixth and last purification
It is given a coiling motion
By vivid yellow and conch-shaped red engines,
This gallery like the broad inside of rainbows
Which rejoice in low thunder over the purification of
    water,

Trumpeting Staines water triumphantly from spinning
    conches to all taps.

MY FATHER'S TRAPDOORS

I

Father led me behind some mail-bags
On Paddington Station, my grief was intense,
I was a vase of flowing tears with mirror-walls,

He wore a hard white collar and a tight school tie
And a bristly moustache which is now ashes
And he took me behind the newsprint to kiss me hard,

The travelling schoolboy,
And his kiss was hungry and a total surprise.
Was it the son? Was it the uniform?

It was not the person, who did not belong
Not to father, no.

II

He drove a hole-in-one. It flew
Magnetised into its socket. He'd rummy out
While all the rest shuffled clubs from hearts.
He won always a certain sum on holiday

At any casino; called it his 'commission'.
He could palm cards like a professional.
He had a sideboard of cups for everything

From golf and tennis to public speaking.
He took me to magic shows where people
Disappeared and reappeared through star-studded

Cabinets with dark doors, and magicians
Chased each other through disappearance after
    disappearance.
He sat down in front of my dead mother's mirror

And disappeared himself, leaving
Only material for a funeral.

I looked behind the dressing-table
Among the clooties of fluff and the dust,
I looked under the bed and in the wardrobe

Where the suits hung like emptied mourners,
I looked through the shoes and the ironed handkerchiefs
And through a cardboard box full of obsolete sixpences,

I looked in the bathroom and opened the mirror,
Behind it was aspirin and dental fixative,
I looked through the drinks cabinet full of spirits,

And I found on the top of the chest-of-drawers
Where there was a photograph of my dead mother,
My living self and my accident-killed brother,

A neat plump wallet and a corroded bracelet watch
And a plate with one tooth which was hardly dry,
And I looked down the toilet and I turned

All the lights on and I turned them off,
But nowhere in the bedroom where he sat down
And fell sideways in a mysterious manner

Could I find how he did it, the conjurer
Had disappeared the trapdoor.

IV

It was easy to disappear me.
He was doing it all the time.
I did not return that bristly kiss.

On my fourth Christmas there were so many toys
I disappeared into them thoroughly,
There was a silver crane on my mother's counterpane

It was faulty but I did not want it returned,
I have reappeared and so has it,
Nearby and grown-up in the Falmouth Docks,

And there was a conjurer's set
With ping-pong balls that shucked their shells
From red to amber, amber to green,

With a black-white wand that would float,
And half-cards and split rings as tawdry
As going up on the stage among the trapdoors

And meeting Maskelyne close-up, his cuffs were soiled –
White tie and tails should be spanking clean,
My father's would have been, and I hoped

The conjurer would not kiss me,
It would disappear me.

V

He could wave his wand casually
And I would reappear elsewhere;
Once in bed at ten cuddly with mother

He waved a wand in his voice
And I got out of the silken double-cabinet
For ever.

VI

The rough kisses come round the door.
I give rough kisses myself, I am as bristly.
I am not a woman or a little boy.

And I can frighten her or make her disappear
Temporarily so she has to go to find herself
Again in the mirror somewhere;

But having learned this I am careful not to do it.
I do it less than I did.
I did not ask for this bearded equipage.

VII

It has taken me a long while
To appreciate this wedding-tackle at its worth.
My father gave it to me like a conjuring-set.

I do not use my wand to disappear you,
I am rather too fond of disappearing it myself,
But I also use it to empower us both,

It is the key to a wonderment openness
Like turning inside-out harmlessly
Among lights, turning

Over in bed into someone else.

VIII

The conjurer in his soup-and-fish
Vanishes into his cabinets,
His rival reappears, they cannot bear

To be together on the stage
Not while they're dressed in their power
Of black whiteness with starched bows

And cuffs that make the hands flash
While explaining here's a new trick:
The Chinese Cabinet.

It is a silk tent with a front door
As black and tall as Downing Street.
This must be a special trick, shall I expect

Mr Major to ride out on a white horse?
Three people with slant eyeliner have erected it,
They are dressed as spirits who seem

Of the one sex which is both sexes,
And this cabinet is not coffin-like,
No, not at all, what coffin

Would be painted with sun, moon and stars?
A Grand Mandarin with a little drum comes in,
And throws an explosive down as conjurers will

So that the tent shivers and collapses –
Yes, it is a wardrobe that has disappeared all the clothes,
The white tie and tails, the sponge-bag trousers, the
    soup-and-fish,

For someone is coming through stark naked
And it feels good to him
For he is laughing and the mandarin bows as if proud of
    him,

He who touches everywhere for all clothes are gone,
Why, he's in the buff and happy as Jesus save that
His lean rod is floating out just as it should,

Floating like my own, pleased to be like him.

XXII

ABYSSOPHONE
(1995)

THE MOTHS

Palpitations – the moth-beats
Of the heart in the clambering weather
Wrestling with itself.

The moth lies down on the windowpane full of light
In its bath of lights.

I look out of the window past the moth
Like some gigantic inhabitant rising from its unconscious
    mind.

What does the unconscious mind of a moth resemble?
The conscious mind of a devoted naturalist.

That is why the moths come to him like inhabitants
Of his unconscious when he lays his white sheet down in
    midnight
Over the grass and shines his car's headlights on it;
They speed to their baths of light.

And here come more moths over the estuary,
They stagger over the roof of the house of light built
    without hands,
And they settle in its garden of white lawn.

Before he thought of blacking his face they came to him,
To its whiteness, and sipped from the fountains in the
    pores.

Now they come to his body-heat
When he lies down in his bedsheet.

They will eat him like candy even to the bones,
He will fly away on their wings;

None of the wicked will understand,
But the wise shall understand.

A SHELL

The shell the skeleton of all the waves.
Lacking a sea view
I place it on the windowsill

Which watches the drizzle along the canals,
The chained doors of the Green Inn,
And the commercial district where there are no theatres.

On some magnetic points of the iron footbridge
I thought I could estimate by a certain note
The city river's depth;

During the demolitions
When the copper ceiling of the theatre fell
Bells sung in all the padlocked churches.

They took it away for a military bandstand
That green resonator. I return to my shell
As though it were my wife.

Was Lot's wife, bones and all, turned to salt?
She would stand there, a pillar, until the next shower.
The old buildings are showing their bones in this leached-
    down city.

I pick up my salt shell, and listen
To its hushing tune like the city's, listen
To city-air tossed here and there

In all its wave-shaped singing opus-chambers.

CAT AND TREE

There is a fragrant and spiky small tree
In bud, into which the birds descend.
It is the cat's bird-machine.

He stands poised with one paw
Resting on the slender vibrant trunk, like a cellist
Testing the hall's atmosphere through his G-string before
He starts to play.

Birds descend and ascend, untroubled, pause
On a bough a while to contemplate and mute
Guano, they rise up having done so
With the cat like a black shadow at the trunk's foot.

There is a detonation from the docks, and the birds rise
And scatter like a black substance torn to fragments,
The cat merely lays his head back on his shoulder and
    watches
For the echoes to subside among the ship-machinery.

The echoing birds slip back one by one
Into his bird-machine; now they will scare less.
He pushes his stare forward and enters the slaughter-tree;
It is all cat now along every bough, as the spider
Lays a paw to her harmonium of gossamer.

PURE CHANCE

The trees were dark as bears, and moved disturbingly,
And made one think of uneasy bones
Digging their way out. Indoors,

The pretty wooden gospels, ludo,
Snakes and ladders, that make visible
The tiny throws of chance,

The disposition of the powers,
As the trees do, heavy breathing in the oaks,
Nothing but green lungs and air. Are they

The powers? They are very close to them.
He takes his dice board under the oaks in the park
To improve his lot; the snakes may glide

Out of the boards and wreathe the oaks,
The green snakes becoming invisible in the leafy ladders;
Thus the pictures flat on the boards grow solid:

Snakes and laddering branches, the snaky wind
Coiled into the oaks, hissing. He walks free of them
Out of the wood on to the meadows of pure chance.

SEA-EYE

He knew a clergyman he could say anything to,
But nothing changed inside him; it was horrible
That there was no horror,
None of the horror that melted him
So that his belly plucked like a saurian in a tar-pit,
And if he melted deeper inside it was to white,
To pure, liquid boy,
His thick, secret sauce. This was what he wanted:
Deep feeling; so, instead of the vicar he went to see
The one-eyed old man with corded forearms
On the beach who had furnished
His entire cottage with chairs and tables
And bookshelves washed up out of the sea
And the boy brought him books
And that made him friendly so he took out his eye
Which scared the boy satisfactorily, and, staring at him
With one dark moist orb and one cavernous gristle
That old man further melted the boy to his essence
With the horror of his tales that all ended
With his losing his eye by the deliberate action
Of a young boy who has come to listen to his stories,
But the sea had rinsed that socket clean; and once
They were rowing, and he paused on his oars
And wiped his brow and took his glass eye out
And rinsed it in the ocean and dropped it
So the dark-irised ball went dwindling down
And the boy jumped in and swam down after it
And scooped it up just as it touched the sand
And brought it back triumphant glaring in his palm
And tossed it to the old man who caught it saying

'Not Popeye but Sea-eye'; the diver felt the whole ocean
Running through his clothes, undressing him;
Sometimes the old man wore instead a smooth sea-pebble
   in his socket.

FAMILIAR

The cool seriousness
Of the cat's gaze while the stars rise
And dry leaves catspaw past the windows,

Contented maestro who proceeds
By ritual gestures, his eyes blazing
With that interior self-monument of gold:

Linked with all tigers, striped
For their passage through the long grass invisibly,
Voiding immense stalings that are volumes of passion
At the four corners of the green garden;

Like an enchantress too
Walking her battlements passionately
And chucking out her chamberpot at the four castle-
   corners,

Familiar with an angel
Who has pouncing wings and the miaow
Of a choir of ten thousand from the one pair of catlips.

XXIII

ASSEMBLING A GHOST
(1996)

ESHER

The two suns,
The sun in the sea, the sun in the sky:
The bicycle of summer.

Do I deserve it,
Shirt open to my breastbone as I ride?

My shirt billowing like more lungs,
Like sunny clouds
On my summer bicycle,

The dawn wind
Smelling like a scrubbed deck.

Later, the sky of an uncolour –
Pale as a grey cat's fur,
Or ancient glassware
Rubbed misty in the desert.
Do I deserve it?

The garden birds flow up out of the lilac,
The gulls
Hang up by one wing and wheel around.

The bicyclist with all Esher
In his shirt, kept
Warm and sunny there.

BIBLIOPHILE

Because of Falmouth
He has more Bibles than he has shirts.
He will search out Jerusalem with candles.

Falmouth seems undersea,
Or it brims with the understructure of the clouds,
With invisibly salted water and mist

Which webs everything into one great mansion,
A mansion turning all the time,

An invisible manor-house greater than any human
    home.

Staircases, dungeons, great slam-gates,
Sequent chambers, draughty galleries, speed past me,
Secret passages disclosed, lifts on their hawsers,

On their salt ropes ascending
Momentary high towers whose shafts
Exclaim with sunshine and open to the foundations.

What does the Bible give to an unbeliever?
The Bible has fullness.
Fullness stops the mind being wiped

By Falmouth, that is my prayer
As I shut my shirt to my chin and open my Bible
Every time the clouds

Blow in from the East, on that East wind
Which has holes opening in it, bible-deep.

DAVY JONES' LIONESS

There was a siege of dreams
Of needing or wanting
To buy a new watch; almost
It slipped away as I paused
By the Xmas display of actual watches, spoke

To the woman serving in dark suit
And pearls, of the beauty
Of the pearl display on dark velvet
(Meaning herself also)

We agreed they were pretty
And what a pity it was
That men did not wear them. I informed her
I had gone out in the heavy male
Serpentine beads and they interested the women
Just as they liked my sporting
A pigtail, and she said

She could see that, and why had I
Not put them on to visit her? this was unspoken,
And now she paced
Like a small dark lioness,
Her movement round the shop
Had been increasing, I could not
Keep track and she seemed
As she moved to roar subsonically
Through the open maw of her black suit
While I told her that a stranger
In the pub had kissed me because

I wore beads and she did not know
That men could, and I said yes,
As you see, they can; but,

Said the dark lioness, does that
Include pearls? she was pacing now
Up and down the jeweller's stairs while I
Looked again at the watches, remembering my dream
Of needing a watch and she watched me
Because it was a dream in which
I had remembered my dream, and this was why
She came and roared at me
Soundlessly in her dark. The bijouterie
With its beauties shedding
Their light everywhere was now charged
With the subsonic breath of pearls;

It was like lions in an aviary,
It was the singular oyster-shop of pearls,
Of pearls and glittering innuendo;
The slime of the sea necklaced round
The long neck of the dark assistant,
The cabinets full of ticking salt
Sea-jewels telling me the tide was rising;
This was Davy Jones' Locker
Full of ivory-treasures, tides and gems,
That is the watch of watches, and she?
Davy Jones' Lioness from the Orient
Now wearing pearls that gathered
Like rain under the sea.

ENÝPNION

A bee in the library
Of elm books and oak books,
Holly shelves,
Ivy shelves,
The drowsy-house,
The dreamlike slumber in books;

Polishing the windows
Of the drowsy-house
That open to and fro
One sees out of the leaves;

I open the book and its honey runs over,
The supple binding polished with beeswax,
The dark-veined pages,
The whispering leaves
Inscribed with sentences that hum
In the amber twilight,

A gentleman's library
In which to drowse
That is full of Virgil
Who has retired,
Who has finished with all
Heroes larger than beesize.

LEATHER GOODS

I feel emptied by the thunderstorm. She
Looks as I feel. He takes me behind the shop
To show me the source of the leather with which
He makes his wonderful supple skirts, waistcoats,
Tabards, luggage, including doctors' bags. I must
Conceal the origin, he says, handing me her skin
Perfectly tanned, hanging it over my arm, it is heavy
As the ulster of a big man, the hands bear nails
Which are as fresh as any person's living,
I cannot see the expression, her hair
Brushes the planking. He tells me

It was a pleasure-steamer wrecked
Off the Manacles and the bones
Gently rolled out of them and their leather
Brine-tanned in a volcanic undersea stream
That was sulphurous;

'The diver into that wardrobe,
She came in one evening, when I was closing,
With a beautifully supple Gladstone bag, out of it pulled
A total body-suit with nails complete and a zip
"I can deliver five hundred," she said;
"The leather breathes, but is warm still
In sub-arctic chills," "There's
Little call for this degree
Of warm clothing here," I said,

'"Then shut your eyes," she said. I felt
A little soft cool hand steal
Into my own, it was comforting. "Let me take
Just the hands, six dozen at first, see how they go . . ."

'Under the sea the teeth rolled
Away like pearls as the gums rotted, scoured
Into white sand. The hair
Continued growing all those years, hiding the wreck
Like a head of hair itself, with full tidal tresses;
Out of that undulant harvest the diver plucked her
    fortune.'

from ASSEMBLING A GHOST

MS POTTER

A smile painted red
Signifying mastery of oral sex,
Teeth white as the Moon,
And an amazed 'Oh!'
From the warm blackness –
Having shown that chord of colours:
Red, white and the deep
Black of her spoken merriment;

Now she sits down at her wheel
In her death-clothes
Creating the algorithm
Of the Potter who made us all
With her belly-art, and winks
And throws down clay
With a slap on her spinning
Wheel, and she catches it
With her fingers as it
Shoots away in loops –
And immediately form rears up,
A low vase of hers spins in
Pulses from shallow to deep
And back again, storing darkness
In the bowl of the vase, then
Dismissing it, thumb-forcing
The shadow out of the bowl in
This messy cave with
Its mud-splashes, puddles,
A hissing tap. Her smock
Is filthy-stiff. There is a streak
Of clay across her cheek while
The zinc perfume of the stinging earth
And high velocity mud shoots
Off the wheel-rim, this makes the place
So real that almost every gesture now
Hypnotised by the wheel falls
Into the ritual,
The vase deepening
Like the night-sky forming
In the potter's thighs
Her fingers digging
In the spinning void
That falls exactly
Into the tall vase-walls:
Central night, with stars of wet clay;

I needed to spin my heirs
On her wheel
Like a meteor-swarm, the children
Pushing and shoving to get in
The stout thumb and the gracile fingers
Opening the door in her death-clothes

A door is opened
To the yard and birds
With the cool faces of virgins
Pace over the threshold, pick their crumbs
From the bread-rolls tall as vases.

I sit patiently on the uncomfortable
Stool made of a late-mediaeval
Crosshead; the heiroglyphs are swarming
Again as she peddles at the wheel, the hypnotic vase
Pulsing with shadow, then shallowing
To a vibrant bowl; she is interested
In the brown and carrot-shaped
Amphoras made of Nile mud; this is how
The wines of Egypt were transported;

She, by chucking and spinning
Has constructed just such a bottle; I cannot help it –
I picture her at her wheel of light and shadow;
It needs to be oblivion wine from such a bottle.

NUDE STUDIES VI: THE HORSE

She is in love with the canoe-faces of horses,
Their violin smile. Riding them
Naked skin to skin

Is to sail close to the symphonic brink of the known
    world.
It amazes her that entering the pub
Of kisses, basket meals, stout decals, accelerando

Chatter, is to plunge
Into a rubbish-tip of bright plastic and broken
Radio-sets still working though they

Have been thrown away; yet after a beer or two
It is eating one's Good Food inside a Christmas Tree;
And this marvel is nothing

To the sonorous breathing of the horse
She rode yesterday skin to skin
Up to the vast water-note

Of the reservoir from which the horse
As from a harp plucked water; the ripples
Of his drink reached out easily to the far shore.

BOY'S PORRIDGE

I

She serves me my round plate of porridge
Pocked with craters. It is the Full Moon
I am eating, smiling up at Mum. 'Where
Does porridge come from?' 'Down the chimney, son.'

'Why *morning* porridge?' 'It is the Moon.
We don't eat it at night. It is out of reach.'
The Moon like Santa Claus
Delivering sacks of cold porridge down the chimney.

II

My next-day's breakfast plate riding high,
Brightening the clouds. Mother pins
Her moonstone to her collar to serve me
My boy's porridge; like a full moon rising
Through maternal skies, it rides her breath.

There is cinder-snapping as the hearth-fire cools;
I go out into the night to watch the scudding
Ashes in the sky, and the round clinker riding
That burns with a cold fire. As I return

Hungry for porridge the sun rises over the sea:
Fleets of jellyfish bump in the tide
Like salty bubbles in moon-porridge
Set to boil on the hob.

WHEAL CUPID

Thunder over lake, a beating
Of wings over the skin
Of the lake, two blue dragonflies
With thunder in their wings
Thunder; whose shaking
Is in the lake.

Two sky-skinned dragonflies
Bent like twin tempered blades
Shuddering, sip
From each other;

Tempered dragonflies reined
Into a smooth loop, thunder
Negotiated with wings
Darting, then stone-still;
Hoop spins over the lake;

The feet of the dragons
Running through thunder

Their lightning plashes everywhere.

ABATTOIR BRIDE

Slow-working in the slaughterhouse
On a showery day. He holds out
A bloody fillet in his icy hands.
I pop with sweat. Bleed out, sparkle!

There are flies like lacquered idols, skulls
The size of sand-grains humming like nuns,
Exquisite religious sculpture vibrating
To the note of that god-gong, the sun,
Flies carved again as with knives, risen
Out of the food-chest with ivory clasps,
Shut into the meat, it seems, by him let out
With his shining knives and his shadow of flies,
His marriage-property, sturdy and obscene.

And there is a leaf-marriage too, the sun lying
In panels and yellow shadows on the path,
The flies in intermediary shady swarms
Celebrating the marriage of meat and sun;

And this little rain marries all the leaves;
The sealed chamber, this vagina
Is like a bird flying
Through the rain, drenched,
Beak wide as a fledgling straining for the worm;

He has opened many creatures, this one
Opens itself, alive, without violation,
However loud the sun, with its darkening flies.

THEY COME

They come flickering down the lane
In their black-white,
White-black shirts and skirts
As the moon changes
White to black and back again,
White shirts, black waistcoats,
A lick of white petticoat
At the hem of a black skirt
Flickering down the lane,
The human flowers
Are black-white, white-black.

On the body, like amazement gathering,
The matters that arrive of themselves:
Hair breaks on chest, balls drop,
Voices break heartbreakingly, hips
Gather and round their pillars, and on the smooth
    chest
Tiny magnolias bud.

The homes turbulent
With strange new body-perfumes,
The black-and-white courtship moon-engine
Comes flickering down the lane.
How many of them meet there?

All? Or none? the white moonlight
Flickering through the branches.

'Development,' they say, as when you hold
A polaroid and watch the picture, the person
Stepping into the white space, like
The person you know stepping off the train
On to the platform; you saw him before
In his grandfather, his aunt.

The bones, white as photography
Hold the image of him for a certain time;
It fades off them to appear
Elsewhere, like a spirit, clothing itself
In black-white, white-black for the meeting in the
    lane.

XXIV

ORCHARD END
(1997)

ORCHARD END

Apple-trees coralled behind
The warm stone walls that help
To ripen them. We discuss

In whispers the spiritous dark
Within the fruit, the boughs
Librating their poundage
Like heavy bosoms in a green shirt.

As an eye sleeps each apple
Sleeps in its seamless lid
Until I bite into the black, turning it
To white, saying
'Let there be light.'

COLLECTED

I toast Browning
As I drink up this
Apple-juice. On my plate

A stump of apple, slowly browning.
In the grill, the toast
Is browning, nicely.

He would have relished
This March morning
With the gusty showers

And the great rotund
Thunder-carriages rolling in
Over the brown and activated

Fields. Here comes a cart
Heaped with freshly-dug potatoes,
Earth-apples fresh from the field:

They are browner than brown can be
Because of their smell, which is like

A brown light. Each tuber

Is a lighted lamp of earthsmell,
Bob Browning! a lamp
In which burns the oil

Of distilled field. I return
To the huge brownstone hearth
And take up Browning's

Collected bound in doe
And drink a glass of brown ale
To wash it down, brown

As the pelt of potatoes
Clotted with mothering
And greening from the brown

In tendrils '. . . With such hair too . . .
'Used to hang and brush their bosoms . . .'

AT THE WINDOW ON THE WORLD

(King's Head, Falmouth)

The King's head, chopped off,
Has rolled to the foot of the stairs
The moss-moused stairs
That mount to the Church of Charles the Martyr,
North door.

Watching the whole world passing
In the window of the pub
From right to left to the Moor, from left to right
To the Docks, the beer calling out of them for me
A new compendium of humanity, how it walks,
Not what it says;

Sitting in the visionary window of the pub
Among the laughter, beer, mellow lights,
Everything friends and beer-coloured, watch out
Up the flight of stone steps to the tall dark doors

Which are open on blackness
Like a hole in the church rock for the people's refuge
From such as I, where I sit in the Head of the King
Like a tipsy watchman,
For the bride and groom are signing the register in there,
Signing in the vestry twilight,
And as soon as the pen lifts from the last signature,
The bells call out.

On the church steps
Four bridesmaids in royal blue are hanging about.
The limousine has driven up shining and parked shining.
The fronts of the dresses of the bridesmaids
Are ruched like the hulls of marvellous fruit;

And I'll drink to the Bride
Through the visionary window when she appears
As she does now and the bridesmaids in a simultaneous
    salute
Flare open their parasols of royal blue and twirl them
    about.

It was most sexual
When the Bride appeared
On the arm of her scarcely-noticeable groom, like
A great white bird folded on its perch,

Or like a waterfall out of a mountain
Manifests from the shadow of the granite porch –
Crystals ringing each like a bell itself –

And steps out and stands on the steps pouring white
Among her blue maidens whose dresses signify
That by the magic of the Bride
The whole earth can blossom in maidens
(This is the Spirit conceived in the depths
Which emerges after signing the register
Like light breaking out of the rock
Into the upper air as the flowers do everywhere)

Their floral dresses bloom in a long thoroughfare
The women of the family who now press forward
Like more flowers bursting from the rock;
As the bridesmaids live in their dresses

Unborn children live in the women's fountains
Waiting to be born to the sound of bells and flowers
As the shining track of the Bride brushes past them.

Why on their way down the stairs from the hole in the
     churchrock
To the black and shining limousine do they turn back
And enter the pub, why does the wedding-party
Flow in and commandeer the bar and press
Towards my window with their shaving lotions and scents
     and grey toppers?
Why do these visions press towards my window,
How can I have deserved to be introduced to the Bride
Whose veil is pinned back to allow her smiles
Access to us all? Who am I
That they should come to see me, and to the sound of
     bells
(Which makes it difficult audibly to refuse drinks)
Offer me their electricity elixir
In champagne glasses that chime like handheld churchbells
And brim with bridal spume?

NUDE STUDIES III: THE SPELEOLOGISTS

The unclean and desperate interlopers
Filled the table, the nude men
Full of meat and sin,

Furnished with a formidable bottle
And a ferocious overbite, devouring
The curry omelettes; in their presence
All ghosts melt down to a pile

Of grease and rags.

The early-morning sapsuckers went on tapping
At the trees outside, finding the door of the forest
Into their banquets. A thrush,

Bloodying a worm, sang after,
Whistling in an almond-tree.

The party consisted of robust speleologists
Who had shaken off any demon's nightgame
And penetrated the darkness on their own terms,

For whom the clock merely stitched
Its ticks through the night
Creating no stars.

The men were hungry because of yesterday,
When the limestone cliffs had cast a welcoming coolness.

The only thing was to banquet nude
On the strongest curries of meat
Transformed into liquid fire,
They needed to fill themselves with fire
And empty themselves

So that they became like the caverns
Lighted in their limestone guts with beating flambeaux;
They ate by curry-light in that solid nude encouragement
As if they could never be filled again
So extensive were their galleries

In the long crepuscular room smelling
Of woodshavings, curry and glue of craftsmanship,
Concrete and cockroaches, each penis
Stiff as a golden fingerstall. They guffawed
About the sale of underground
Building-plots. It was a room
In which a Bible brought in at once sprouted mildew.

SQUELETTE

The dainty skeletals of feet
Are stepping down, and the shining shin-bones
Follow, and then the whole

Body of bones.
O tall skeleton
Crowned with extra bones

And further bones arranged about its person
Like the bones of a crinoline
Or a chandelier in four flounces

Stepping down the loft-ladder
Into the white-gloss corridor
Sheer as the interior of a bone

This is the squelette
Of an ex-wife so powerful she
Has bones left over and to spare

Or is remains of two people
Too fond ever to leave
Their intermingling, grinning

At it; surmounting all,
The mitre of small bones
Like those of a baby self

With the pendent skull
The size of an orange
That beats on the breastbone

As the bones stride; I follow
The bone-music like whetting knives,
These bones so white

Against the wall they'd be lost
But for the intercostal
Shadow-flicker that attends

Progress towards the white sash-window;
Its fingering bones grip
And fling up

It steps out
On to the black slant roof-slope
Slides down with a farewell wave

From the curious engine
Of one calcite hand;
It drops in a disarticulated

Bone-shower lightly on the green,
Green lawn, these bones land lightly,
And of their own accord

Separate, peck and coo
Now a white flock of doves.
I slide the easier way

Down the gutter-pipe,
I find my jacket-pocket
Brims with birdseed

Which I scatter to feed
The erstwhile bones;
They devour so hungrily.

Down the whitened corridors
More bones proceed to dovemaking, hitch
Their shinbones over the white windowsill,

They are all the same person, one adult
Skull, more bones than are needed,
None so dead they cannot proceed to doveship

And shake far-reaching ghost-breezes out of their pinions.

XXV

FROM THE VIRGIL CAVERNS

(2002)

ARRIVALS

The spider in her draughty great halls
  hanging by her fists
    from the rafters,
A few dried leathers
  and wings like cracked windshields
    dangling from the radii;
Harley Davidson chassis without engines
  hollow as bongoes;
    washing machine in energetic renewal,
Revision, a cube of hasty
  hurricane water hurrying,
    a tornado shaking
In my father's scullery
  wearing white like his doctor
    whose white coats
Have to be washed somewhere,
  bring him close to the ghost
    every rotation a whiteness;
My father turning up at Paddington
  in his car, for a surprise,
    smiling at his fingertips
Like a conjurer with his four-wheel cabinet
  laughing at his traffic adroitness
    like a conjurer
Producing himself from the shiny coachwork;
  today he lost the way:
    all the streets wept
So well know to him;
  his knowledge went,
    his engine stopped,
Emptied. I know
  how it was,
    he showed me something else
That belonged to both of us
  with the engines stopped
    and the halls draughty,
Close to the ghost;
  his knowledge went, and mine followed,
    catch it before
It leaves like a ghost,
  on these stepped verses;
    on these stairs met together,
These radii.

AT THE OLD POWERHOUSE

(Kingston on Thames)

A swan stretching
  its neck like a javelin speeds
    a couple of metres
Above the roughened river,
  the stridor of its breath-shaped
    wings like the creaking
Of a supple switch, a whipstock;
  descending further, the swan steps
    across the water in five
Giant strides, in five
  mighty braking steps, settles
    its own foldings
Among the waterfoldings, tucks
  its wings into its armpits, shrugging
    them in, and yachts onward
As a serenely-sailing ornamental waterbird
  reborn out of the turbulent and draughty
    air-voyager;
The river glitters like errant electricity
  and a watermusic floats downstream,
    a jazz funeral no less
With a band and a catafalque and a small black barge
  full of golden instruments;
    the powerhouse draws itself up
To attention like the old soldier
  it is; I expect smoke from the broken
    chimneys, from the colossal
Hearth-chambers, but those
  are swifts coiling on the air
    as the music coils
In the air that rushes
  sonorously through
    the river-doubled
Trumpets and trombones.

FROM THE VIRGIL CAVERNS

'The change of perception is godlike.'

Shirokov reported
          in the *Independent on Sunday*
                    (2 May 1993) on the true
Use of the cave paintings;
          the theory is that the boys
                    entered the Distant Hall
Crawling on their stomachs
          through the mud
                    which represented dying
Through the synaesthetic ordeal
          of the lower death-passage
                    where the animals seemed
To come alive, prancing
          in the extended senses
                    of the Distant Hall
Thus creating in the candidate
          his own particle
                    of shared subconscious
Which they brought out unbroken
          into the world
                    through the other fissure, a Yoni
A few feet higher where they are clothed
          with exterior cunt like a waterfall
                    that fits them for society.

I

Also the stone track
          of a spiritual acrobat
                    there are clefts
And vaginal openings giving forth
          a floor of jewels
                    and many formations;
There are spires
          rising from the floor and pulling
                    from the ceilings
And often as they meet
          they meet as folded curtains
                    draped on strong bars

Or as semi-transparent screens
            pleated and folded,
                        a lamp
Shines as a rose through this alabaster.
            These bijouteries
                        in formation
In a cavern like a garage
            of old Chevrolets carved
                        in wet marble appear
In the flow of water
            covering everything,
                        appear to be rushing forward and
They are not in fact
            perfectly still since
                        like freeze-frame
They are moving through
            the millennia too slowly
                        for any movement to be seen,
Though in their stillness
            they bear about them the look
                        of racing through a mild rain-shower
Of mother o'pearl, speeding
            down pearly thoroughfares:
                        bring your lamp
To the cavern
            they are immediately present,
                        and wet, and rosy
With their presence.

                        II

The wet clock of stone
            seems stopped
                        but all the surfaces
Are moving under the water
            an inch
                        in a thousand years
The rafts of jade
            and mats of creamy alabaster
                        owned by China
And stopped under England;
            and the water-bright
                        stalactites or linghams

Slide as slowly
            downwards by the same clock
                        in the caverns
Where hollow spires
            spring up everywhere;
                        the maternal water-sculptures
Inherent in the rock
            constantly in bloom
                        from within the stone;
The caves are filling up
            with exceedingly slow
                        spires and mirrors:
The travelling church of the giants
            comes to approximate stillness
                        in this rosy rock.

III THE ARRIVAL

So many of the walls
            depict robed guides:
                        figures painted in ores
And looming through the ever-wet
            walls; shining statues
                        upon whose heads
The waterfalls plash.
            For the humans
                        whose smoky lamps paint
Their ceilings in sfumage
            there are swifter guides,
                        Wills-of-the-wisp
Skimming the surface of the
            underground lake
                        guide the penetrant oars
And there is slow lightning
            pointing the arches, electricity
                        from the dunes
Rolling overhead . . .
            there is an echo
                        like rubberlined doors
Squashily opening and closing, for
            there is a ceremony
                        hiding round every corner;
And there are pillars of limestone
            whose table-top is hollow
                        and contains

A serving of mud; collected for centuries,
            small altars of mud
                        so heavy it is pure; everything
Here weighs heavy with purity; the sand
            underfoot drifts heavy
                        because it is so pure,
Washed and rewashed
            in the constant distillation
                        of the cavern waters;
The air is heavier here
            because of purity, and the great
                        striding arches
Are pure in form because water
            has worn them that way.
                        Close to these pedestals
In the presence of offered mud
            the walls are more nearly
                        transparent, and the guiding figures
Have approached nearer the surface,
            nearer to stepping forward
                        through the stone,
About to show their faces,
            wiping away the limestone crusts,
                        like rubbing sleepy-sand away
With the backs of their pebbled fists;
            a virgil has burst
Through the rock-grain with its scents and lotions;
            whomsoever it is, a presence
                        passing through the Virgil Caves,
Passing through all the perfumes of Rock.

IV THE INTERIOR MOUNTAINEER

The hills hollow and chiming
            like bells
                        to the gigantic labours
Of water building
            its limestone cathedral,
                        excavating bells
From their native rock;
            the notes of them
                        fitting each to each,
In their millions the first congregation;
            the city of stone and water
                        creating itself

And telling us all about it
            from larynxes larger than
                        terrene cathedrals
And from tabernacles reaching
            round the world
                        where milliards sing
With each shower and gather
            into subterranean waters;
                        and larynxes small
As holed pebbles
            lined with crystals
                        like radio sets
Broadcast the cavern look
            to lie
                        on hills that are
Caverns inside, small enough
            to take home (you could not
                        take the hills home),
And listen to them there
            natural trannies
                        tuned to the water-stations
Or right down to the dust
            that is dancing
                        to mountain vibration;
And the dust
            of the great bass explosions
                        in slate quarries whose air
Is full of stone
            broadcasting. The face
                        of this climber
Is streaming
            with creative water
                        as he swings himself down
Through the roof's point
            into the great hall
                        via the shakehole or doline
The water falling over him
            like an armour of glass
                        his faded boilersuit charged
Shining and new
            as dew is, ringing its bell.
                        Above us, on the exterior slopes,
Beyond the rock-roofs
            these woods are thickly
                        stocked with stout pigs.

RESERVOIRS OF PERFECTED
GHOST

(From the Virgil Caverns)

Acres of the sky having
    floated down and settled in the woods,
        the bluebell canopy spreads beneath
The green capes of the trees;
    heaven is so full of sky
        it cannot hold it – it falls
Into the woods, and spreads, heaven
    skygazing in its woodland cavern;
        bend down and pluck with admiration
A juicy stem; the blue bell
    salivates glass-juice on your fingers;
        lift this flower to your nose
It smells not at all!
    it is all of them that smells:
        the sun reaches through the leaves
And lifts the perfume out, gently
    from these masses, so as not to break it; keeping
        the shock of the blueness
As it issues from underground;
    heaven must have gone deep,
        to arrive so.

TSUNAMI

The tidal wave
    it rushes upon the coast
        so fast everything
Seems still, hangs for a moment
    like veined stone
        over the off-white hotels –
It speeds-in faster than tigers
    running, its body striped
        with currents and bannered
Armies of kelp, this great Crystal
    Palace toppling overhead,
        inside you can see

The boarding-houses and chapels
        twisting over and over,
                the arms of the dock-cranes
Knotting and unknotting
        inside the glossy flank;
                inscribed on the wheeling
Precipices are shining
        whirlpools deep
                but stable as if drilled,
Snaky corridors;
        he dives into one
                of these vaginas
Before the wave-head
        champs him up
                in foaming teeth,
And he is crest-carried along
        like a pilot
                in his cockpit,
Pilot of Leviathan, while she
        roars and falls
                without ceasing to fall.
He is buoyed
        in his personal maelstrom
                and makes a safe touchdown,
Face-skidding
        on blackmirror mud
                that is salty
And without horizon, or circumference,
        like God's Hinder Parts;
                the hunched green wave far-off
Is still pouncing under its cape
        and shouting as it goes
                and shuddering still
As I am shuddering.

ELDERHOUSE

(Falmouth Café)

Elderly and most
        dignified in her whitesugar
                coat, rinsing the plain

China cups for the dishwasher,
                I requested tapwater
                                in an ordinary tumbler
And this started a procession
                of courtesy-gestures, in turn:
                                ran the tap over the back
Of her hand until it was cool,
                turned it off, off on
                                to give me the clearest
Available; I thanked her
                with my best smile, to which
                                she replied 'Have you
A pension-book? if you have,
                go to the British Legion,
                                they will give you a free
Meal . . .' I smiled and said
                I would do this in
                                a couple of years, and smiled
With more care and repeated thanks
                keeping my voice slightly
                                high and elderly
Which it was anyway though I did not quite
                have the pension-book, not quite;
                                smiling we parted,
She like a white officer, and I had
                                contacted a friendship
Of those who have grown old
                and offer me a glass
                                from the elder house of waters
With a ceremony that was private and kindly meant,
                drawing the water, in white, as if
                                she had been and was still
In service in a great house
                Among the waters;
                                the friendship of those
Who learn to grow old
                where our rooms are readying,
                                old as waters.

LAWN SPRINKLER AND LIGHTHOUSE

(at the Lizard)

A water-sprinkler seen in the seaward meadow,
    a complex ghost-pulse
        seen, low in the meadow
By lighthouse-beam:
    a dew machine,
        a complex ghost-pulse
Beaten out by the beam
    sweeping the meadow
        a screen of mist against which
The lighthouse beam pumps carousel,
    the screen pulsing in itself,
        and the beam swinging across,
The cycle of each drawing
    together, and drawing apart:
        the sprinkler's almost invisible
Dewy head bowing to the great beam.
    white shadow of the spray
        of the water-ghost vanishing
And appearing again
    in a new place,
        pacing out its ghost-circle
Under the orbit of the lighthouse,
    in the beam, white, faint
        like faint chalk
On a dusky board, in the shadow
    of the whirling beam, felloe
        whirling round its nub
Above; below the spray beating in
    several soft arcs of a shining house traced
        under the lighthouse,
And with a turn of the clouds
    the full moon with its clouds
        full of its light.

LIMESTONE CAT

for N.R.

I

I throw a pebble in the lake
   I see the shape
      of a sitting cat
In the moment it leaves
   my hand, enthroned cat
      it breaks the roof
Of the lake, the one pebble
   fills the surface
      with its shape:
The vibrating depths
   organise themselves
      into that shape –
In the lake's dark
   the stone cat comes
      to life, prowling
Like a night-companion. The mass
   of waters forms itself
      round the small host
Which enters the church of waters
   and alters them, each ripple
      is aroused in a purr-shape,
Which touches the lake's rafters,
   in invisible chanting.

II

I search the shore for another cat
   to throw after the first
      and find only
Buddha-stones – I throw
   Buddha in a pebble and again
      the whole lake
Reorganises itself, something calmer
   sits down in its centre, but the cat-ripples
      prowl round
The seated sage who ripples
   in his own time,
      Buddha and cat who

Seeks his lap
      through the whole lake,
            cat and Buddha –
The same water in different
      sequences, cat prowls
            like a walking-master
Who can with gold discs
      see in the lake-dark,
            Buddha sits.

III

I find a pebble
      like a child sleeping
            a stone baby curled
Up into itself; if I throw it back
      into the cradle of waters
            it will wake up the cat,
Then the Buddha, then itself
      in child-signatures, wet echoes,
            as it rearranges the water,
Anything, it depicts
      anything:
            Catlake, Buddhawater,
Sleepingchildlake;
      I threw a cat-pebble in
            to alter the religion
To alter the water, like a woman
      pinning a cameo to her collar;
            the folds of her dress,
The coiler, fall
      into a new pattern,
            of its own accord,
Shaped by everything.

HUGE OLD

(from the Welsh Virgil Caverns)

These are the huge old
    may trees so full of flowers
        they seem already woven into gardens
On Hay Bluff
    the air like childhood air:
        on the Pilgrim mountains
Silkier.
    Trees pour ghost
        from tree to tree;
The torrents of scent
    splash into flowers, the flowers
        splash back again into scent;
Each small flower blows
    sweet smell like a swirling fanfare:
        the health of it
Is like low thunder, the great
    escarpment bending forward
        with a pressure of silence;
The silence is scented even in the core
    of the wind-shadow.

BUZZ

I feared the miracle
    of the next day's waking,
        my bed was jammed against the wall
On my right, there was wallpaper
    with a vibratory pattern I forget,
        it went 3D and on the
Other side was a sinister organist
    playing his metals: it is now
        the organs on my right side
That are vulnerable, groin and pancreas.
    I wanted mental marvels
        from simple sleeping pills
And caffeine tablets,
    got some from laburnum seeds,
        safe when dried.

I fixed a little box with a buzzer in it
          on my bicycle-front to ride to school with,
                    to signify I was being charged up
Or electrified by the journey, batterybuzzer;
          the bicycle bell was for emergencies
                    that would break the trance,
Like the navigator natives on Darwin,
          a little flap of cloth would recharge
                    the whole person's perceptions:
I did this by buttoning and unbuttoning
          my shirt as I rode; it was rare
                    and to be remarked upon
To see an open shirt
          on the way to Esher;
                    I am still the boy riding there
Or as far as Guildford
          among the buzzing, the coloured
                    and tactile images. Once
I stopped at a cinema on the way:
          a woman in ample Victorian dress
                    slipped and fell into a garden pond
In which she sat enraged, her beige skirt
          struck shit-colour instantly,
                    with a shine –
What a vision! even women could get
          sexy-wet, especially women; Jesus
                    offered living water to the women
At her well, but these were cunni-waters
          and her own element and familiar.
                    Come and be well! my skin
Was transparent as water
          with that vision of exterior cunt.
                    She offered her pond,
The woman in the flowing shirts,
          and in the Song, the woman lover
                    is a fountain of living waters.
I could not send these visions away,
          not for long anyway,
                    they were an ultimate for me.
The Sin is not the visions,
          but is quenching the visions:
                    quench not the Spirit (1, Th. 5.19);

I knew something too of
            the dry water of the alchemists
                    it was the vibratory
And streaming atmosphere my mother
            could make in bed, and she was wise
                    with the bouquet of her skin,
Her dreaming breath, and mine.
            How that woman of the pond
                    glittered in her new clothes;
What is that dream
            you are having this instant;
                    how her jet necklaces shine
Like stars that are dark
            and bright at once;
                    out of her belly
Living water, water
            that will not be quenched.

DENTIST-CONJURERS

The dentist-conjurers,
            initiates into the white robes;
                    because of all their signs –
The sharp white coats,
            the surgical smiles and smells,
                    the subtle tools that clink
Into sonorous dishes,
            the fountain of circular water
                    you spit into, and that the tooth
Is gone, only a footprint remains,
            and the bite gone –
                    you allow them into your mouth
With their condom fingers.
            Time is altered, the teeth
                    enlarged into mountain ranges;
A rubber touch to the lip
            it strolls on the edge
                    of cruelty, the deep
Black torture-chairs
            their cushioned comfort
                    awaiting pain, that see-saw
And swing on the same touch,

a small sharp pain
                into the gum secures
Against a fully-developed pain
                in the darkness like a magician's hat
                                turned inside-out
That is your mouth in which
                wispy shadow-rabbit shapes are
                                reflected from the instruments
And their rubbery touch,
                and then a rending, profoundly
                                unfelt though it might be
That the anaesthetic breaks
                and cancels, atrocious pain,
                                the brink that is everywhere
But not here, not in this mouth
                which is a shadow-play,
                                a dreaming-place of
Snapping rafters, shattered stone;
                It is my pain but feels like another's hurt,
                                borrowed calm, and I walk
Away with one lip caught up painless
                in a snarling invisible hook
                                with a ferocious lisp
But strengthened with fresh biting power
                in a perfect gummy shell
                                eating as an oyster eats,
Flap flap the
                digestible pap now rules
                                O.K.?
Where does the pain go?
                everywhere but in this room
                                of bright light
And comfortable deep torture chairs.

BODY, MIND AND SPIRIT

Working in a little tent
                the Healers, three of them,
                                under the cast-iron rafters of the echoing
Exhibition hall;
                my daughter Z
                                went into them

And emerged shining
          like Moses off the Mount,
                    would never tell me
What happened in the
          off-white tabernacle
                    that shone her up so;
I knew it was supposed to be not touch,
          but meridians of wildfire, of bio-energy
                    speeding over the skin like a
Shunting yard at night.
          I approached the Chief Clairvoyant:
                    she took one look at me,
This old lady and said:
          'You're a Glory-Boy. What do you want
                    of us, Glory-Boy . . .'
I was taken aback. Was it really
          or entirely that I wanted
                    Own Glory, or was it truly
To extend spirit into body
          and body to spirit. As she berated me
                    I saw her clairvoyance
By my own:
          a great butterfly or moth has fastened
                    itself to her brow
At the 'third eye', and its wings were
          beating over her forehead,
                    as if to fly.

APPRENTICE

My father at the bonfire
          in the garden, under the great
                    sycamore tree near the laburnum
Into which I climbed
          to poison myself with
                    its green fruit, black fruit;
The tree of a knowledge
          that peeled scales
                    from my eyes –
Illumination and sickness
          in the tiny studs;
                    my father demonstrating

The unreeling snake
        he had made visible in the wind,
                demonstrating to me the demons
And daemons of the smoke in the garden
        polished up by the perilous laburnum;
                demonstration of the horses
Of fire stampeding in their smoky stables,
        the doors of smoke opening and slamming
                on the lighted interiors;
The great magician working
        and the sorcerer's apprentice working
                clapping the planks together
To lift into the blaze the juicy boughs;
        his cacky or khaki shirt opening and closing
                in the heat
Spiritual earth of soldier's shirt; his
        invisible beard and robes
                tinctured into visibility
By the laburnum's permission
        showing me the world that came
                on the wind that was him;
(My mother conducted me
        between the surfing of the poplars
                telling her tales of them
Simply of themselves on the wind, to and fro
        exchanging stories of gentle monsters,
                favourable green phantom fountains.)
My father rushed the wind
        turning the solid wood to fluid smoke
                that travelled over the world
Crying out laburnum! from
        the clouds where I can see to this day
                his white merlin shadows in the clouds,
And he tends his bonfire
        that removes still
                innumerable further scales from
My apprentice eyes.

XXVI

SHEEN

(2003)

TOM AS SUPERNATURAL PRESENCE

(For Tom) OB 9.9.99

A Guinness erect on the bar
  like a straight-backed pint
    of black cat, full
Of black lights;
  the young black cat, he
    is a dream-presence
Like a Guinness; it was as though
  the sealed books of his heart
    burst open; he shot out
His bolts of warmth
  into my lap, the locked volumes
    burst their clasp;
It binds me to him,
  he does it
    more than once,
To ensure our friendship;
  then he glides down
    and scuds away
Leaving my feelings aglow:
  a bonfire of animal heat
    right up to my midriff.
I have seen him retexture his coat
  to make it fascinating;
    it glows subvisibly;
Or he causes each hair
  to declare itself separately,
    each like a black ray
From an invisible star; as though
  it were the nerve-endings
    he combed with his tongue,
The plantations of blackness
  rippling as with a night-breeze in
    the moment before the first
Star becomes visible;
  and then a swift glance
    from the gold eyes
Like a ship floating painted black, lined
  with its great cargo
    of pleated gold-leaf;

Or in the shadows
at the stair-foot
this pair of jewels
Floating a few inches above
the carpet, as though darkness
were crouching to inspect
For night-mice
at the house-root.

SPIRITUALISM GARDEN

Eating on the edge of death,
the brink —
green laburnum.
Black laburnum seed, the green forbidden
the black full of power
sharpening the presences
Of the garden by shifting of perception,
the plants and trees
offering their substances
To make their spirits visible
in soft green seeds in rows
which are death;
They must be dry and black
rattling in the pods
and I carried the black seeds about
In a white box
which would tell me all
from second month onwards
That happened beyond
the portals of the worm
to my siblings who were dead
Evolving into the apple-trees
of Orchard End and its laburnums;
I climbed up the laburnum ladder
For my lessons,
I sat in a tree
eating the black seed of my siblings
Using their eyes
to see the garden
with everything on the trembling

Edge of being seen, foetus, foetess,
                colloquy with my garden siblings,
                        green spiritualism;
The seasons change as I eat
                the black seeds, seeing.

SOLID PRAYERS

Sex as solid prayers
                full of stars!
                        a high degree of reality
In the starry turning dome-stage where
                she struts her funky stuff,
                        rain, skin and sweating slightly
To shine, making
                a heiroglyph with each
                        ritual unconscious gesture
Saying
                I am here
                        I am here again
I am here still,
                I am here there everywhere;
                        she turns up her shine
Of the three colours which are gates:
                black oral, white smile,
                        rouge lips; also
I know her from her gait
                which struts
                        marching astride
Her pelvic cask,
                she swings on her gates
                        everlastingly, all smile
Her smile everywhere
                the barrel full of womanly ale,
                        hale and bellowing like a whale
As she blows and puts her tongue out
                meaning
                        I can fellate you with this.

IN THE YEAR OF THE COMET

The roads are long metallic
     rays of stars,
          the comet is a great
Frozen lake flying in the sky, vibrating
     reeds, ice-waterfalls and all,
          a lake of frozen pitch flying,
A salt marsh flying;
     a thunderclap from the blowhole;
          the spray flies up in a cloud
in which a rainbow hovers
     like a comet's trail
          we are passing through,
An entrance to the comet
     in seven colours, thundering;
          that winter
We cut steps in the gigantic ice
     and went in and out of the house
          by the lavatory window,
Cut steps and paths
     in the frozen pitch
          and in the saltmarsh:
Our upstairs room
     was called the Gynoecium
          because it was hers,
And she cleaned its wide-curving windows
     so we could look out
          while we were in bed
In the comet's spectrum halls.

HENRHYD WATERFALL

Is like the bow window
     of an ancient ship
          sunk in its vale;
In this drought
     only a little flow
          tumbles into the air
Off the high lip of rock
     and the captain's
          stateroom windows are

Blind stone. There is still
          a hint of rainbow
                    in the gulf
A rainbow scent
          or sensation in the
                    presence of the cliff
Which at spate cascades
          bending its stout rainbow
                    in mid-air
Like the shining mainspring
          in a clock
                    of seven colours
Its tensions
          demonstrated
                    by its colours;
But today you see
          the fall's foundation
                    of rock, the dry
Nether underpinning
          of the famous rainbow.
                    The Fall
Has followed us home
          and the boulders abound,
                    and the stone of the hotel
Walls seem underpinning
          for rainbows; a fly
                    from the falls
Hanging suddenly on the clear
          outside bedroom window glass
                    seems a seed of that water's
Withdrawn force, a seed
          of that water's force;
                    it lands straddled on the glass
Flexing its rainbow waxes
          like a black star
                    with its legs stretched
A visitor of the black underground water
          and its batwings
Like a draughtsman's
          perfect equilibrium
                    of flying forces, like a
Denotation water
          captured and controlled
                    in an insect virility;

One of the thirsty parched mariners
      that glide through the stone fissures
           powered by secret rainbows,
The colours on the air
    of the speed
        of the ship's still wake
at Henrhyd Falls.

AFTERGLOW LABORATORIES

I poured the dry sand
      from one broken milkbottle
         to another –
Peterstone with all his eyes open,
      the stone made of eyes,
           at Llandudno, in the Great Orme,
In a cliff-cavern floored
      with dry sand
        like an alchemist
with his dry water
      ora et labora: the pouring
        was a kind of prayer-work
I poured and repoured
      in the little warm cavern or cell,
        poured flexible rock,
Dusty rock
    with a light in it
        once I slipped on the turf
The Orme rolled me
    to the brink of the cliff
        on the narrow pathway
Down from my sandlab,
    one of my laboratories.
          I had at home another laboratory
Made of fused sand, the glassware –
    how did I gather
      this impressive scene
Of crystalline tubes,
      flasks, retorts,
        fractionating columns
(An emblem of slowing the breath)
    chromatography-stripes,

a kind of action-painting,
The look of the glass furniture, the luminosity of
the delicate transparent machinery
mattered a lot:
The transparency meant truth,
the battles of the home revealed,
boiled up in these test-tubes
Like glass magic skeletons
that healed with their fluid dance
their scudding drops
Made into the figures of a glitter-science
whose haunting solvent-smells
of ether, of acetone tuned
Into a glass trance-device
that bypassed
my father's angers
My mother's distresses.
She combed her distresses
my apparatus absorbed them,
Sent them out on the air like
dry water, and the great books
absorbed the anger
With their hexagonal sigils,
for I most loved Organic Chemistry,
its sonorous smells,
Its linked potencies.
At Cambridge, none of the laboratories
were mine, all were competitive
None contemplative,
my vocation was alchemist not chemist,
my laboratories were everywhere;
Also I could not follow
that other ritual of fertile mud
called Rugby Football, of chemists
Kicking a leather egg,
much to my father's disappointment.

XXVII

A SPEAKER FOR
THE SILVER GODDESS

(2006)

LUCKBATH

'We need the mud'
C.G. Jung

Blackening the white garments
    in order to transfer
        their radiance inwards;
Covering himself with estuary mud
    in order to achieve the inner glory;
        clothing the soul
In its shining garment
    by defiling the outer:
        he is changing skins,
He strips the old filth off,
    the radiant new season begins;
        the reek of fruct and filth
Was unbelievable and its look
    unpredictable,
        the monster-look,
The shambler clothed in tree-shit,
    balsmic cascades,
        the body-of-smell reborn;
Nevertheless, the clean twin still visits
    drawing-rooms, not in his Hyde
        but in his snowy Jekyll,
But an invisible forest enters the room too,
    Hyde concealing himself
        in bushes and swinging
From tree to tree;
    silent Hyde; from his seed
        spring great oaks.

THE PARADISE OF STORMS

Pepper and salt stubble, little
    white crystals mixing with
        tiny black ones, this crystalline
Scum expounds into its beard,
    the waves of beard
        flowing out of the skin
Ceaselessly, day and night, registering

                    by a small agitation of growth
                              as the trees do
The presence of women
                    and the growth-properties
                              of the weather.
Thus the beards, and the trees:
                    this one knows that a woman
                              waited under it for an hour today
During the rain; if we took
                    a slice of its trunk
                              and looked carefully
At the fattening of the cambium
                    which registers the shower we would see
                              a small figure with a furled
Umbrella. In a man
                    that would be a barbarity.
                              Can I read that lady
In the unfurling of my beard?
                    But the tree-rings should be read
                              without broaching the bark
For the perfume of a tree
                    compiles its experience
                              as it matures . . .
The great detective pauses
                    under the tree full of eyes
                              in the garden of the murder-house
And the name of the butcher
                    passes into his mind
                              like a whispering witness,
He lays his hand on the culprit's shoulder
                    whose beard reeks bloody murder
                              and an *at-last-I-am-caught-and*
Can-rest blend of scents. Now
                    the paradise of storms passes on,
                              showering in every skin.

MOTH-ER

A sudden rose-garden in the bedroom.
          I pad my way
                    through this labyrinth

To where she is.
                  As we kiss and touch our quick
                        windows open to the sky,
Which signal to her, finish.
                  Every dusk she eats a moth, it is
                        a winged key to the invisible,
It trembles on her tongue,
                  accepting her
                        as though she were the night
And the stars would bloom in her mouth
                  when this tiny
                        giving-of-all was enacted,
By moth-kiss, by moth-death. This
                  was her sin,
                        she had got her sins down
To this small murder
                  and the eating up of this
                        little star-map . . .
Her figure reclining in violin shape,
                  a little bonfire on the tongue,
                        her dozing body pulses
As though the skin were moths,
                  their tones. She
                        sees through her skin
With a moth's eye and with
                  its radio tuned to moth-death,
                        the final broadcast . . .
Completely insupportable,
                  the quicksilver-flutter,
                        the burst of rank juice
Like a turpentine, like tasting
                  a painter's brush in starlight . . .
Which paints stars
                  arranged in their cupolas
                        like whispering galleries
Crowded with white-faced watchers.
                  She licks this brush for luck:
                        the stars
Painted across the moth's back
                  reappear in heaven.
                        Now her skin is soft
As as many moths as she's consumed, fitted together
                  in galactic designs of touch;
                        this is the secret she gives to me,

The winged jewels built into a temple,
      with her last breath
           as conscious mind and the unconscious
Rush together, and the stench or perfume
      in her last breath seeks above
           its constellation of the Mother,
Moth.

NUDE DESCENDING

The Saint has multiplied her limbs,
      every thread of drapery a nerve
           feeling into each corner of the room
As she descends the stairs, the nude, clothed
      only in her vapours, her great
           power-sleeves, even
In the banal condominium
      now full of grace felt out
           by her;
With each fresh step a new set
      of feelers is created, or wings, for her
           auric fields resemble
The gold grain of a moth-wing;
      if we did not know that here
           is a nude descending we would believe
We were in the presence of a queen of moths
      and her perfumes which were also light
           like clothes
And provisional ears and muslin
      radio-dishes. Since
           this gracious passing-through,
Epiphany, was mediated by the odours
      we do not now need
           any contrived pomps,
For each breath of air,
      each lung-full,
           is a palace.

MY PRINCE

His name translated meant
    Infant Snow, Babysnow,
        The Japanese Prince;
He was almost a young man, with
    his olive oil skin
        and his charcoal business suits;
I wanted him to be transparent,
    and he was trying, not opaque
        or too Japanese,
Since I was sweet
    on his sister the Princess
        which seemed to be plain sailing
In her mind: it was our uneasiness,
    the young man's and mine, which remained.
        Would he become my friend
or would he stay completely
    a Prince of Blood with no affections,
        I would have liked such
A courtly friend; and what I had to offer, why,
    his sister was sure of what that might be, even
        if I wasn't, and I was to
Marry her; why should the Prince
    suspect us?
        All we did, she and I
Was to sit together in one of the palace
    halls, it was wonderful.

XXVIII

THE HARPER

(2006)

BALL LIGHTNING

A waterfall in a vaporous glade,
    Ladders of vapour
        propped against the apple-trees
Everywhere.
    The devotion in the old dog's face
        as he gazes round and round
His mistress's garden.
    The pleasant, salt-silvered
        old house.
The loaf on the slate shelf,
    the patient ferment.
        An agate ball of lightning floats
Out of the charged orchard
    like an apple-ghost
        offering itself in turn
To our lips: house,
    dog, lover, woman,
        out of the girdle of trees
Shedding their windfalls
    in shining cascades like waterfalls;
        she got a look from it
That now she wears
    random and swamping,
        and so do I
In the smell of apple-mortality
    which is sweet,
        there are tears like windfalls
Dried on our cheeks;
    this apple-mush, these tears
        the real home of all,
Fruit, dog, woman, lover,
    ceaseless waterfall and ancient house,
        vaporous stairs that
Wait for our ascending.

CORNISH PERSEPHONE

The little Christmas tree asserts
      its pagan presence
         aglow with electric bulbs
In the shapes of flowers, dew, castles, St Nicolas,
      all of them bursting light from within;
         then, suddenly it takes hold
And becomes a person;
      the pine-perfume lovingly reaches
         out of it, soaking up
A tincture of radiation
      from the small light-engines.
         It is as though
The fairy on the peak,
      the star welding at the tip of her wand,
         has created the foliage
By rolling her green dress down,
      and stands there,
         with the tree her whole garment,
Gifts about her feet,
      the star fissioning on her wand,
         visiting us
In a green shape at the steep year's end:
      the Giantess in her lair,
         the Cornish Persephone,
She spends the dark months
      struggling towards us
         with her light held up
Like a Christmas Tree, light-bursting.
      She is away, or so it seems
         during the New Year –
In March and most of April too
      she is struggling towards us
         through the mineral mire,
And through the oiled lakes underground
      and through the cities of ore
         more capacious far
Than the small towns of our Duchy;
      our underworld is a Birmingham of rocks
         through which she toils
Emerging at a mine-tip in flowers
      on Goonhillie, St Day,
         and as she rises it is like

An electricity you see because you feel it;
        When she is with us
                people live in sunlight
As the blessed do visible and invisible too
        for the seven other months –
                all trees shake their presence out:
Leaving her consort in the living rock,
        she rises learned
                from her imprisonment.

THE RAINBOW

The great reservoir
        hangs up inside itself;
                it reflects a sky
Corroded like zinc,
        in its pewter-coloured surface
                a small squall
Patches the water
        into roughened metal:
                you shall perceive
All the colours of the world
        in the cold gust crossing:
                to sip
At a tumbler of its water is
        to set open a glass of dream.
                A clew of sunbeams hangs
Suddenly in the brimming glass,
        sipping this water at her lips
                charged her
With its reflections,
        moistened her yoni
                with nude water,
And she felt a rainbow
        of pleasure
                shining through the squall
Within her,
        up there,
                and in her reservoir.

TRIAL BY MALLET

He was lean, fast-moving,
    darkly-handsome,
        wore white-and-black
Like me; I had to fight
    this younger man
        in the long and arch-roofed room
Like a storm-drain, ancient brick
    scrawled over
        with white lime crusts
And hedgehogged with pencil-stalactites.
    It was raining solid rods,
        water-curtains muffled
The entrance-arch, inside
    the shelly pendules started
        to drip clear water.
A third man in formal dress was present,
    he carried, for the *coup de grâce*,
        a lunar penknife blade,
Its small scythe flashing
    in the ambiguous light
        of two torches
Struck flaming in iron brackets.
    We each grasped
        the thick stems
Of the iron-bound mallets;
    it was Trial by Mallet, I could see us
        as we would be
If this duel began,
    crushed bone creaming
        in the black cloth it rent,
Two men moused by the cats-clawed mallets.
    One of us demanded
        a limit on the tally
Of blows, our umpire
    grinned like that cat
        and shook his head,
We could almost see the pleased tail swish
    under his tailcoat;
        this shared glimpse
Made me remember
    that my opponent was also my friend,
        near to a brother,

By trade a pilot
          full of strategies, vitality, navigations,
                    so why did we plan to fight
In this storm-drain underground,
          whose body was to be flushed
                    out to sea on the flood?
My friend, I thought,
          the storm is coming on, with thunder, soon
                    we shall be fighting
Knee-deep in its torrents.
          I caught his eye, and as one man
                    we turned towards the umpire
For answers, the mallets heavy
          as our children's heads.

TRUE WASP

On the twentieth of this November
          I noticed wasps
                    eating a toad flattened by cars –
They were tearing away
          strips of toad-skin
                    braided to the asphalt;
Later the same day I saw
          a dead mouse opened by its own gas
                    with wasps studding its backbone:
It was their season,
          turning horror to vigour;
                    turning eyes downwards
I saw wasps pinching
          fine ginger crumbs
                    from a reclining dogturd;
By the sweet hum of the small power-station
          I was caught in our mother the rain
                    and still the wasps came weaving
Between the drops slow as syrup,
          never struck and always steady,
                    entering the machinery
To collect light from the cables,
          winged vessels distilling sharp venom
                    in the great wasp

Nesting hum of the transformers
        painted yellow and black, separating
           bitterness from light.

CORE

We cannot hear the voice
    of this machine,
        they scan the unborn
With ultra-sound –
      Will the foetus not be bonded
        to this song,
Will inaudible whistles not
      become its mother?
         Is whistling at girls
With ultra-sound not wrong?
      A transparent window opens
        suddenly in their bellies
Disclosing a buddha-face
      in shadows on a VDU
        semaphoring its arms
Below the belt:
      through the swiftly-transparent
        muscle-skin walls
A sudden clear glass appears
      and suspended there
        the star
Of fivepoints shines
      within the apple-womb
        weaving her fingers,
Beating at her temple walls:
    the Core;
        or, the sixpointed male
Waving to us
    through the skin and flesh.

AUTUMN LOVELETTER

The skin-of-the-earth-shining
   as you walk towards the tree
     which has exuded
A sheening envelope of sap;
   it is like a door
     opened in the trunk
And, inside the door,
   something to drink.
     I move closer, and think,
After Bunyan:
   'In this Land the Shining Ones
     commonly walked,
Because it was
   on the borders of heaven.' The aroma
     and the fragrance of new thoughts
Were perceptible in these designs
   of balsams and barks . . .
     What is a Grail-Winner?
Why, any man who frees the waters
   in the woman by her consent, which means
     he is a rainmaker
As she is. He knows
   from a bad temper in the sky
     that the rain will soon
Come down here: irritability
   above the barley-fields
     seldom persists, it relents
In heavy and opulent showers. The barley-beard
   pierces every drop that falls . . .
     A bird fighting its shadow
On a whitewashed wall,
   coming at it
     with beating wings, stabbing
Beak and claws . . .
   that apple-tree's fruit
     with stars in its mansion
Shall serve as meat for all;
   the thrush energetically
     excavating the last ones
In the tree,
   taking boxer's stance on the apple-domes
     and stabbing into them

With swift wet strokes . . .
        at Maenporth the woman
                climbs out of the plasm,
Out of the darkened tabernacles,
        and there is
                the golden-glow
Of the heroic skin, alive
        with its inexcusable hazard. She
                drops her soiled robes
As she comes, the black
        off the golden glow,
                the mudworks full
Of emergency eyes
        that marvel at her form . . .
                the nectar of the tree
Is flowing from the doorway
        under the shining lintel:
                any tree, mound,
Standing stone
        can take you thus inside, if you have
                freed the water, the nectar.
Now the pelvic cups tilt and kiss
        and are of the same pulse. We see
                the various flowers
And flower-gardens we are made of
        inside – the carnation
                of the heart,
The daffodil banks
        of the spleen,
                the jasmine kidney. We watch
Free cities of flowing nectar;
        all the citizens in polished carapace
                feast at its banks:
This is the start
        of Unbottle, or Autumn,
                when the pleasure
Of smells
        is at its most
                perilous.

THE HARPER

Shiny waterbeetles
      scribe the pond, each one
            the centre of its circular signature,
Each one the centre
      of its circular harp;
            these harps collide
Sending out graven improvisations,
      sketches, line-drawings
            and scrawling signatures,
All the same signature,
      never identical,
            now an ellipse,
An egg drawn on water, a one system
      with two beetle-centres . . .
            the woman swimming
At the heart of her harp,
      swimming in her evening clothes
            that make fresh signatures,
Entering the music like Ophelia
      but a strong swimmer,
            in her presence
The music bends,
      turning over and over
            in its helicals,
Her orchestra skirt and blouse
      winding conches and sails;
            how the cloth clings
In a lover's chord . . .
      Her love is the fresh
            and talkative spring she
Couples with,
      and in it layers herself,
            clothes scribing out
The depths of the river . . .
      the woman swimming looks up
            and the whole woodland pond
Is reflected in her eyes,
      her hair twining and searching
            in the signature:
Woman harpist clothed in the forest brook.

PIANISM

Fluid pianism. It was as if
      he sat down at a waterfall, it flowed
            over his fingers and they wrestled
With the disappearing water; the piano's
      frame and strings reappeared
            from moment to moment in the busy
                    water
Then disappeared in a sudsy flux of brilliant
      current, or were marked across by some
            new breeze of tributary torrent but
The sheerwhite style was creaselessly present:
      something in the speed; his hair flowed too
            down to his shoulders and was a part
Of the music seen as well as heard,
      its sound matched the brilliance
            of his hair-gloss and the white foam
Flowed over the piano's terraced ledges
      down his legs and over the stage
            into the audience soaking them with
      Liszt.

THEME-DREAM

Touching my tongue
      to her hole, there was
            an electrical jolt
Like the stud
      of a powerful torch battery,
            the kind that goes on
For ever; then there was an electrical theme-park
      seen through the skin
            full of invisible but melodious
Carousels; ferris wheels and booths of chance,
      and this was a dream clothed by
            the actual visit
We had made that afternoon.
      The children ran ahead
            between the model buildings

One-tenth the size, there was Pisa leaning
          and the munificent Swiss chalet
               full of accordion mirth
On self-changing records ever-lasting
          to which the girls were dancing
               before the David
Of Michelangelo
          like a golden calf;
               they danced with joy
Because of his neat genitals
          like a draw-string shammy bag
               with a weasel peering from it:
The two were only nine at that time,
          this the only wedding-muscle they'd seen,
               so sweet and neat they danced
And then the voice above of splitting-open drowned
          the Switzer jollification, and the axe
               of thunder sang in the black
Cloud towers, the snaking blue fire
          played about the shammy-bag
               of valiant David
In the pouring rain.

ORCHARD END II

In the rainshower
          under the green skirts,
               sheltering with my mother;
Beneath the oak
          the sudden magistery
               of the oak smell,
The oak coming forth
          with a hiss in the leaves,
               as the oak comes
Into the rainfall
          the ground darkening
               and then puddling with mirrors,
Stepping out into the world of the oak,
          into the world changed
               by the oak-elixir, charged,

The rain lowers herself on the oak
        and the oak comes
                into the rain
By the house called Orchard End,
        either because it was the end
                of the great orchard of Malden,
Or the end of paradise
        that was expected to fade
                as one grew up,
But it didn't
        because of the oak coming forth
                under my mother's shade
Which has since
        become the oak-shade.

LAST POEM

Buzz-saw cry of the gannet,
a ghost of water,

his outside child

The next station is God
Mind the doors!

Alive in those shadow-streets

NOTES

'Phlebas the Phoenician': the title is from Part IV of *The Waste Land*. This poem was incorporated into a six-part version of 'Lazarus and the Sea', which was never published. Published in *Chequer* 2, 1953.

'Dr Immanuel Rath': inspired by Josef von Sternberg's 1930 film *The Blue Angel*, about a repressed teacher who becomes enslaved by a manipulative nightclub singer. Published in *Delta* 2, 1954.

'Guardian': published in *Delta* 3, 1954.

The Collector: Redgrove's first volume bears the date 1959, but publication was actually delayed till January 1960 in the hope of being the 'Choice' of the Poetry Book Society.

'Lazarus and the Sea': see John 11. When Redgrove was conscripted into the army at the age of eighteen he had a breakdown, was diagnosed as schizophrenic and subjected, as the standard treatment of the time, to fifty 'insulin comas' by withdrawal of blood-sugar. He has written that when he started to write poetry he wondered what authority he had, and realised that he had 'died' fifty times. This is the poem that resulted.

'The Collector': this poem is the subject of one of Redgrove's most resonant and oft-repeated anecdotes: 'The first time I slept with a woman . . . such a peace and silence came into my conflicting head! Then into that peace came of itself a measured statement, and this was my first poem.' The earliest extant draft is only four lines:

> 'Caught in a fold of the living hills he failed.
> Extending his amiable senses he found
> The mist that glittered like a skin
> The horny rocks and the alien soil.'

'Memorial': on Christmas Eve 1957 Redgrove's younger brother David, just short of his twentieth birthday, was killed in a fall, trying to climb into the hotel bedroom window of a friend who was locked out of her room.

'Variation on Lorca': adapted from 'Alma Ausente', Lorca's elegy for the bullfighter and writer Ignacio Sanchez Mejias. Redgrove effectively elides the Mediterranean detail and references to Mejias's maturity, to create an elegy for David, who was a soldier.

'Being Beauteous': adapted from Rimbaud's prose poem of the same title.

'Mr Waterman': performed on BBC TV *Monitor* by Kenneth Griffith, 1962.

'In Company Time': written when Redgrove was working as a scientific copywriter for Glaxo Kline. The prose section is a sample of his actual copy. The poem celebrates the birth of his first son, Bill, in July 1958.

'The Force': in the summer of 1963 Redgrove and his family stayed at a B&B owned by Mrs Tyson in Borrowdale, Cumbria.

'The House in the Acorn': this poem was inspired by Dame Julian of Norwich: 'he schewyd me a lyttille thynge the qwantyte of A <u>haselle Nutte</u> lyggande in the palme of my hande & to my vndyrstandynge that it was as rownde as any balle. I lokede theropoun and thought whate maye this be and I was aunswerde generaly thus it is alle that ys made.' (Amherst Manuscript Folio 99)

'The Ferns': 'Three things made this poem. It happened to be the dead of winter and the window glass was so cold that to breathe on it was to get instant frost-ferns. I had been reading about some Greek philosopher, I think, who said everything was water, and I had not understood this but wondered what it felt like to believe it. And the third thing was that I had been reading – fact or fiction, Conan Doyle or Dr Beebe, I don't remember – about an astonishing dive five miles deep into the ocean. One of the characters at the bottom of the sea was having a bad time and could not help knowing how deep he was. He thought of the steamer as far above him as the highest clouds in the sky were above that steamer and still could be clouds – five miles. This seemed so astonishing to me that it all came together in this poem, The Ferns, a poem of transpiration, translocation and flow.' [PR]

'The Sermon': performed on radio by Donald Wolfit and on BBC TV *Monitor* by Michael Hordern in 1963. 'This figure of the Dispossessed Parson works with me more and more. He implies so much social organization, so much of schooling, so many elaborate churches to which people no longer return. And for the individual me, he's the sign of an active religious sensibility (I believe) that can't stand churches. As Jung say somewhere, the Western Church, despite its admirable exfoliation of externals, has quite failed to show the image of the inner God to the inner man. God should haunt the pages of "The Sermon" in glimpses and brushes, if it works at all as I thought.' [PR]

'The Case': this poem was published separately as a pamphlet with the title 'The God-Trap' and the following Introduction:

'"The God-Trap" started with my hearing Verdi's *Requiem*. I don't know whether my view of this marvellous music is an orthodox one, it had a very violent effect on me. I seemed to hear a plea for the eternal rest or punishment of all sinners and it was, naturally, sung in the confident words of orthodox religion. The singers on the other hand were not the high calm voices of much church music, but rather the full-blooded singers of opera, seemingly fully aware both of their sensuality and their mortality – and they were scared stiff by what they were singing, although they put a bold face on it.

Such people could not help making love as they sang, I felt, whatever words they were singing.

'And I too was very disturbed by this, because I saw for the first time how you could believe in a God separate from his creation, frowning down upon it. Loving both God and the creation, one's being would be split in two.

'Later I came across Hermann Hesse's *Steppenwolf* and when I encountered the following passage, I felt again as if I were living in the two worlds simultaneously: "Man is not by any means of fixed and enduring form . . . He is much more an experiment and a transition. He is nothing else than the narrow and perilous bridge between nature and spirit. His innermost destiny drives him on to spirit and to God. His innermost being draws him back to nature, the mother. Between the two forces his life hangs tremulous and irresolute. . . bourgeois 'man' is a transient agreement. . . a compromise. . . an experiment with the aim of cheating both the angry primal Mother Nature and the troublesome Father Spirit of their pressing claims, and of living in a temperate zone between the two of them."

'I happened too to be reading a little about Manichaeism, which as I understood it meant exactly this dualistic split between the glory of created things, which were evil, and the glory of God the Creator, who was good, and during my reading I was surprised to learn that Mani, the founder of this "heresy", was often known as "The Son of the Widow". I was surprised because I had already begun to write "The God-Trap", and my cast was settled. It comprised a Widow and her son, and the Son was searching for a Father.

'The clinching thing, though, as far as this poem was concerned, was an actual happening. We were visiting one of the great national trust houses near Harrogate. It has a wonderful walled garden. It was in this garden that I saw an elderly woman – she was about sixty – wearing a cotton dress with a floral pattern that spread great flower-blooms over her motherly figure. She was standing by a great bank of flowers, her eyes half-closed, leaning back slightly, and saying, quite softly: "Oh, this is life. . . what a shame we have to die . . ."

'The figure of this woman haunted me and I had to work it out. She seemed so in love with the gardened earth I wondered what God she could have and whether he were apart from it, and if he were God in heaven, up there, how she could possess both him and the flowering earth. What could there be in the death of this woman, for others or herself, but terror and absence, the spirit and the flowering body taken apart, the white from the yolk.

'And I thought of the son of such a woman, she perhaps pious and widowed, he sent almost by hints, misunderstanding of her piety on a mythic quest for God, the missing father, and how his inherited senses and his inherited piety would be as great as hers, and how he might court his destruction in his search, and where he would find his equilibrium, his compromise, Hesse's "temperate zone", and the poem seemed to give its answer; that his fate would be a modern fate, a Faustian fate, in his striving to command absolute experience, but the outcome would be the same as that of King Oedipus in the old story.

'And lastly I wondered if I had ever met an actual person such as this, and where he would be found if I had not. For I saw that I was trying to write an elegy for him, a requiem, and one for a split in Man's consciousness, and then I found that I had noted, as if by chance, this paragraph from some journal:

'"'Clinic Director: This is schizophrenia. The boy was close to his mother: a widow after a very unsatisfactory marriage. His illness, which must always have been latent, accelerated when she died. . . He suffers also from hysterical blindness, and cannot open his eyes. They have remained closed for the ten years of his illness. . . He likes to spend his time in the garden and likes also to be called "Father". He never replies when he is so called, but only smiles a little, and turns away. . . I have noticed that such cases, which are nowadays very widespread, often seem unwilling to be cured.'"'

On the evidence of Redgrove's drafts, this 'clinical report' is his own fiction. 'Then-shall-ye-see-and-your-heart-shall-rejoice-/And-your-bones-shall-sprout-as-the-blade . . .': Isaiah 66.14 as quoted in John F. Potts's translation of Swedenborg's *Arcana Coelestia*. I have been unable to identify any of the other quotations.

Work in Progress: this volume was published by a small press, 'Poet and Printer'. Although it bears the date 1968 it actually appeared in the spring of 1969. It contains many of the poems subsequently published in the Routledge collection *Dr Faust's Sea-Spiral Spirit*; the three poems reproduced here are not in that volume.

'The Old White Man': adapted from 'The White Monkey' in *The Dragon King's Daughter: Ten T'ang Dynasty Stories*, Longman Foreign Languages Press, Peking, 1954.

'Quasimodo's Many Beds': Redgrove wrote about this poem to his analyst, John Layard: 'I'd take its meaning two ways. The truth is somewhere in between. Either Quasimodo is revealing something important to the girl, that she should love more widely, and if she does indeed love, his quirks are no deformities; or the girl is waiting for Quasimodo to stop playing about and make love to her properly. *It doesn't really matter to the poem which.* The situation is there, and it's the reader's own business to decide which of the two persons in the poem he thinks is right, if either is. Also it may behove me as recipient of this poem (or "active imagination") to consider my own psychological situation as reflected in the poem. Nevertheless the poem tries to be a discrete entity, a little machine that tells a tale. All it wants to do is to tell the tale. The moral is up to the reader. As a writer, I am still reflecting on the moral. It is a voyage of discoveries.' The poem reflects the crisis in his first marriage.

'Christiana': see John Bunyan, *The Pilgrim's Progress*, Part 2, Chapter 3. The poem is dedicated to Redgrove's first wife, Barbara, and was written shortly after their separation in 1969.

'The Moon Disposes': 'Barbara and I mending our broken ring on Cornish sands, our world displayed and observed under the just dominion of the Moon.' [PR to Dilly Creffield] Written in 1966, when Peter and Barbara moved to Falmouth from Leeds.

'Young Women with the Hair of Witches and No Modesty': 'Dilly Creffield at her most glamorous and provoking, in the company of her children.' [PR to Dilly Creffield]

'The Youthful Scientist Remembers': 'A poem about the blessed lascivious humour of women. A poem of innocent surprise on the young man's part.' [PR to Dilly Creffield] In draft this poem is dedicated to Barbara.

'The Idea of Entropy on Maenporth Beach': the title echoes Wallace Stevens's 'Idea of Order at Key West'. The epigraph is from Baudelaire's 'La Géante': 'It is she, black but shining.' The poem is dedicated to John Layard, and the first draft was written during a sleepless night on an overnight train, after hearing Layard lecture. Subsequently Redgrove had analysis with Layard for about eighteen months. This is the first poem in which he openly explores his 'alternative' sexuality, and he regarded it as a turning-point in his work.

'The House of Taps': dedicated to Penelope Shuttle.

'The Haunted Armchair': 'Redgrove solus, as invincible virgin.' [PR to Dilly Creffield]

The Hermaphrodite Album: a collection of poems by Redgrove and Penelope Shuttle, in which the authors of individual poems were not identified.

Sons of My Skin: this was Redgrove's first Selected Poems, drawing on his collections up to 1973. It also contains a number of otherwise uncollected poems, from which these have been chosen.

'The Oracle': 'He' in this poem is John Layard.

'Sam's Call': based on a family anecdote from Redgrove's Art School colleague Derek Toyne.

'Dog Prospectus': Redgrove wrote this poem after an unhappy experience at Colgate University, New York State.

'Tapestry Moths': Hardwick Hall is a great Elizabethan house in Derbyshire, famous for its extensive windows and its tapestries, which

Redgrove visited in 1973. He probably had in mind a tapestry representing a fruit seller (actually female) in the Entrance Hall.

'Dance the Putrefact': broadcast on Radio 3 in 1975.

'God Says "Death"': mire-drummer: bittern.

'Living in Falmouth': Trelissick is a garden, now owned by the National Trust, near Truro, Cornwall. The Carrick Roads is a large natural harbour navigable from Falmouth to Truro.

'Excrementitious Husk': St Cuby is a church at Cuby, near St Austell in Cornwall, restored in the nineteenth century.

'Rev. Uncle': "Obby 'Oss' alludes to the ancient festival held on Mayday in Padstow, Cornwall, which Redgrove describes in *The Colour of Radio* and *The Sleep of the Great Hypnotist*.

'Tall Hairdo': goffered: fluted. St Materiana's is an eleventh-century church at Tintagel, Cornwall.

'At the Street-Party': 'The biblical echo to the smelling of the son is Genesis 27:27; Isaac blessing Jacob disguised as Esau.' [PR]

'Gwennap Cross': near Redruth in Cornwall.

'The Cave': codling is both a species of apple and a species of moth that feeds on apples.

'From the Life of a Dowser': a dowser is a water-diviner. 'Fenten ow Clyttra' is Cornish for sparkling well.

'Renfield before his Master': Lola Montez (1820–61) was an Irish-born dancer and mistress of King Ludwig I of Bavaria. Redgrove pasted into his journal a newspaper clipping with a photo of her and the caption: 'Lola Montez shook up San Francisco with her spider dance and set the citizens gawking by walking two greyhounds on a leash while a parrot perched on her shoulder. She smoked cigars, gambled in forbidden saloons and claimed to be the illegitimate daughter of Lord Byron.' 'The *karast* is literally the god or person who has been mummified, embalmed, and anointed or christified', Gerald Massey, *Ancient Egypt the Light of the World*, p. 218. This is one of many details that Redgrove derived from the works of the Victorian Egyptologist Gerald Massey, to whom he dedicated both *The Apple-Broadcast* and *The Man Named East*.

'Silence Fiction': loosely based on C.G. Jung's account of a dream which, he said, led to the discovery of the collective unconscious: *Memories, Dreams, Reflections*, London, Fontana, 1967, p.184.

'Call': dedicated to the poet Frances Horovitz, a close friend of Redgrove, who died of cancer in 1983.

'In the Pharmacy': dedicated to a student of Redgrove's at Falmouth School of Art.

'The Green Tower': the church is St Euny's in Redruth, Cornwall, which is near the hill of Carn Brae, site of Neolithic and Iron Age settlements, and a medieval castle.

'The Quiet Woman of Chancery Lane': there are a number of pubs with this name and sign, immortalised by Hardy in *The Return of the Native*, but not in Chancery Lane, the main thoroughfare of London's legal quarter.

'The Funeral', 'Warm Stone for N': Redgrove's mother Nancy (or Nan) died in 1980.

'Cloudmother': dedicated to Derek Power, the first Chair of the Falmouth Poetry Group.

'Local': dedicated to Gerald Massey (see note to 'Renfield before his Master'). 'The Quiet Woman': see note to 'The Quiet Woman of Chancery Lane'.

'Pneumonia Blouses': nenuphar: water lily.

'Horse Looking over Drystone Wall': a response to one of a number of photographs of the Scilly Isles by the Falmouth-based photographer Simon Culliford, to whom the poem is dedicated.

'Thunder-and-Lightning Polka': dedication: J.H. Barclay was a retired biscuit-manufacturer from Bootle, who collected Redgrove's work and was one of his most devoted readers.

'Into the Rothko Installation': Redgrove wrote this poem spontaneously as a response to the Rothko Room at the Tate, and was subsequently invited to contribute a poem to the gallery's anthology *With a Poet's Eye* (Tate Gallery, 1986).

'Summer': 'Shivering Mountain' is Mam Tor near Castleton in Derbyshire. This passage is based on notes Redgrove made during a visit there, sixteen years before the poem was published, an extreme example of his method of 'incubation'.

'Stench and Story': 'the Roads': the Carrick Roads (see note to 'Living in Falmouth).

'Eight Parents': Redgrove's father died in 1989.

'My Father's Trapdoors': Maskelyne: the name of a family of stage magicians. The one Redgrove saw as a boy must have been Jasper Maskelyne, 1902–74. 'Soup-and-fish': colloquial term for men's evening dress.

'Esher': a town in Surrey, six miles from Redgrove's childhood home in Kingston on Thames.

'Davy Jones' Lioness': an unusual example of a poem that was directly inspired by a dream.

'Enýpnion': this Greek word, more usually transliterated 'enupnion', means dream.

'Leather Goods': there is a shop in Falmouth which sells leather retrieved from shipwrecks, but not to my knowledge human skin. 'Manacles': notoriously treacherous rocks off the Lizard peninsula, Cornwall.

From 'Assembling a Ghost: Ms Potter': inspired by the death of Redgrove's first wife, Barbara, in 1994.

'Wheal Cupid': the name of a disused mine at Lelant, near St Ives, Cornwall.

'Orchard End': the name of Redgrove's childhood home in Kingston on Thames.

'Collected': 'With such hair too. . ./Used to hang and brush their bosoms': from Robert Browning's 'A Toccata of Galuppi's', stanza 15.

'Squelette': see note to 'Assembling a Ghost: Ms Potter'.

'Limestone Cat': dedicated to Neil Roberts, critic, biographer and editor, who showed Redgrove a petrified cat in a Derbyshire pub.

'Spiritualism Garden': when Redgrove was ten or twelve years old his mother confided in him about, and possibly made him complicit in, one or more abortions. He became preoccupied with the thought that the foetuses might be buried in the garden at Orchard End.

'Afterglow Laboratories': in 1941 Redgrove was evacuated with his mother and younger brother to Llandudno in North Wales. 'Ora et labora' (Pray and work) was the motto of Taunton School when Redgrove was a pupil. It has recently been changed to the corporate-sounding 'Offering more'.

'Nude Descending': see Marcel Duchamp 'Nude Descending a Staircase'.

'Orchard End II': see note to 'Orchard End'.

'Last Poem': transcribed by Penelope Shuttle from Redgrove's hand-written draft.

INDEX OF TITLES

INDEX OF FIRST LINES

Carriages sealed, and marked 'reserved', 246

Caught in a fold of living hills he failed, 14

Cloth woven on a loom whose spindle-weights, 190

Clouds and mountains were invited, both the conscious, 275

Coat over arm I step off the moss-silenced stairs, 30

Darkness is a power. She haunts with power, 124

Dawn, his first day, 131

Dearly beloved. I should say, Friends, 70

Death as pure loss, or immutability, 277

Dipping into the Tate, 315

Down the small path to the winding marsh, 299

Dreaming of a dog, whose nostrils, 243

Eating on the edge of death, 450

Elderly and most, 435

Even the bicycle-oil smelt of daffodils, 215

Father led me behind some mail-bags, 388

Final things walk home with me through Chiswick Park, 37

Fluid pianism. It was as if, 476

For a moment take into your two hands, 380

Frog-leap plops into the sandy water, 184

Generations of black snowflakes, frail and durable, 157

God says 'Death' in a gentle voice, 187

Grown-up idiot, see the slow-motion of him, 68

Hard rubber in its silk sheath like a nightie, 312

Having immured his new bride, 83

He is very impressive. I am very impressed by him, 133

He knew a clergyman he could say anything to, 398

He stands under a bright sky, 227

He switched on the electric light and laughed, 100

He was a good husband to his family, 4

He was eight when he started earning, 232

He was hounded from one bride-chamber, 373

He was lean, fast-moving, 470

Her bronze hair beaten into a bearded face looking backwards, 209

Her dress rushed and glistened as she went, 183

Her great thoroughfare, 359

Her menstruation has a most beautiful, 333

He's been somewhere far away for ten minutes, 47

His dead-white face, 316

His name translated meant, 463

Humming water holds the high stars, 109

I am a gardener, 74

'I am afraid for the meat', 107

I am frightened. It makes velvet feel too tall, 109

I chuck my Bible in the parlour fire, 241

I don't want to play, 17

I feared the miracle, 440

I feel emptied by the thunderstorm. She, 406

I have always loved water, and praised it, 100

I know a curious moth, that haunts old buildings, 142

I lay in an agony of imagination as the wind, 11

I love the cold: it agrees with me, 45